VISIONS *of* Freedom

WILFORD WOODRUFF AND
THE SIGNERS OF THE
DECLARATION OF INDEPENDENCE

Michael De Groote
and Ronald L. Fox

Cover and book design © 2015 by Covenant Communications, Inc.

Published by Covenant Communications, Inc.
American Fork, Utah

Copyright © 2015 by Michael De Groote and Ronald L. Fox

All rights reserved. No part of this work may be reproduced by any means without the express written permission of Covenant Communications, Inc., P.O. Box 416, American Fork, UT 84003. This work is not an official publication of The Church of Jesus Christ of Latter-day Saints. The views expressed within this work are the sole responsibility of the author and do not necessarily reflect the position of The Church of Jesus Christ of Latter-day Saints, Covenant Communications, Inc., or any other entity.

Drawings and Engravings of the Signers of the Declaration of Independence (Images in chapters 11 thru 66)

Drawings from
The Declaration of Independence by William H. Michael Government Printing Office 1904
Josiah Bartlett, Carter Braxton, Samuel Chase, Abraham Clark, George Clymer, William Ellery, Button Gwinnett, Lyman Hall, Benjamin Harrison, John Hart, William Hooper, Stephen Hopkins, Samuel Huntington, Francis Lightfoot Lee, Thomas Lynch Jr., John Morton, Thomas Nelson Jr., William Paca, John Penn, Caesar Rodney, George Ross, James Smith, Richard Stockton, Thomas Stone, George Taylor, Matthew Thornton, George Walton, William Whipple, William Williams, James Wilson, and George Wythe

Engravings from
Biography of the Signers of the Declaration of Independence by John Sanderson, Philadelphia 1823.
Samuel Adams, John Adams, Charles Carroll of Carrollton, William Floyd, Benjamin Franklin, Elbridge Gerry, John Hancock, Joseph Hewes, Thomas Heyward Jr., Francis Hopkins, Thomas Jefferson, Richard Henry Lee, Francis Lewis, Philip Livingston, Thomas McKean, Arthur Middleton, Lewis Morris, Robert Morris, Robert Treat Paine, George Read, Benjamin Rush, Edward Rutledge, Roger Sherman, John Witherspoon, and Oliver Wolcott

Printed in United States of America
First Printing: April 2015

25 24 23 22 21 20 19 18 17 16 15   10 9 8 7 6 5 4 3 2

ISBN 978-1-60861-227-7

For Barb, Kate, and Ellie
sine qua non
—MDG

For the Waddell Family:
Wayne, JoAnne, Glenn, Michael, Chris, and Scott

and for
Robert Trythall, Frank, Merlyn, and Max Poppleton
Their dedication, commitment, and example changed my life forever

and also for
the Hardy Family and their ancestors, Josiah Gile Hardy and son Warren, who assisted in building the St. George Temple and who did the endowments for two of the Signers of the Declaration of Independence
—RLF

Contents

Preface VII

Timeline VIII

Prologue XIII

Chapter 1 I Have a Mother There 1

Chapter 2 Redeeming the Dead 4

Chapter 3 A Temporary Temple 11

Chapter 4 "The vary thunders of heaven"—A Temple in St. George 15

Chapter 5 Priesthood and Patriotism 20

Chapter 6 Discerning Dreams and Visions of Freedom 23

Chapter 7 Doing the Work for the Signers and Other Eminent People 29

Chapter 8 The Vision's Legacy of Modern Temple Worship 33

Chapter 9 Wilford Woodruff's Last Testimony 37

Chapter 10 "Independence Forever" 39

Chapters 11 to 66 Biographies of the Signers 41
The biographies of the fifty-six Signers of the Declaration of Independence are in alphabetical order, with the exception of Samuel Adams's, which was placed before John Adams's to give a better chronological overview of the American Revolution.

Epilogue 210

Appendix 1 Extracts from Wilford Woodruff's Journal 211

Appendix 2 Extract from John D. T. McAllister's Journal 214

Appendix 3 Extract from a Discourse by Wilford Woodruff 215

Appendix 4 Extract from John D. T. McAllister's Journal..........................217

Appendix 5 Extract from Joseph West Smith's Journal............................218

Appendix 6 Extract from President Wilford Woodruff's Remarks................219

Appendix 7 Extract from President Wilford Woodruff's Discourse...............220

Appendix 8 James Godson Bleak Family History Account.......................221

Appendix 9 The Temple Work (A Full Listing of the Signers, Presidents, and Other Eminent Men and Women)..224

Appendix 10 The Declaration of Independence..................................233

Bibliography..236

Source Notes and Abbreviations Used 244

Endnotes...245

Acknowledgments

Vicki Jo Anderson, author
Thomas G. Alexander, author and historian
Brent Ashworth, historian and collector
Michael Bedard, artist
Richard E. Bennett, historian
Bill Bleak
Anthony Christensen, Anthony's Antiques
Thomas Coon
Craig L. Foster, LDS Family History Library
Reid N. Moon, Moon's Rare Books
John Murphy, Brigham Young University Library
Paul Swenson, Colonial Flag
Ronald W. Walker, historian

Richard E. Turley, Jr., Glenn N. Rowe, William Slaughter, Emily Utt, Brittany Chapman, and the staff at the Church History Library
The Church of Jesus Christ of Latter-day Saints

Julie Fisher, Brad Westwood, and the dedicated staff of the Utah State Historical Society

The National Archives
National Portrait Gallery
Library of Congress
Salt Lake City Library
Salt Lake County Library System
The Deseret News

Samantha Millburn, Margaret Weber, Mark Sorenson, and the rest of the staff at Covenant Communications

Preface

To truly do the Signers justice would require fifty-six books of this length and mining source materials across the country for each of them. Naturally Thomas Jefferson, John Adams, Benjamin Franklin, and a few others have demanded extensive biographies and will continue to do so. Other Signers left behind fewer records and enjoyed less attention.

Of necessity, much of the Signers' biographies are dependent upon secondary sources. We discovered that many of those secondary sources rely on early biographies, such as Charles Augustus Goodrich's *Lives of the Signers to the Declaration of Independence*, published in 1829 when one of the Signers, Charles Carroll of Carrollton, was still alive.

For the section about Wilford Woodruff's visions of the Signers, much more source material was available for examination. For example, we were able to examine Wilford Woodruff's 1877 journal and see his entry about the temple work he did for the Signers and other eminent men. A close examination of the document showed how for decades authors and historians have accidently omitted one of the eminent men: Robert Fulton, who invented the first commercially successful steamboat.

We could also see Woodruff's fingerprint in a smear of ink on those pages. Things like this help ground the reality of what Woodruff experienced.

This book tries to retain the original spelling, capitalization, and punctuation of the original sources. This is why, for instance, one chapter is called "The Vary Thunders of Heaven." Even though, technically, Woodruff had two visions, he spoke of them as if they were one experience. For the most part, this book will refer to the encounters with the Signers as a vision in the singular.

The appendixes have all the different accounts of Woodruff's vision in full and the first full listing of all the Signers, presidents, and other eminent men and women for whom temple work was done as a result of that vision.

We have worked on this project for several years. Ronald L. Fox worked on the photographs, special research efforts, and other central issues related to the book. Michael De Groote did the main research and the writing. We discussed and worked on together on all aspects of the book in a partnership that, we hope, produced a book readers will find interesting and inspiring.

It wasn't an isolated project, however. Many, many people helped us along the way and are mentioned in the acknowledgments. We couldn't have done this without them. That being said, we take responsibility for the contents of this book. Any mistakes are ours.

In addition to those mentioned in the acknowledgments, we want to thank Wilford Woodruff for listening and paying attention. In his time, he struggled for understanding and revelation and was rewarded with a vision of temple work that expanded our view of the eternal and infinite love of God.

We also want to thank the Founding Fathers themselves. They risked everything to follow promptings, not for greatness for themselves but for principles and perpetuity. They were, as Wilford Woodruff said, "the best spirits the God of heaven could find on the face of the earth."

Timeline of America
1700 and 1800s

LONG EVENTS

1754–1763—The French and Indian War

1775–1783—The Revolutionary War

1790–1840—The "Second Great Awakening" religious revival

April 1846–February 1848—Mexican-American War

March 1857–July 1858—Utah War

April 1861–May 1865—U.S. Civil War

1706
January 17—Benjamin Franklin born

1722
September 27—Samuel Adams born

1732
February 22—George Washington born
December 28—Franklin publishes first Poor Richard's Almanack

1734
January 20—Robert Morris born

1735
October 30—John Adams born

1737
January 23—John Hancock born
September 19—Charles Carroll of Carrollton born

1743
April 13—Thomas Jefferson born

1752
Franklin conducts kite experiment about electricity and lightning, honored by Royal Society for his work

1754
The Albany Congress, Franklin proposes plan for colonial union, which is rejected by the various colonies' legislatures

1764
April 5—The Sugar Act taxes passed by Parliament

1765
March 22—The Stamp Act taxes passed by Parliament
May 29—The Virginia Resolves oppose Stamp Act because it was enacted without representation
October—The Stamp Act Congress meets, petitions Parliament to repeal Stamp Act

1766
March 18—Britain repeals Stamp Act
May 16—Boston learns Stamp Act repealed

1767
June 29—Parliament passes the Townshend Acts, taxing imports of glass, lead, paint, tea, and paper

1768
February 11—Samuel Adams writes Massachusetts Circular Letter protesting Townshend Acts
May—British warship HMS *Romney* arrives to intimidate Boston
June—John Hancock's sloop, *Liberty*, seized for trying to avoid import taxes
August—Boston nonimportation agreement

1770
January 28—Lord North becomes prime minister of Great Britain
March 5—The Boston Massacre, six people killed by British troops
April—Parliament partially repeals Townshend Acts, leaving the tax on tea

1772
June 9—HMS *Gaspée* attacked, looted, and burned by colonists
November 2—Samuel Adams organizes a "committee of correspondence"

1773
May 10—Parliament passes the Tea Act, giving East Indian Tea Company a huge financial advantage over colonial smugglers
December 16—The Boston Tea Party

1774
Benjamin Franklin questioned before Parliament
March 31—First of the Intolerable Acts passed in retaliation against Boston, British warships close Boston Harbor
June—Thomas Gage attempts to bribe Samuel Adams
June 17—Samuel Adams calls for a Continental Congress
September 5–October 26—The First Continental Congress meets in Philadelphia

1775
March 23—Patrick Henry's "Give me liberty or give me death" speech
April 18–19—Battle of Lexington and Concord begins the Revolutionary War, Paul Revere warns Samuel Adams and John Hancock to flee British troops
May 10—The Second Continental Congress convenes in Philadelphia

June 15—George Washington chosen as Commander in Chief of the Continental Army
June 17—Battle of Bunker Hill
July 5—Olive Branch Petition approved by Continental Congress to send to King George III, who doesn't look at it

1776
January 9—Thomas Paine's *Common Sense* pamphlet published, galvanizes public opinion toward independence
March 17—British army leaves Boston
June 7—Richard Henry Lee's resolution for independence
June 11—Committee appointed to draft Declaration of Independence, includes John Adams, Benjamin Franklin, Thomas Jefferson, Robert Livingston, and Roger Sherman
June 12–27—Jefferson drafts the Declaration of Independence
July 2—Continental Congress votes for independence
July 4—Written Declaration of Independence approved
July 8—The Declaration of Independence read publically in Philadelphia
August 2—The bulk of delegates sign the Declaration of Independence
August 27—British rout Washington's troops on Long Island
September 11—Staten Island Peace Conference, Lord Richard Howe offers reconciliation but can't accept independence demanded by John Adams, Benjamin Franklin, and Edward Rutledge
December 26—Crossing the Delaware River, Washington captures Trenton, New Jersey

1777
May 27—Button Gwinnett dies of wounds from a duel
June 14—American Flag stars-and-stripes design adopted by Continental Congress
September 26—British occupy Philadelphia, Congress flees before they arrive
November 15—Articles of Confederation, the agreement on how to run the federal government, is adopted by the Continental Congress
December 19, 1777–June 19, 1778—Continental Army, with Washington, winters at Valley Forge

1778
February 6—France signs an alliance with the United States
June 18—British leave Philadelphia, Continental Congress subsequently returns
December 29—British capture Savannah, Georgia

1779
September 23—John Paul Jones captures the HMS *Serapis*

1780
May 12—British capture Charleston, South Carolina

1781
March 1—Articles of Confederation is recognized as ratified
June 4—Thomas Jefferson almost captured at his home in Monticello
October 19—Washington defeats Cornwallis at Yorktown, Virginia, the last decisive battle of the Revolutionary War

1782
March 20—Prime Minister Lord North resigns

July 11—British leave Savannah, Georgia
December 14—British leave Charleston, South Carolina

1783
September 3—The Treaty of Paris officially ends the Revolutionary War
November 25—British troops leave New York City
December 23—Washington resigns as Commander in Chief of the Continental Army

1787
May 25–September 17—Constitutional Convention in Philadelphia
September 17—United States Constitution signed in Philadelphia
December 7—Delaware first state to ratify Constitution

1788
June 21—Constitution officially established upon New Hampshire's ratification, the ninth state to do so

1789
April 30—George Washington inaugurated as the first president of the United States

1790
April 17—Benjamin Franklin dies
May 29—Rhode Island finally ratifies Constitution, the last of the original thirteen states

1791
February 25—First Bank of the United States created by Congress
December 15—Bill of Rights amendments ratified

1793
October 8—John Hancock dies

1797
March 4—John Adams inaugurated as second president

1799
December 14—George Washington dies at sixty-seven years old

1801
March 4—Thomas Jefferson inaugurated as third president
August 26—Robert Morris released from debtors' prison

1803
Benjamin Rush becomes president of Pennsylvania Abolition Society
October 2—Samuel Adams dies

1805
December 23—Joseph Smith Jr. born in Vermont

1806
May 8—Robert Morris dies
June 8—George Wythe dies from poison

1807
March 1—Wilford Woodruff born
August 17—Robert Fulton's *North River Steamboat* makes its inaugural run

1808
June 11—Bulah Woodruff, Wilford Woodruff's mother, dies at age twenty-six

1809
March 4—James Madison inaugurated as fourth president
November—Aphek Woodruff marries Azubah

1817
March 4—James Monroe inaugurated as fifth president

1818
October 28—Abigail Adams dies

1820
Missouri Compromise over slavery
Joseph Smith Jr.'s vision of God the Father and Jesus Christ

1821
Woodruff starts working in a mill

1825
March 4—John Quincy Adams inaugurated as sixth president

1826
July 4—Thomas Jefferson (83), then John Adams (90), die on the fiftieth anniversary of the Declaration of Independence

1828
Woodruff becomes friends with Robert Mason

1829
March 4—Andrew Jackson inaugurated as seventh president
Book of Mormon published

1830
April 6—The Church of Christ, later called The Church of Jesus Christ of Latter-day Saints, is organized

1831
William Lloyd Garrison begins antislavery newspaper, The Liberator

1832
Woodruff moves with his brother Azmon to Richland, New York
November 14—Charles Carroll of Carrollton, the last living Signer of the Declaration of Independence, dies at age ninety-five

1833
December 29—Woodruff hears Mormons preach
December 31—Wilford Woodruff is baptized in Richland, New York

1834
May—Zions Camp, a group of Mormons including Wilford Woodruff, march from Ohio to Missouri

1835
January 13—Woodruff leaves Missouri on first mission

1836
February 23—Battle of the Alamo begins
March 27—Kirtland Temple dedicated

1837
March 4—Martin Van Buren inaugurated as eighth president
April 13—Woodruff marries Phebe Whittemore Carter
May—Woodruff leaves on a mission to New England

1838
July—Woodruff called to be an Apostle

1839
Aphek Woodruff, Wilford Woodruff's father, is baptized
April—Woodruff ordained an Apostle by Brigham Young
August 8—Woodruff goes on a mission to England
December—Martin Van Buren tells Joseph Smith Jr. he can "do nothing" to help the Mormons who have been expelled from Missouri

1840
January 11—Woodruff arrives in England
March–August—Woodruff and others baptize almost 1,800 people
August 15—Joseph Smith preaches for first time of baptism for the dead

1841
March 4—William Henry Harrison inaugurated as ninth president
April 4—John Tyler inaugurated as tenth president
October 5—Woodruff back in Nauvoo from mission
October—Woodruff first hears of baptism for the dead
November 8—Nauvoo Temple baptismal font dedicated

1842
March 17—Female Relief Society of Nauvoo founded
April 21—Woodruff baptized for his deceased mother, Bulah
August 26—Woodruff baptized for his friend Robert Mason

1843
November 11—Wilford and Phebe Woodruff sealed "for time and all eternity" by Hyrum Smith
December 2—Woodruff received his endowments from Joseph Smith

1844
June 27—Joseph and Hyrum Smith murdered in Carthage, Illinois
August 8—Brigham Young accepted by majority of Mormons as leader
Woodruff president of European Mission

1845
March 4—James K. Polk inaugurated as eleventh president

1846
April 13—Woodruff back in Nauvoo
April 30—Woodruff and Orson Hyde dedicate Nauvoo Temple
July 21—Mormon Battalion begins march

1847
February 16—Brigham Young talks about how spiritual adoption needs further revelation
July 24—Brigham Young arrives in Salt Lake Valley

x

December 27—Brigham Young sustained as President of the Church

1848
Woodruff on mission to East Coast
Seneca Falls Women's Rights Convention held

1849
March 4—Zachary Taylor inaugurated as twelfth president

1850
July 9—Millard Fillmore inaugurated as thirteenth president
Council House in Salt Lake City completed (part used as a temporary temple)
September 9—Utah Territory organized by Congress
September 29—Fillmore appoints Brigham Young Utah territorial governor

1853
February 14—Salt Lake Temple groundbreaking ceremony
March 4—Franklin Pierce inaugurated as fourteenth president

1855
May 5—Endowment House, temporary temple, dedicated, used for twenty-two years

1856
Woodruff becomes Church historian
First convention of the Republican Party, held in Philadelphia
October–November—Rescue of Willie and Martin handcart companies

1857
March 4—James Buchanan inaugurated as fifteenth president
Supreme Court's Dred Scott decision declares blacks do not have citizen rights
July 24—Mormons learn the U.S. government is sending an army to quell their nonexistent rebellion
September 11—Massacre at Mountain Meadows

1858
Transatlantic cable laid
June 26—Johnston's Army marches through Salt Lake City

1860
December 20—South Carolina declared its secession from United States

1861
March 4—Lincoln inaugurated as sixteenth president
April 12—Civil War begins at Battle of Fort Sumter
October—First transcontinental telegraph completed

1863
Lincoln issues Emancipation Proclamation abolishing slavery in rebelling states
July 1–3—Battle of Gettysburg

1865
April 9—Civil War ends with Robert E. Lee's surrender to Ulysses S. Grant at Appomattox
April 14—Abraham Lincoln assassinated
April 15—Andrew Johnson inaugurated as seventeenth president
December 18—Thirteenth Amendment abolishes slavery

1868
Fourteenth Amendment ratified, recognizing blacks as citizens

1869
March 4—Ulysses S. Grant inaugurated as eighteenth president
May 10—Transcontinental Railroad finished at Promontory Summit in Utah

1871
August 23—J.D.T. McAllister assists Hayden Wells Church in doing baptisms for the dead for Signers of the Declaration and a few U.S. presidents
November 9—St. George Temple site dedicated by President George A. Smith, First Counselor to Brigham Young

1873
March 10—St. George cornerstone laid

1876
July 4—Declaration of Independence Centennial celebration
August 9—John M. Bernhisel performs baptisms for the dead on behalf of most of the presidents, including Martin Van Buren (Woodruff is present at the same time in the Endowment House in Salt Lake City)
November—Woodruff and J.D.T. McAllister work on endowment ceremony text

1877
January 1—Completed parts of the St. George Temple dedicated by Brigham Young
January 9—First baptisms for the dead performed in St. George Temple
January 11—First endowments for the dead
March 1—Woodruff is assisted by 154 women in doing temple work for 130 women from his family
March 4—Rutherford B. Hayes inaugurated as nineteenth president
March 10—Woodruff marries Eudora Lovina Young
March 23—John D. Lee executed for his part in Mountain Meadows Massacre
March 30—Woodruff performs endowment for Robert Mason
April 6—Completed St. George Temple fully dedicated
April 8—Woodruff becomes St. George Temple president
April 13—Woodruff sealed to his deceased father
August 15–August 16—Likely dates of Woodruff's two recurring dreams/visions of Signers of the Declaration of Independence
August 18—Woodruff compiles a list of Signers and other eminent men and women to have their temple work done
August 21—Woodruff baptized by John D.T. McAllister for 54 of the 56 Signers of the Declaration of Independence and also other eminent men (work for others, including eminent women, also begun this day)
August 29—President Brigham Young dies, and John Taylor, as senior Apostle, succeeds him as Church leader

September 16—Woodruff's first-known public description of the visions of the Signers given in the Tabernacle

1881
March 4—James A. Garfield inaugurated as twentieth president
September 19—Garfield dies from an assassin's bullet, Chester A. Arthur inaugurated as twenty-first president

1884
May 17–19—Logan Temple dedicated

1885
March 4—Grover Cleveland inaugurated as twenty-second president
November 10—Phebe Whittemore Carter dies, Woodruff can't attend funeral because of persecution over plural marriage

1887
Edmunds-Tucker Act against plural marriage passed
July 25—John Taylor dies, Woodruff succeeds him as senior Apostle and Church leader

1888
May—Manti Temple dedicated

1889
March 4—Benjamin Harrison inaugurated as twenty-third president
April 7—Wilford Woodruff sustained as President of the Church

1890
September 24—Woodruff issues Manifesto ending plural marriage

1893
March 4—Grover Cleveland inaugurated as twenty-fourth president
April—Woodruff mentions the vision of the Signers in two sessions of the dedication of the Salt Lake Temple

1894
April 8—Woodruff announces in general conference that he received revelation to end the practice of spiritual adoption
November 13—Woodruff helps organize Utah Genealogical Society

1896
January 4—Utah becomes the forty-fifth state

1897
March 4—William McKinley inaugurated as twenty-fifth president
December 12—Woodruff mentions the vision of the Signers during a stake conference

1898
February 15—The *Maine* explodes in Havana Harbor, bringing on the Spanish-American War
April 10—Woodruff mentions the vision of the Signers in his last talk at general conference
April 25–August 12—Spanish-American War
September 2—Woodruff dies in San Francisco, California

PROLOGUE

They came to him.

One died in a duel. Another was poisoned by his nephew.

There was a smuggler, a preacher, and a poet.

There were slaveholders, and there were abolitionists.

Some were the richest men in America, and some couldn't afford new clothes. But all of them came together with one purpose.

They had triggered a revolution of freedom a century earlier—and now, in a gleaming white temple among red, stony cliffs in an isolated town in the West, the Signers of the Declaration of Independence were coming to a seventy-year-old man. And he was asleep.

They needed his help, these men who were the "best spirits the God of heaven could find on the face of the earth."[1] They needed liberty again. And they were laying the groundwork for yet another revolution—one of even greater magnitude than the first—in which Wilford Woodruff, an Apostle of The Church of Jesus Christ of Latter-day Saints and president of the St. George Temple in southern Utah in 1877, would set them free.

* * *

Freedom and liberty were not a rallying cry for the Patriots of 1776 alone but also for Mormons a century later. Both felt they had laws and magistrates thrust upon them without proper representation, though the irony of the situation lay in the 1876 Mormons feeling that their arm of oppression came not from the British but from their fellow Americans. The Mormons believed deeply in the hope and promise of freedom inaugurated in the Declaration of Independence and codified in the United States Constitution, but they fought a seemingly endless battle to enjoy those blessings because greed, corruption, and other unrighteousness had led the Federal government and its appointees in Utah Territory to stray from the path the Founding Fathers had laid out.

And so the Mormons celebrated the centennial of the founding of the nation with mixed feelings because of the effect the current state of the nation had on them.

The Church of Jesus Christ of Latter-day Saints has as one of its basic principles the idea of change—of continuing revelation. Its members believe in repentance and that all people are children of a Heavenly Father who loves them and

The Cradle of Liberty, Independence Hall Philadelphia, Pennsylvania, 1991; photograph by Ronald Fox

XIII

Wilford Woodruff, Pioneer Park dedication, July 24, 1898; one of his last public addresses before his death; by Charles Ellis Johnson, Ronald Fox Collection

wants to help them. In the second century since the founding of the United States, Church members have moved on from the hardships of earlier years, and they have allowed those who misused them to do the same, viewing them as brothers and sisters in God and a group who has overcome and learned from their mistakes. The mistrust between American Mormons and their country is gone—except, perhaps, for the same distrust the Founding Fathers hoped all Americans would perpetually maintain: the distrust of power.[2]

As the Church continues to grow and change through continuing revelation, its understanding of its purpose here on earth increases. Along with members' responsibilities to spread the gospel to the world, perfect themselves, and help those around them, the responsibility to redeem the dead weighs heavily on their minds, and temple work continues to intensify. When Mormons first built temples in Utah, they thought differently about their purposes, though some things haven't changed, such as men and women being married for time and all eternity and members performing baptisms on behalf of dead family members.

Other practices have changed—expanded by practical experience and especially revelation, even through visions.

Wilford Woodruff stands at the center of the changes in the Church, having paved the path for how Church members perceive the eternal family of all mankind and how they view the freedoms brought forth through the Founding Fathers. He was foreordained to this cause. His experiences in life prepared him not only for visions of the Signers of the Declaration of Independence but also for an understanding of the significance of what they demanded from him.

Woodruff's intense interest in seeking out his own family history and his untiring efforts to perform proxy ordinances for them was an act of love. The divine guidance he received expanded that love to include more people than his family circle. His revelations ending plural marriage and the now-little-known practice of spiritual adoption, along with his all-important vision of the Signers, set the stage for an understanding that made Mormons integrate the temple more fully into their worship and broaden their understanding of the reach of Christ's Atonement, power, and love.

The Signers of the Declaration of Independence helped teach Wilford Woodruff that families are what the temple is all about.

Chapter 1
I HAVE A MOTHER THERE

In 1841, when Wilford Woodruff first heard the Prophet Joseph Smith speak about doing vicarious work for the dead, one of the first things he thought was, "I have a mother in the spirit world."[3]

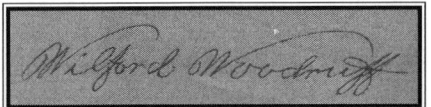

But he had no memory of her.

Woodruff was only fifteen months old when his twenty-six-year-old mother, Bulah, contracted spotted fever and died in June 1808. Woodruff's father, Aphek, remarried seventeen months later to Azubah, who had six children—four who died before reaching adulthood.[4]

Death surrounded Woodruff as he grew, and it shaped his life.

Death was also part of one of the first dreams he considered to have come from God.

Woodruff was eleven years old when he dreamed of a great gulf through which everyone in the world had to pass and drop their worldly goods before they could move on when they died. In the dream, he saw an aged man. "The man looked very sorrowful," Woodruff said. "I saw him come with something on his back, which he had to drop among the general pile before he could enter the gulf."

A few years later, after Woodruff moved to another town with his father and stepmother, he ran across a man he recognized as being the aged man from his dream. "I knew him the moment I saw him," he said. "His name was Chauncy Deming."

Deming died a few years later, and Woodruff attended the man's funeral. When the coffin was being lowered into the grave, Woodruff again remembered the dream. "And that night his son-in-law found one hundred thousand dollars in a cellar belonging to the old man," he said.[5]

For Woodruff, the lesson was that God could use dreams to tell people truths—and one of those truths was how the grave separated people from the things of this world.

* * *

As Woodruff grew older, he became a "seeker," someone who looked for God to send new Apostles and prophets who would bring back, or restore, the original Christian church. In 1828, Woodruff was twenty-one and working at his aunt's mill when, in a nearby town, he met a visionary man, another seeker, named Robert Mason.

Mason told Woodruff about a vision he'd had of an orchard. In Mason's vision,

Top: Signature of Wilford Woodruff; scan from a temple dedication ticket by Ronald Fox

Bottom: Aphek Woodruff, father of Wilford Woodruff, Salt Lake City, Utah 1860, photo by Edward Martin, Ronald Fox Collection.

1

the trees bore no fruit, died, and fell to the ground. Then, from the roots, new trees instantly grew and bore fruit. Mason reached out and grabbed some of the fruit, but before he could sink his teeth into it, the vision ended. Mason said the Lord's voice explained the meaning of the vision: He couldn't find the original Christian church because it wasn't yet upon the earth.[6]

Mason finished recounting his vision by telling Woodruff, "I shall never partake of this fruit in the flesh, but you will and you will become a conspicuous actor in that kingdom."[7]

On December 29, 1833, Woodruff went to a local schoolhouse to hear two Mormon missionaries, Zera Pulsipher and Elijah Cheney, preach. Upon hearing their words, Woodruff's search came to a close. He believed he had found the Restoration of the original Christian church and that a living prophet named Joseph Smith Jr. was leading it. On the last day of 1833, Wilford Woodruff was baptized into the Church of Christ, which would officially be called The Church of Jesus Christ of Latter-day Saints in 1838.[8]

One of the first people Woodruff thought of after he was baptized was Robert Mason. He wrote him a long letter telling him about the true gospel, and Woodruff said Mason received the news with joy—but died at the age of eighty-six, before he could be baptized by someone holding the authority Mason had so long sought.[9]

Mason held the fruit in his hands but didn't taste it.

Woodruff ate it whole.

Less than five months after he was baptized, Woodruff traveled with Zion's Camp to Missouri. The expedition, led by the Prophet Joseph Smith, was ostensibly to bring relief to members of the Church who were being persecuted in Missouri, but the camp journeyed and then disbanded without reaching its end goal. Even with the dissolution of the camp's purpose, the experience had life-changing effects on Woodruff.

Joseph Smith, Jr., circa 1844; National Portrait Gallery, Washington, D.C., from the Community of Christ Church; photograph by Ronald Fox

In January 1835, a little over a year after he was baptized, Woodruff left Missouri on a mission to preach the gospel in Arkansas and Tennessee. After his two-year mission, he was called to the First Quorum of the Seventy and married Phebe Carter. Just a few months later, in the summer of 1837, he was called on his second mission, this time to the Fox Islands near Maine.

During his mission, Woodruff was called to be a member of the Quorum of the Twelve Apostles. He didn't find out about the call until a month later in August 1838. Not only had he found a church

2

with Apostles, but he was to become one of them. After Woodruff's mission, Brigham Young finally ordained him to the apostleship in April 1839, and four months later, Woodruff was off to England on yet another mission.

He arrived in England on January 11, 1840, and eventually helped about 2,000 people join the Church. He did not personally see, however, what was going on at home while he was an ocean away. Much to his grief, his first child, Sarah, died, but he found consolation in hearing that his first son, Wilford, was born.

And Joseph Smith preached for the first time on baptism for the dead.

Brigham Young, circa 1840s, from the book *Route from Liverpool to Great Salt Lake Valley*; by Frederick Piercy & James Linforth, 1855

Chapter 2
REDEEMING THE DEAD

The first time Joseph Smith publically mentioned baptism for the dead was in an August 15, 1840, funeral sermon for Seymour Brunson, a member of Nauvoo's high council.[10]

Woodruff didn't hear it preached until after he returned from his mission to England in October 1841. He later recalled the event: "He [Joseph Smith] called us together and told us that the Lord had revealed to him a principle whereby we could go forth and redeem our dead. It was like a shaft of light from the throne of God to our hearts. It opened a field as wide as eternity to our minds."[11]

The doctrinal foundation for baptism for the dead rested on several New Testament concepts. First, Jesus was emphatic that baptism was necessary for salvation; for example, in Mark 16:16, Christ says, "He that believeth and is baptized shall be saved; but he that believeth not shall be damned." In Peter, it mentions how Christ, in spirit, "preached unto the spirits in prison" (1 Peter 3:19). And in 1 Corinthians 15:29, Paul used the Corinthians' practice of doing vicarious baptisms as part of a list of proofs that there is a Resurrection.

By revelation, Joseph Smith came to understand how those who didn't have a complete chance to accept the gospel of Christ in this life would have that chance in the next. Members of the Church could be baptized on behalf of the dead—giving them the opportunity to accept not only the gospel of Christ but His saving ordinances as well.

As with all doctrines, understanding came line upon line. At first, people went down to the Mississippi River to be baptized for dead relatives, but few or no records were kept. Additionally, women and men were baptized for both sexes, and they continued to use the river for baptisms until they could build a temple in which they could perform the ordinance. Their enthusiasm and joy for the revealed truth trumped order.

Most of the time, Latter-day Saints in Nauvoo (and later in the West) were baptized for deceased family members, such as aunts, uncles, nephews, and parents, but they were also were baptized on behalf of friends. On rare occasions, those "friend" baptisms were for historical heroes. One reason they performed these types of baptisms was because genealogical work was still a

Top: Joseph Smith, Jr., circa 1840s; 19th century engraving based on Maudsley

4

Nauvoo, Illinois, circa 1843; from the book *Route from Liverpool to Great Salt Lake Valley* by Frederick Piercy & James Linforth, 1855

difficult and expensive proposition, so it was hard to find their own family members. It was much easier to gather readily accessible information for famous people. Another reason had to do with early members' admiration and respect for heroes, people they probably thought would have accepted the gospel had they known about it or been alive after the Restoration.[12]

In 1841, there were several such baptisms. Nehemiah Brush was baptized for his "friends" Anthony Wayne (a Revolutionary War general) and Zebulon Pike (a famous explorer).[13] James Adams was baptized for an unrelated "friend" who shared his last name: John Adams, one of the Signers of the Declaration of Independence.[14] Sarah M. Cleveland was baptized for her "friend" Martha Washington.[15] Martha Washington's famous husband, George, had his baptism performed for him multiple times, including once by the Prophet Joseph Smith's brother Don Carlos.[16]

Other notable proxy baptisms included Benjamin Franklin, James Madison, James Monroe, Thomas Jefferson, William Henry Harrison, and Marquis de Lafayette, among others.[17]

The practice of baptizing for the dead outside a temple took place from August 15, 1840, until October 3, 1841, when Joseph Smith said, "There shall be no more baptisms for the dead, until the ordinance can be attended to in the font of the Lord's House. . . . *For thus saith the Lord!*"[18]

Woodruff was on his way back from his mission to England when Joseph Smith gave this sermon, but he may have read the account in the *Times and Seasons* newspaper a few weeks later.

Martha Washington; 19th century engraving

George Washington; 19th century engraving

5

The wait to resume baptisms for the dead didn't last long, however, and on November 8, 1841, Joseph Smith and Brigham Young privately dedicated a wood baptismal font in the unfinished Nauvoo Temple's basement—which was exposed to the elements. After a shed was built over the font, the font was more publically dedicated on November 21. Baptisms for the dead were performed that day for about forty people, and Woodruff was there and helped perform the confirmations.[19]

The construction of a stone font to replace the wood one or other construction-related reasons may have led some, including Woodruff, to later resume performing baptisms for the dead in the river.[20]

For example, in March 1842, Woodruff saw Joseph Smith perform some of these baptisms in the Mississippi River and later followed the Prophet's lead, performing with his wife, Phebe, and others vicarious baptisms for family members, including his mother, Bulah, who died in 1808, and his dead friend Robert Mason.[21]

A non-Mormon who was living in Nauvoo, Charlotte Haven, wrote in May 1843 about a river baptism. She was on a walk along the river with others, watching sheets of ice floating by. "Then we followed the bank toward town, and rounding a little point . . . we spied quite a crowd of people, and soon perceived there was a baptism," she wrote. "Two elders stood knee-deep in the icy cold water, and immersed one after another as fast as they could come down the bank. We soon observed that some of them went in and were plunged several times. We were told that they were baptized for the dead who had not had an opportunity of adopting the doctrines of the Latter Day Saints. So these poor mortals in ice-cold water were releasing their ancestors and relatives from purgatory!" She came closer and could hear some of the names of the dead for whom people were being baptized. "And you can imagine our surprise when the name George Washington was called. So after these fifty years he is out of purgatory and on his way to the 'celestial' heaven!"[22]

* * *

Woodruff had more than the ordinance of baptism for the dead on his mind. Joseph Smith introduced the temple endowment to select members of the Church beginning in 1842. The endowment was, as its name implies, a gift of knowledge and power from God and built upon earlier vestiges of the ordinance that were part of the Saints' worship in the Kirtland Temple.

The endowment taught truths in symbolism and ritual. It gave a sweeping view of the context of human history within the eternities of God's purposes. It was a depiction and symbolic reenactment of the journey of mankind that culminated with a symbolic reunion, effectuated by Christ's Atonement, with God the Father in His celestial kingdom. In it was an overview of the life of each individual, the history of God's intervention in time, and the exaltation of those who made and kept sacred covenants with their Heavenly Father in the name of Christ. It gave eternal perspective and deeper meaning to everyday life.[23]

At the laying of the southeast cornerstone of the Salt Lake Temple, Young publicly defined the endowment as follows: "Your *endowment* is, to receive all those ordinances in the House of the Lord, which are necessary for you, after you have departed this life, to enable you to walk back to the presence of the Father, passing the angels who stand as sentinels, being enabled to give them the key words, the signs and tokens, pertaining to the Holy Priesthood, and gain your eternal exaltation in spite of earth and hell."[24]

The endowment also bound the Apostles and other faithful members of the Church together. On November 11, 1843, Wilford and Phebe were sealed as husband and wife "for time and all eternity" by Hyrum Smith.[25]

Less than a month later, on December 2, Woodruff received his endowment in the second-story assembly room over Joseph Smith's Red Brick Store in Nauvoo. Phebe received her endowment on December 23.[26]

Joseph Smith continued to learn more about proxy work for the dead and expanded it. In the same way husbands and wives could be eternally sealed together in this life, husbands and wives who had died could also have a marriage sealing performed on their behalf.[27]

The connections between husbands and wives and children were like a spiritual priesthood chain. Joseph Smith described it as a "welding link" and then said it was necessary "that a whole and complete and perfect union, and welding together of dispensations, and keys, and powers, and glories should take place, and be revealed from the days of Adam even to the present time" (D&C 128:18).

The work of redeeming the dead required the work of people on both sides of the veil. Those dead in spirit "prison" needed to have the gospel of Christ taught to them. To gain the full blessings of accepting Christ, they needed to accept His ordinances—and those ordinances needed to be done on their behalf by someone living. The full implications of this doctrine were only beginning to reach people's understanding, but Joseph Smith gloried in it. "Brethren, shall we not go on in so great a cause? Go forward and not backward. Courage, brethren; and on, on to the victory! Let your hearts rejoice, and be exceedingly glad. Let the earth

Nauvoo Temple, Nauvoo, Illinois, circa 1845; Church History Library Collection

break forth into singing. Let the dead speak forth anthems of eternal praise to the King Immanuel, who hath ordained, before the world was, that which would enable us to redeem them out of their prison; for the prisoners shall go free" (D&C 128:22).

As part of connecting and sealing people together, Joseph Smith also taught what became known as the law of adoption. The idea of adoption, in this context, reflected the understanding that was just beginning to come forth about connecting people in a grand, eternal family or kingdom. Active members of the Church were often not sealed to their own ancestral families because they didn't want to risk having their ancestors reject the gospel. They were afraid that such sealings would be futile and empty gestures, connections to dead branches of their family trees as far as priesthood and eternal exaltation were concerned. Their lack of understanding because the depth of redemption had not yet been fully revealed led them to be sealed to leading General Authorities—both living and dead. The practice created expanded families and a spiritual kinship between the living members of the Church.[28] "Through this heaven family, all of humanity could be interconnected in indissoluble bonds—the broad kinship group was the actual structure of heaven," historian Samuel Morris Brown wrote. "The Mormon heaven family provided a network of eternal belonging for the Latter-day Saints."[29]

Joseph Smith, Jr.; 19th century engraving from a painting by D. Rogers, 1842
Frontispiece, *A Journey to Great Salt Lake* by Julies Remy

It was the structure of heaven. It was an eternal network.[30] It was like a great family tree, except the practice of adoption was like grafting branches into family lines that had accepted the gospel instead of staying attached to family lines that had rejected it.

When Joseph Smith was martyred at the hands of a mob in a jail in Carthage, Illinois, on June 27, 1844, Woodruff was, like most of the Twelve, away on a mission—this time as part of a campaign for Joseph Smith to become president of the United States. By August 6, 1844, Woodruff and most of the Apostles were back in Nauvoo, and they had asserted their priesthood right to leadership over the Church.

In the years that followed, the Apostles supervised the finishing of the Nauvoo temple and the administration of the endowment to eager members of the Church. Woodruff once again left on a mission to England—this time taking Phebe with him. It wasn't difficult for him to affirm the

Hyrum Smith;
19th century engraving from a painting by D. Rogers, 1842
Frontispiece, *A Journey to Great Salt Lake* by Julies Remy

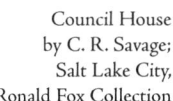
Council House by C. R. Savage; Salt Lake City, Ronald Fox Collection

authority of the Apostles in England when so many in that country had joined the Church under their watch.[31]

Woodruff and his wife returned to Nauvoo on April 13, 1846, and, already, many members of the Church were on their way west. Young, as President of the Quorum of the Twelve, had led the efforts and had even used some of Saints' recently created family groups, through the adoption process, to structure the exodus.[32] Woodruff didn't waste time in following the Saints into the wilderness. By the end of the month, his three full wagons had crossed the river and were facing west.

But there was one more task for him to complete before he journeyed on.

In the evening, on Thursday, April 30, Woodruff and fellow Apostle Orson Hyde gathered with about twenty other elders to hold the first meeting to dedicate the Nauvoo Temple. Although the temple had been in use in part and dedicated in part, this was the culmination of presenting a finished temple to God. The next day, they held a public dedication session, followed by a final dedication on Sunday. In that dedication service, Hyde took a vote to sell the temple to help finance the emigration of poor members of the Church to the unknown West. The plan to raise large sums by the sale never succeeded. It was eventually sold for $5,000, a fraction of its worth, in the spring of 1848 but then burned to the ground in October of that year after an unknown arsonist set it on fire.[33]

The Nauvoo Temple fulfilled prophecy, redeemed the dead, and braced the Saints for the trials ahead. It had served its purpose. It would be thirty-one years before Woodruff would participate in the dedication of another temple—1,500 miles distant, far away in the West.

Almost six years after arriving in the Great Salt Lake Valley, on February 14, 1853, the Saints broke ground for another temple. It would be forty years before they would complete it, so in the meantime, they needed somewhere to perform temple ordinances.

The Endowment House on the northwest corner of Temple Square; Ronald Fox Collection

They performed endowments and marriage sealings upstairs in the Council House—a government building finished in 1850. On February 3, 1854, Woodruff led two of his children through the endowment in the Council House.[34]

Six months later, on August 4, the foundation work began on a temporary temple or, as it became known, the Endowment House.[35]

Chapter 3

A TEMPORARY TEMPLE

The Endowment House,
Salt Lake City;
Ronald Fox Collection

The Endowment House was built in the northwest corner of Temple Square in Salt Lake City and was dedicated on May 5, 1855.[36] There was nothing grand about the appearance of the building—it was the

structure's use that made it special, and for twenty-two years, it was the closest thing the Church had to a temple.

In 1873, after the Saints began construction on the St. George Temple, Young explained how some ordinances "must be performed in a Temple that is erected expressly for the purpose" while other ordinances could be performed without a temple. "We can, at the present time, go into the Endowment House and be baptized for the dead, receive our washings and anointing, etc.," he said.[37]

Baptisms for the dead, the endowment for the living, and marriage sealings for both the living and the dead could be done in the Endowment House, but sealing children to their parents, doing adoption sealings, and doing endowments for the dead had to be performed in "a Temple prepared for that purpose."[38]

"No one can receive endowments for another, until a Temple is prepared in which to administer them," he said. "We administer just so far as the law permits us to do."[39]

Before the St. George Temple was built, the Endowment House was not a center of ongoing worship for most members of the Church. People rarely returned after receiving their endowment and being married. There was no need—except, perhaps, to perform a few baptisms for the dead or to be sealed to a plural wife.[40]

But that would change.

Woodruff bucked the trend, and whenever he was in the Salt Lake Valley, he spent more and more of his time officiating in the Endowment House,[41] performing endowment and sealing ceremonies for the living.

Woodruff had a deep interest in his own dead relatives and gathered many

St. George Temple
under construction;
Utah State Historical Society
Collection

11

John D. T. McAllister, early St. George Church leader; 19th century engraving, Ronald Fox Collection

records while on his missions in England. He performed a large number of their ordinances in the Endowment House in June 1869.[42]

* * *

Historian Brian H. Stuy did yeoman's work investigating what proxy temple ordinances were performed in the Endowment House for prominent men and women. He found that Signers of the Declaration of Independence and former presidents of the United States had baptisms done on their behalf in the 1870s before the St. George Temple was completed.[43]

Haden Wells Church, whom Joseph Smith baptized into the Church in 1841, showed his own concern for the Founding Fathers. In the Endowment House in 1871 and in 1872, he performed baptisms for the dead in behalf of twenty-nine of the fifty-six Signers of the Declaration of Independence and for several presidents of the United States.[44] John D.T. McAllister was the recorder and confirmed Church for several of these baptisms on August 23, 1871, including hard-to-forget names such as Benjamin Franklin, Andrew Jackson, and James K. Polk. Not all the other names of the Signers baptized and confirmed that day were instantly recognizable, but Church likely explained to McAllister and the others present who they were.[45]

Another Signer, Oliver Wolcott, had his baptism performed by a descendant on September 13, 1872.[46]

John M. Bernhisel, a physician and representative of Utah in the United States Congress between 1849 and 1863, also did baptisms for the dead on behalf of several prominent people.[47] On June 25, 1873, he was baptized for abolitionist and journalist Horace Greeley (Greeley had died eight months earlier after unsuccessfully running for president against Ulysses S. Grant). Greeley became acquainted with the Church when he visited Salt Lake City back in 1859.

Bernhisel was also baptized for William Henry Seward, who, as Andrew Johnson's secretary of state, was most famous for his role in the purchase of Alaska from Russia in 1867. Bernhisel also performed a baptism for George Clymer, a Signer of the Declaration of Independence from Pennsylvania.[48] The next year, Bernhisel was baptized for philosopher John Locke, President Millard Fillmore, writer Washington Irving, and Signer Benjamin Rush.[49] In 1875, he added Charles Carroll of Carrollton to the list of Signers he had baptized.

John M. Bernhisel, Utah's First Congressional Delegate; John M. Bernhisel baptized by proxy many of the Founding Fathers; Ronald Fox Collection

12

The year 1876 was the centennial of the signing of the Declaration of Independence. Bernhisel celebrated it in his own way by being baptized on behalf of many of the Founding Fathers and other political leaders.[50]

On August 9, 1876, Bernhisel and his daughter Mary performed baptisms on behalf of most of the presidents and first ladies of the United States. Among those presidents was Martin Van Buren, who was a very unpopular figure among members of the Church because of his refusal to help the Mormons against Missouri's state-approved persecutions in the late 1830s. James Buchanan, who died in 1868, was another unpopular president for Mormons because he sent an army in 1857 to quell a nonexistent rebellion. Bernhisel did not do Buchanan's proxy baptism.

Woodruff was also in the Endowment House on the day Bernhisel performed these presidential proxy baptisms. Woodruff didn't mention the baptisms of presidents when he recorded the day's events, but he did mention that 500 baptisms for the dead were done that day, along with his being proxy for thirty-three marriage sealings for the dead. So it was possible he could have known of the baptisms, given their unusual nature and the smallness of the Endowment House.[51]

A few weeks later, on August 23, Bernhisel was again at the Endowment House. This time he concentrated on having baptisms performed for the Signers of the Declaration of Independence and also the signers of the U.S. Constitution.[52] He did not redo the baptisms for the two Signers he had already been baptized for, Carroll and Rush, nor did he do the work for James Wilson and John Adams—perhaps knowing Adams's and Wilson's work was done previously in Nauvoo.

There is no indication Bernhisel knew of Church's 1871 and 1872 baptisms of many of the Signers. The way records were kept and submitted and checked at that time meant work was often duplicated.

The Endowment House was used from 1855 until the St. George Temple was dedicated in 1877. On October 25, 1876, a few months before the St. George Temple was dedicated, a letter from the First Presidency stated, "In the days of our

Signing of the Declaration of Independence; from a painting by Jonthan Trumbull, 1817; 19th century engraving

St. George Temple original spire; Utah State Historical Society Collection

poverty, and while we had no Temple in which to administer ordinances for the dead and to give endowments and to perform sealings and other ordinances for the living, the Lord permitted us to erect an Endowment House in this city—. This we have used for many years, and many ordinances have been administered therein; but there are other important ordinances which have not been, and cannot be, administered, except in a Temple built and dedicated to the Most High for that purpose. Such a Temple we now have so far completed at St. George that we can commence attending to these ordinances there."[53]

In its thirty-four years of use, the Endowment House had stayed busy. There were 134,053 baptisms and confirmations done on behalf of the dead and 68,767 marriage sealings performed for both the living and the dead. The unofficial count also had 54,170 endowments for the living.[54]

Later in the next year, after President Young died, President John Taylor allowed the Endowment House to be used for the aged and infirm and for young people being married. It was finally closed and torn down in 1889 after Woodruff became President of The Church of Jesus Christ of Latter-day Saints.

Brigham Young, circa 1868; Utah State Historical Society Collection

Chapter 4
"THE VARY THUNDERS OF HEAVEN" —A TEMPLE IN ST. GEORGE

When Apostle Erastus Snow heard Young announce the building of a temple in St. George on January 31, 1871, he shouted, "Glory; Hallelujah."[55] His exuberance reflected the love he had for the hardscrabble pioneers who stuck it out in the desert.

And desert it was. A poem by Charles L. Walker described St. George when it was first colonized:

> They said the land it was no good,
> And the water was no gooder,
> And the bare idea of living here
> Was enough to make one shudder.
> Mesquite, soaproot, prickly-pears and briars,
> St. George ere long will be a place that everyone admires.[56]

The St. George Temple progressed faster than the temple being built in Salt Lake City. President George A. Smith, First Counselor to President Young, dedicated the site on November 9, 1871.[57]

A few years later, on March 10, 1873, the cornerstone was laid.[58] Work continued until November 1876, when Woodruff left Salt Lake City to travel to St. George with President Young, Assistant Counselor in the First Presidency George Q. Cannon, and other General Authorities of the Church.[59]

Not only were they going there to dedicate the temple, but they were also going there for the winter and the prophet's health.

When Woodruff and Young's party reached the town eight days after leaving Salt Lake, Woodruff called the view of the gleaming temple "a glorious sight."[60] The next few months saw continued work on the temple, and Woodruff, along with McAllister, wrote the ceremonies for work in the temple.[61] In the same way the Nauvoo Temple was dedicated and used in part before its completion, the St. George Temple had enough work completed on the baptismal font and the endowment ordinance areas that a partial dedication could take place.

On New Year's Day 1877, about 2,000 people gathered in the temple's basement at noon. Ten members of the Quorum of the Twelve Apostles were present.[62]

Young's rheumatism in his feet was so bad that three men had to carry him around in a chair, but he was still present.[63]

Woodruff offered the first dedicatory prayer at 12:30 p.m. from the upper step of the baptismal font. The experience may have reminded him of the

Wilford Woodruff, August 23, 1844, age 37 years; earliest-known documented image of the Nauvoo period; this is the first publication of this image; daguerreotype by Lucien R. Foster; Ronald Fox Collection

St George Temple near completion; Ronald Fox Collection

day in 1841 when he was at the public dedication of the baptismal font in the unfinished Nauvoo Temple.

At the St. George Temple dedication, Woodruff reminded those gathered around him that they were blessed with a privilege few since the days of Adam had ever enjoyed—the blessing of entering a temple of God. Then he prayed: "O our God we thy sons and daughters have assembled to gether in the Name of thy Son Jesus Christ within the walls of this Temple this day for the Purpose of dedicating and Consecrating a portion of this house unto the Lord Our God that it may be Holy and acceptable in thy sight. May the prayers of thy People ascend into thine ears O Lord, and be heard and answerd upon their heads."[64]

After Woodruff prayed, the choir sang a song by Charles L. Walker titled quite simply "Temple Dedication Song":

And down the stream of times great river,
How many million souls have sped
No ray of hope bid them deliver,
Themselves nor ee'n their kindred dead
(Chorus)

Glory to God! O Praise the Lamb!
Let all the Angelic Legions sing.
The Temple of our God's completed
Hossanna! praise the Lord our King.[65]

The group then moved upstairs for further prayer and dedication. At the end of the dedication service, the prophet Brigham Young rose from his chair and stood painfully at the pulpit.

"What do you suppose the fathers would say if they Could speak from the dead?" Young said. "Would they not say we 'have lain here thousands of years here in this prison House waiting for this dispensation to Come. Here we are bound and fettered in the association of those who are filthy.' What would they whisper in our Ears? Why if they had the power the vary thunders of heaven would be in our Ears if we Could but realize the importance of the work we are ingaged in. All the Angels in heaven are looking at this little handful of people."[66]

Young also announced the schedule for temple ordinances: Tuesdays and Wednesdays would be for baptisms for the dead. Thursdays and Fridays would be for sealings and endowments. The division was necessary because the endowment ceremony used some of the space utilized by the baptistry.

And then he said, "Amen," and appeared to be finished before wondering aloud whether those present were satisfied with the dedication services. Then he thundered,

"I am not half satisfied and I never Expect to be satisfied untill the devil is whiped and driven from off the face of the Earth." He gave the pulpit a solid blow with his knotty hickory cane as he spoke, whacking it as if he were cracking it across Satan's skull, and left deep dents in the new finish that are still in the soft wood of the pulpit today.[67]

Woodruff later summarized his feelings in his journal: "This is a vary important day to the Church and Kingdom of God on the Earth."[68]

* * *

Eight days later, on Tuesday, January 9, the first baptisms for the dead in the St. George Temple were performed. It was noon when Woodruff stepped into the font to baptize Suzie Amelia Young Dunford for her deceased friend Mary Sheppard. Charles Walker wrote in his journal about the experience: "Brother Brigham, lame as he was, by the aid of his crutch and stick ascended the steps up to the font and witnessed the first Baptism. I stood near the font, and watched them baptize and could not refrain from shedding tears of joy on beholding the commencement of so great a work."[69]

Woodruff baptized the first 141 people. He and Young then performed the proxy ordinance of confirmation for those first people baptized. No endowments for the dead were performed that day. In his journal, however, Woodruff described the events of the day as being "the day that the first ordinances of the Endowments for the dead was performed in the Temple of God in St George."[70]

Because he would sometimes skip writing in his journal for several days and then go back later and fill in the missing days, it isn't clear whether he made a mistake when he began writing on this day. It is also possible that he looked at the temple ordinances holistically—as the total number of ordinances being part of one endowment. Even today, members of the Church look at the individual ordinances as separate acts—but the idea of redeeming the dead is broader. No one ordinance would do. As Woodruff wrote in his journal in 1868, "It will take all the ordinances of the gospel of Christ to save [one] soul as much as another." This applied to the living and the dead.[71]

Baptism, confirmation, the Gift of the Holy Ghost, ordination to the priesthood (for men), washings and anointings, and the endowment were all necessary for salvation.

Brigham Young, circa 1870;
Ronald Fox Collection

17

The first day endowments were performed on behalf of the dead in the dispensation of the fulness of times was on Thursday, January 11. Woodruff simply noted sixty-three endowments were performed for the living and ten for the dead.[72]

The opening of a permanent temple in St. George and the need to perform endowments for the dead changed the whole nature of temple worship and gave members of the Church many more opportunities to return to the temple.[73] They wanted to have endowments performed for their deceased family members, who were members of the Church but died without having the temple ordinances performed. Children who died were also sealed to their parents.[74]

The work of redeeming the dead began in a fuller measure than was previously available in the Endowment House in Salt Lake City, and adoptions were again performed. By 1893, a little more than 13,000 adoptions had occurred.[75]

St George Temple with current spire; Utah State Historical Society Collection

After the preliminary dedication, temple construction continued over the next four months. In this time, Young asked Woodruff to "write out the Ceremony of the Endowments from Begining to End,"[76] codifying the ordinance more fully.

A month after the temple dedication, Woodruff wore the first fully white suit in a temple—featuring "doe skin," or soft wool pants and vest.[77] He continued to do the temple work for his own ancestors but wondered how he was ever going to get so many endowments done for the women in his line since none of his wives were there to help him work on the family. At the time, it was the practice to have only family members do the proxy ordinance work for deceased family.

With revelation, which Young confirmed, Woodruff determined that nonfamily members could act as proxy for deceased people. So, on his seventieth birthday, March 1, 1877, 154 women from St. George helped him do endowments for 130 women from his family—including several who were previously sealed to him as plural wives.[78]

* * *

The month was eventful for Woodruff. He was sealed on March 10 to Eudora Lovina Young, a daughter of President Young and Lucy Bigelow Young.[79] Woodruff saw his first adoption ceremony on March 22,[80] and the next day, John D. Lee was executed by a firing squad for his part in the 1857 massacre at Mountain Meadows.[81]

On March 30, 1877, Woodruff acted as a proxy for the first time in performing an endowment for the dead. He did the work for his old friend Mason, who at last could taste of the fruit of the gospel through the ordinances of the temple.[82]

The Forty-Seventh Annual General Conference of The Church of Jesus Christ of Latter-day Saints was held in the St. George Temple. The main order of business in the 10 a.m., Friday, April 6, 1877, conference session was the dedication of the whole and completed temple. President Daniel H. Wells, second counselor to President Young, offered the dedicatory prayer.[83]

Two days later, Woodruff was appointed to take charge of the temple and preside over it as its first temple president.[84]

The spirit of Elijah—turning the hearts of the fathers to the children and the children to the fathers (Malachi 4:6)—was beginning to burn, and the new St. George Temple was its torch.

Chapter 5
PRIESTHOOD AND PATRIOTISM

Two weeks after the final dedication of the temple, Woodruff and Phebe were both sealed to Woodruff's father.[85] It was his heart turning to his father.

On June 16, 1877, his heart would suddenly turn to his children as Woodruff was struck with a sudden pain in his stomach at 1:00 p.m. Three hours later, he perceived the spiritual reason when he was handed a telegram his son David Woodruff had sent about another son, Brigham Woodruff:

"Logan
June 16, 1877
To Wilford Woodruff
St George.
Brigham Woodruff was drowned in Bear River near Smithfield 1 oclok to day. Body not found.
—David Woodruff."

Woodruff's son Brigham Young Woodruff had been hunting close to his home when he drowned. The body wasn't found until six days later, seventy miles downstream.[86]

"He was a good young Man, virtuous, Temperate, Honest, and lived his Religion," Woodruff wrote in his journal. "He had received his Endowments. I have felt Calm, Composed, and reconciled in this bereavement. I have thought that as I was doing so much for the dead here in the Temple in St George, that it might be necessary to have one of the family in the spirit world."

* * *

At 10:00 in the morning on July 4, 1877, Woodruff and much of St. George gathered in the St. George Tabernacle to celebrate Independence Day. McAllister read the Declaration of Independence, then Woodruff gave the keynote oration.[87]

The fact that the Saints could celebrate the founding of the United States while also looking for the country to be punished for its sins against them showed the conflicting feelings they had about the nation. Woodruff prayed during the first dedication of the St. George Temple back on New Year's Day that the nation be broken in pieces, yet here they were, celebrating the birth of freedom and the Founding Fathers.

Just before the centennial year of 1876, he wrote in his journal:

U.S. Flag, circa 1896;
Ronald Fox Collection

20

This is the Commencement of the Centennial year of the American independance.[88] *At the Commencement of the Centaury 1776, and through the Revolutionary war the United States Government was Composed of an honest, industrious, Christian People, and the Leaders were pure true, virtueous, honest industrious Statesmen who labored hard to promote the interest, & welfare of the whole people, and to Establish a free Republican Government. This they did accomplish, and Esstablished laws and a Constitution which was a glorious Legacy to their posterity.*

But Jan. 1, 1876 finds a great Change has Come over the American Government. Virtue has departed from the Land, and Corruption occupies its place. Honesty has been driven from Evry department of Government from the presidential Chair, the Halls of Congress, from Evry Department of State, which has reached through Evry State and Territory Except Utah. . . . The seeds of Death and destruction are sown broad Cast throughout the american government, and are ripening for the Harvest.[89]

Declaration of Independence; Stone engraving, National Archives, Washington, D. C.

"They regard the States pretty much as the States regarded England after the War of Independence," Sir Richard F. Burton wrote in his account of his visit to Salt Lake City in 1860. "Theirs is a deep and abiding resentment, which time will strengthen, not efface: the deeds of Missouri and Illinois will bear fruit for many and many a generation. The federal government, they say, has, so far from protecting their lives and property, left them to be burned out and driven away by the hands of a mob. . . . But, more galling still to human nature, whether of saint or sinner, they are despised, 'treated, in fact, as nobodies'—and that last of insults who can bear?"[90]

But bear it they would—celebrating the promise of America and mourning its then apparent loss of the mandate of heaven. The celebration continued as many went to the temple six or so blocks away to help Woodruff do more of his own personal family work. They performed 100 endowments for his ancestors, and Woodruff wrote in his journal, "This was a great surprise to me and a vary pleasing one as it is helping me vary much to redeem my dead."[91]

But even with the day's emphasis on the Founding Fathers and the Signers of the Declaration of Independence, as well as work for the dead, no temple work was done for America's heroes on that day.

* * *

Wilford Woodruff Journal, 1877; Church History Library Collection

Like Joseph Smith, who had been anxious to reveal the temple endowment ordinances to the Twelve before he died, Young felt a similar push to reorganize the stakes and get things in proper order before he left the earth. He pushed himself, and his health suffered as a result.[92]

Before 1877, six of the Apostles were serving as stake presidents. In some areas, there were presiding bishops over multiple communities. In the Weber Stake, they didn't have bishops but, rather, presidents. Other places had acting bishops, and often bishops did not have two counselors. On top of this and other problems, many members of the Church did not officially belong to any ward. Young recognized changes were necessary to bring the Church organization and practice more in line with the revelations of God.[93]

The catalyst for the 1877 reorganization, according to historian William G. Hartley, was the St. George Temple. The temple and its ordinances were an expression of the heavenly priesthood, and the stakes of Zion were its earthly counterpart.[94] Young's dream was to connect earth's organization and heaven's.

The changes began in St. George itself, with the reorganization of the stake there in April, at the same time the temple was dedicated. Young personally released Apostle Erastus Snow as stake president and replaced him with McAllister,[95] who took over the responsibility of presiding over 816 families (4,592 members) dispersed through fourteen wards.[96]

But there were many more stakes that needed reorganization in the Intermountain West—twenty stakes, with 103,793 members in 240 wards.[97]

Woodruff and Snow put McAllister in charge of the temple[98] and left on July 11, 1877, to do their part in the Church-wide reorganization of stakes. They reorganized the Millard Stake in Fillmore, the Beaver Stake, and the Parowan Stake[99] and created new wards. To fill dwindling Aaronic Priesthood quorums (as more adult men were ordained elders in the Melchizedek Priesthood), they gave youth the priesthood.[100]

As they helped fulfill Young's dream of order, Woodruff soon experienced other types of dreams that would change how he viewed work for the dead.

Chapter 6
DISCERNING DREAMS AND VISIONS OF FREEDOM

Religious people throughout the ages have recognized that God has many ways of revealing His will to mankind. Woodruff often looked to dreams for guidance from the Lord, and when he felt a dream had come from God, he would speak about it in the same way the ancient prophet Lehi did in the Book of Mormon when he said, "Behold, I have dreamed a dream; or, in other words, I have seen a vision" (1 Nephi 8:2; see also 1 Nephi 1:16; 8:36).

Dreams were a fulfillment of the Old Testament prophecy of Joel that God would pour out His spirit upon all flesh and "your old men shall dream dreams, your young men shall see visions" (Joel 2:28; see also Acts 2:17).

Woodruff sometimes spoke or wrote about his dreams as visions and sometimes as appearances or visits.[101] But even though he would often record dreams in his journal and try to find meaning in them, Woodruff did not think all dreams were visions sent by God.

In general conference on October 8, 1881, before he became President of the Church, Woodruff spoke about dreams that were just dreams. "I will tell you just about what I refer to," he said. "A man eats a hot supper when he goes to bed; he gets the nightmare; he is chased by a bear; or he falls over a precipice, and as soon as he strikes the ground he wakes up. Now, the Lord had nothing to do with that."[102]

As another example, he told about his dream from the night before, where he was making houses out of glass blocks. He contrasted this with dreams he had had that were fulfilled and visions he had had of the things of God. "Thus we may have dreams about things of great importance, and dreams of no importance at all," he said. "The Lord warned Joseph in a dream to take the young child Jesus and his mother into Egypt, and thus he was saved from the wrath of Herod. Hence there are a great many things taught us in dreams that are true, and

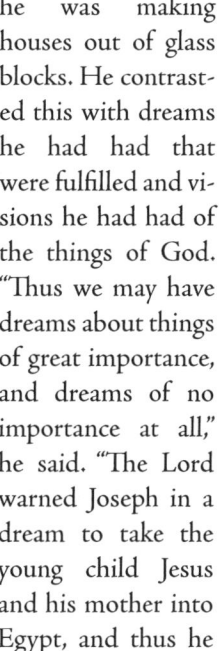

Wilford Woodruff, circa 1885; Utah State Historical Society Collection

23

if a man has the spirit of God he can tell the difference between what is from the Lord and what is not."[103]

Woodruff was aware that dreams from God could include such things as an angel, who appeared and gave instruction (see Matthew 1:19–21 and 2:19–21). They could also be symbolic of larger truths, such as those Daniel in the Old Testament or Lehi in the Book of Mormon experienced (see Daniel 7 and 1 Nephi 8).

And he was aware that dreams from God could occur to change the way people thought, acted, and believed.

* * *

After his month-long trip to organize stakes, Woodruff returned to St. George. The very next day he was back in the temple. Although he lived in a home in St. George, Woodruff may have slept or taken naps in the temple.[104] The sacred building had many rooms that could be used for offices. Accommodations for the president of the temple would naturally also be available for those late-night sessions when he might be too weary to go home or for when he may wish to take a nap. Journal accounts mention beds for these purposes.[105]

When Woodruff experienced his vision of the Signers of the Declaration of Independence, he said it occurred on "two consecutive nights . . . in the Temple at St. George." His journal recorded him doing endowment work on Wednesday, August 15; Thursday, August 16; and Friday, August 17, so it was most likely two of those days. The initial vision probably took place on Wednesday night and the second vision on Thursday evening. Chances are he did not stay overnight in the temple on Friday evening because he may have attended a funeral, and the temple was closed the next day. So, of the three days he spent in the temple that week, it was probably during the first two when he dreamed a dream, or, in other words, saw a vision of the Signers.[106]

Woodruff gave five known accounts of his encounter with the Signers (see the full accounts in the appendixes):

1.) The first account was delivered one month after the experience when he was speaking in the Tabernacle on Temple Square in Salt Lake City on September 16, 1877.[107]

2.) He spoke of it on April 7, 1893, during an evening session of the dedication of the Salt Lake Temple.[108]

3.) He mentioned it April 11, 1893, at another dedicatory session of the Salt Lake Temple.[109]

4.) He referred to it, although somewhat obliquely, during a stake conference in Salt Lake City on December 12, 1897.[110]

5.) The last time Woodruff mentioned the vision was on April 10, 1898—the day he gave his last general conference talk. He died five months later.[111]

Curiously, Woodruff did not directly mention the vision in his journal. But he did write about preparing the list of Signers and other eminent men and women to be baptized for the dead and the exact day the work was done.[112]

So he wrote about all the effects of having the vision on two nights in the temple; he just didn't mention the vision.

It was likely he wrote in his journal after the fact about the days on which the visions occurred and the subsequent work. Although he kept a journal faithfully, he sometimes did not record events on the days they happened.[113]

In this case, he may have hurried through his entry about the days the vision took place so he could get to the long copying work required to record the names he and McAllister did the work for.

Using Woodruff's own accounts (see the full text of the accounts in appendices) and giving the most weight to the earliest version, the visions become clearer.

* * *

In his first public recitation of the vision on September 16, 1877, Woodruff talked about how, for the last 1,800 years, "the people that have lived and passed away never heard the voice of an inspired man, never heard a Gospel sermon, until they entered the spirit-world."[114]

He referred to Young's statement at the January dedication of the St. George Temple about how the dead would, if they were allowed to, thunder in people's ears to get them to build temples and redeem them with temple ordinances.

"We have labored in the St. George Temple since January," Woodruff said, "and we have done all we could there; and the Lord has stirred up our minds, and many things have been revealed to us concerning the dead."[115]

And Woodruff had done all he could, but it wasn't enough.

"The dead will be after you, they will seek after you as they have after us in St. George," Woodruff said. "They called upon us, knowing that we held the keys and power to redeem them."

Flags of the United States; Colonial Flag Foundation; photo by Ronald Fox

25

Then he explained his "night visions" or dreams.[116] They came on "two consecutive nights."[117]

Woodruff said, "They waited on me for two days and two nights," which was an archaic way of saying they visited him over a two-day period, not that they visited him both day and night.

It isn't clear if the dreams were recurring or if each one was unique in its content. When Woodruff described the experiences, he didn't distinguish between the two nights and told the experience as if it were one occurrence. This lends a little toward the idea that the two visions were nearly the same.

He said that in his dream, "the spirits of the dead gathered around me."[118]

In his first account in 1877, he said, "These were the signers of the Declaration of Independence."[119] Two decades later, he added that "General Washington" was part of that group and specified that "every one of those men that signed the Declaration of Independence" was there.[120]

When he talked about the experience, he called it a visit. To him, this was not a symbolic representation that conveyed truth but a group of actual people—spirits of the dead—who had a specific message for him. "You have had the use of the Endowment House for a number of years," they said, "and yet nothing has ever been done for us."[121]

Salt Lake Temple dedication service ticket; Ronald Fox Collection

At least this was what Woodruff remembered of the conversation a month later. His accounts after this did not include any quotes from the Signers. He also didn't indicate who spoke on behalf of the Signers or whether this was a composite statement or an impression or paraphrase of what they said.

In any case, it was an accusation. In 1893, Woodruff said they "argued"[122] with him to do their temple work.[123] It was as if they were saying, "You—the Latter-day Saints—have had the use of the Endowment House to perform your own endowments, but in that house, you have not been able to do that work for the dead. And after all this time, even after building and dedicating a temple where endowments for the dead could be performed, you have still done nothing for us."

They could have mentioned that the Saints had already done baptisms for the dead for them. They also could have mentioned that John Hancock's and William Floyd's endowments had been performed. But they most likely didn't because an endowment for Floyd occurred a second time on August 22, 1877, along with endowments for other Signers and eminent men and women.[124] Hancock's work only occurred once, which could mean Woodruff reviewed the temple records and discovered Hancock's work had already been done.[125]

The Signers continued their argument or application for further temple ordinances. "We laid the foundation of the government you now enjoy," they said, "and we never apostatized from it, but we remained true to it and were faithful to God."[126]

We don't know if Woodruff said anything in reply to the fifty-six spirits who looked into his eyes. He was clearly outnumbered and probably flummoxed. Perhaps he said something similar to the sincere excuses he mentioned in his talk in the Tabernacle a month later. "I thought it very singular, that notwithstanding so much work had been done, and yet nothing had been done for them," he said. "The thought never entered my heart, from the fact, I suppose, that heretofore our minds were reaching after our more immediate friends and relatives."[127]

But the Signers wanted redemption as well. In life they argued for independence; now they were appealing for the binding and connecting ordinances of the house of the Lord.

In his 1898 account, Woodruff said they "demanded at my hands that I should go forth and attend to the ordinances of the House of God for them."[128]

Demanded. Argued. The message was strong. The Signers felt they had been forgotten, which probably hurt since their work had, in some measure, made freedom possible, freedom even to build temples. Now it was time for someone to do something for them that they could not do for themselves.

* * *

It was no accident that those who declared independence would also ask for it. At first glance, the Signers did not come to bring new wisdom. They came for help. But in a deeper sense, they brought the beginnings of a new understanding of temple work, which Woodruff would enhance with future revelation when he became President of the Church.

At the time, though, most members of the Church talked about redeeming the dead as only baptisms for the dead. From 1850 to 1877, there was virtually no mention of doing endowments for the dead.[129] They were not available, so nobody thought about them much.

Except for Woodruff.

When he spoke of redeeming the dead, he went beyond baptisms. He believed the same ordinances that saved people who were still alive were necessary for those who were dead. "It takes just as much to save a dead man as a living man," he said in his 1877 talk about the appearance of the Signers.[130]

And yet Woodruff, as he explained after the vision, had looked mainly after his own ancestors. He had modeled concern for those who had died without the gospel of Christ and had supervised the expansion of vicarious work for the dead, but there wasn't yet an understanding that the saving ordinances of the temple were for all people—relatives and nonrelatives alike. The extent of temple work that seems obvious to today's Church members had not yet been fully revealed, or at least not fully comprehended.[131]

George Washington; painting by Gilbert Stuart, National Portrait Gallery, Washington, D. C.

Declaration of Independence; Dunlap Printing; courtesy of the *Deseret News*

John Hancock, president of the Continental Congress; 19th century engraving

The vision of the Signers changed this in Woodruff's mind, according to historian Richard E. Bennett. "The importance of extending this higher ordinance to this particularly unique group of people, unconnected as they were to any families in the Church, reinforced the doctrine that all the 'worthy dead,' whether family or friend, would be taught the gospel and the ordinances of salvation should be offered to all through proxy work."[132]

In the Salt Lake stake conference in December 1897, Woodruff talked about how only the Latter-day Saints had the power to redeem the dead. "The signers of the Declaration of Independence and the men that laid the foundation of this great American government know full well that there has not been a power on earth where they could apply to have this principle carried out in their behalf, only the Apostles that held the keys of the kingdom of God in this generation," he said. "They have gone to them and plead with them to redeem them because there was no other power on earth could do it, and this has been accomplished."[133]

28

Chapter 7

DOING THE WORK FOR THE SIGNERS AND OTHER EMINENT PEOPLE

To follow the admonition of the Signers in the vision, Woodruff busied himself with their work. On Saturday, August 18, 1877, the temple was closed, and Woodruff wrote, "I spent the day writing."[134] This generic description could have included compiling information, but most likely, it referred to catching up on letters, temple papers, and his journal.

The next day, however, was Sunday, and after a day of meetings, Woodruff worked on the Signers' request. "I spent the Evening in preparing a list of the Noted Men of the 17 Centaury and 18th including the signers of the declaration of Independance and the Presidents of the United States for Baptism on Tuesday the 21 Aug 1877."[135]

Here Woodruff mentioned three classes of people he was going to do the work for, and by the time he wrote it in his journal, the work was likely already completed.

First he compiled the names of the Signers. There were several books published at the time (and the Centennial the year before likely piqued several people's interest enough that the information wasn't hard to find) that had the necessary information for the fifty-six people who signed the Declaration.

The next class of people was the former presidents of the United States and some of their wives. Woodruff gave special attention to George Washington (whom Woodruff later said had appeared to him with the Signers); his wife, Martha; and several of his ancestors. Woodruff didn't, of course, list Ulysses S. Grant, who was still alive and whom Woodruff met two years earlier during President Grant's visit to the territory.[136] He also chose not to include Martin Van Buren and James Buchanan, both of whom were unpopular among Church members.[137]

Wilford Woodruff journal listing of the baptisms done for the eminent people, August 21, 1877; Church History Library Collection

Inside cover of *Portrait Gallery of Eminent Men and Women* by Evert A. Duyckinck, 1873; Ronald Fox Collection

The third class Woodruff mentioned was "Noted Men" of the 1700s and 1800s. Aside from the Signers, most of these noted men came from an 1872 two-volume book titled *Portrait Gallery of Eminent Men and Women of Europe and America* by Evert A. Duyckinck.

Historian Brian H. Stuy examined the list of eminent men Woodruff put in his journal as well as the records of the St. George Temple and compared the lists to the *Portrait Gallery*. Virtually all of the names on Woodruff's list were in the books and even followed the order of the books, which was not alphabetized. Only four names on Woodruff's list were not in the books, so along with the Signers and presidents, there were forty-six other eminent men. Keeping with the books, there was no biographical information put into the temple records that was not also in the books—if a date or place was missing in the books, it was missing in the records.[138] Woodruff even used the book title's description of the men, "Eminent Men," to describe the people in his journal.[139]

Woodruff also compiled a list of seventy eminent women. Many were wives of the Signers, presidents or eminent men, but several stood on their own. Only a few were not in *Portrait Gallery*.[140]

The compilation of the names of the Signers was obvious. They had asked for redemption, but aside from George Washington, there was no reliable record of anybody else asking for their temple work to be done (see Appendix 8 for one account that claims otherwise).[141]

The impulse to do the work for more people outside his family and outside the community of Latter-day Saints came from the growing realization that the ordinances of the temple—all the ordinances—were for all people. Although modern Church practice prohibits baptism for celebrities (unless the person having the temple work done is a relative), at the time, Woodruff had nowhere else to turn to expand temple work. His use of *Portrait Gallery* helped inaugurate the beginnings of a wider view of salvation.

* * *

James Godson Bleak, 16. St. George Temple Recorder. Utah State Historical Society Collection.

On Tuesday, August 21, 1877, Woodruff went to the temple and was baptized for 100 men.[142]

Woodruff first baptized his right-hand man in St. George, McAllister, for twenty-one people, including Washington and the presidents.[143] McAllister then baptized Woodruff on behalf of the Signers and other eminent men. Woodruff's journal and the talk he gave a few weeks later suggested the events occurred in the opposite order—saying McAllister baptized Woodruff first on behalf of the Signers and other eminent men and then Woodruff baptized McAllister.[144]

Whatever the order, McAllister baptized Woodruff for fifty-four of the Signers (skipping only Hancock and Floyd), plus forty-six other noteworthy people, such as Daniel Webster, Robert Fulton, Washington Irving, Henry Clay, Napoleon Bonaparte, Johann Wolfgang Goethe, Lord Horatio Nelson, Sir Walter Scott, William Wordsworth, Christopher Columbus, and John Wesley (see a full listing of the eminent men and women in Appendix 9). Curiously, the temple record listing of the eminent men baptized on that day omitted twenty-five of them. This appeared to be a clerical error, since Woodruff specifically listed the names in his journal. The endowment records of these omitted men also indicated August 21, 1877, as their proxy baptism dates.[145]

After Woodruff completed those baptisms, it was time to do baptisms for the women on the list of eminent women he had compiled. McAllister baptized Lucy Bigelow Young, one of Brigham Young's plural wives, on behalf of the seventy women—including Elizabeth Barrett Browning, Marie Antoinette, Martha Washington, and other prominent women. She was also baptized for several of the wives of men whose baptisms had also been completed that day.[146]

As mentioned before, several of the people who were baptized by proxy on that day had their baptisms previously performed in the Endowment House, Nauvoo Temple, or Mississippi River. It may be that Woodruff didn't know their baptisms had been done (although McAllister certainly knew some were). It may also be that it didn't matter to Woodruff whether the baptisms were done before or not. At this time in Church history, members of the Church were occasionally rebaptized to show renewal of the covenant. People were also rebaptized before they had their own live endowments. Woodruff may also have wanted the baptismal records to be in the St. George Temple for further proof that they had actually been done.

With the inaugural work of the process of redeeming the Signers and other eminent men and women now done, Woodruff charged those present in the temple to complete the ordinance work—to do washings and anointings and endowments for the deceased. "I Called upon all the Brethren & Sisters who were present to assist in getting Endowments for those that we had been Baptized for to day," he wrote in his journal.[147]

Benjamin Franklin; 19th century engraving

Woodruff would never forget the experience.

"It was a vary interesting day," he wrote in his journal. "I felt thankful that we had the privilege and the power to administer for the worthy dead esspecially for the signers of the declaration of Independence, that inasmuch as they had laid the foundation of our Government that we Could do as much for them as they had done for us."[148]

The next day the work continued. McAllister acted as proxy for George Washington and Lucy Bigelow Young for Martha Washington. They did their endowments and then were sealed in eternal marriage on their behalf. Woodruff ordained by proxy both Washington and John Wesley as high priests—a rare occurrence for work for the dead. Usually men are only ordained by proxy as elders.[149]

On Thursday, Benjamin Franklin's work was done, and he was also ordained by proxy as a high priest. McAllister received endowments for Millard Fillmore—a president who was a particular friend to the Church because he had appointed Young governor of Utah Territory—and for Augustine Washington (George Washington's father).[150]

That Friday, August 24, ended temple work for the week. Woodruff ordained Christopher Columbus a high priest by proxy as well. In addition to the beginning work of redeeming the Signers and other eminent men and women, other work was done that week also. There were 356 endowments performed for both the living and the dead and 682 baptisms for the dead.[151]

According to James Godson Bleak's records, that first year, the St. George Temple recorded 30,384 baptisms for the dead and 14,386 endowments for both the living and the dead. By Henry W. Bigler's account in his 1877 journal, that count was 1,166 living endowments and 13,160 endowments for the dead.[152]

The commitment to temple attendance to do the work for the dead was in full swing.

Chapter 8
THE VISION'S LEGACY OF MODERN TEMPLE WORSHIP

The next Monday, August 27, 1877, Woodruff received a telegram that Young, President of The Church of Jesus Christ of Latter-day Saints, was "vary sick." The people of St. George and Salt Lake City, as well as other places in the territory, came together in their various communities at 8:00 p.m. to pray for their stricken leader.

The next day, Woodruff gathered about 100 priesthood holders and thirty women and went to the temple.

They prayed until 2:00 a.m.

They met again on Wednesday, August 29, five hours later, and again prayed all day. Every half hour a telegram came saying how the prophet was doing.

At 4:00 p.m., the final telegram came. President Young, the successor to Joseph Smith, was dead.

Woodruff dismissed the prayer circles.

On Thursday morning, Woodruff left St. George for Salt Lake City to join his Brethren in the Quorum of the Twelve to grieve for their friend and leader. He arrived in Salt Lake on Saturday.[153]

John Taylor succeeded Young as leader of the Church. A week later, on Sunday, September 16, a month to the day since the Signers appeared to him, Woodruff made his first known public speech on the vision.[154]

He spoke in the tabernacle for forty-five minutes to a large congregation of both members of the Church and other people, including General Thomas L. Kane, who had been a friend of Young's and had done much for the Church.

"President Young having now passed away, his labors with us have ceased for the present," Woodruff told the congregation. "He left this unfinished work for us to carry on to completion; and it is our duty to rise up and build these Temples."[155]

He told of the visions of the Signers and said, "I have felt to rejoice exceedingly in this work of redeeming the dead."

Two days later, he helped lay the cornerstones for the Logan Temple.[156]

Young had died—but the work of salvation was alive and well.

Meanwhile, the endowments and other temple work for the Signers, U.S.

Brigham Young, circa 1868;
19th century engraving;
Ronald Fox Collection

33

Wilford Woodruff, circa 1897; Utah State Historical Society Collection.

presidents, and other eminent men and women continued in St. George.

Throughout his life, Woodruff would return to the story of his visions of the Signers to help the Latter-day Saints understand the importance and expanded scope of temple work and salvation.

After President Taylor died in 1887, Woodruff became the leader of The Church of Jesus Christ of Latter-day Saints. He expressed his feelings of humility to Bleak, writing, "Who am I, a poor Miller boy, that I should be honored by all Israel? I don't understand it. If you do, I wish you would tell me."[157]

He later confided why he thought the Lord had chosen him to become Church President: "Because the Lord could not find a weaker vessel."[158]

President Woodruff's administration was one of transition and revelation. He issued the Manifesto in 1890—a public declaration of the end of the practice of plural marriage—and he presided over the dedication of the Salt Lake Temple in April 1893.

Of the Salt Lake Temple dedication, McAllister wrote in his journal on April 7, 1893, how "Prest Woodruff related his manifestations in St George Temple. Referred to his and my baptisms for a number of Notable persons."[159] President Woodruff also spoke about the vision on April 11. McAllister merely recorded that Woodruff spoke about "work done in St George Temple."[160]

Joseph West Smith, a Church member who had come from Arizona to attend the Salt Lake Temple dedication, wrote how President Woodruff spoke in the April 11 session about building more temples and about the vision of the Signers. "While at St. George there was a class of men come to me in the night visions," President Woodruff said, "and argued with me to have work done for them. They were the signers of the Declaration of Independence."[161]

After Young's death and the dedication of the Logan Temple in May 1884, President Taylor felt, like his successor,[162] that further revelation on the topic of adoptions was necessary. There were some discussions, but no clear guidance was communicated to the Church.[163] When Woodruff became President of the Church, he expressed similar feelings about adoption. In a letter written June 8, 1887, he said, "We may not, perhaps, understand it [adoption] now as fully as we should."[164]

Eight days after Woodruff issued the Manifesto ending the practice of plural marriage, he responded to a request from George Q. Cannon, his counselor in the First Presidency. Cannon asked to cancel his adoption to President John Taylor, and the next day,

Salt Lake Temple capstone dedication, April 6, 1892; photo by Charles Ellis Johnson; Ronald Fox Collection

October 15, 1890, Cannon and his siblings were sealed to their late parents instead. Even though Cannon felt a push to be sealed to his own parents, that same day, he had other people outside his family adopted to him.[165]

As Young, Taylor, and Woodruff anticipated, it would take revelation to clarify the practice of adoption. That clarification came to President Woodruff and was announced as a revelation to the Church in general conference on April 8, 1894.[166] "You have acted up to all the light and knowledge that you have had," Woodruff said, "but you have now something more to do than what you have done. We have not fully carried out those principles in fulfillment of the revelations of God to us, in sealing the hearts of the fathers to the children and the children to the fathers."

He spoke about how he sought further light on the temple ordinances and adoption, then said what the new policy was. "I was adopted to my father, and should have had my father sealed to his father, and so on back; and the duty that I want every man who presides over a temple to see performed from this day henceforth and forever, unless the Lord Almighty commands otherwise, is, let every man be adopted to his father. When a man receives the endowments, adopt him to his father; not to Wilford Woodruff, nor to any other man outside the lineage of his fathers. That is the will of God to this people."

It was a new understanding of the priesthood structure of heaven. While Church members had performed temple ordinances for their ancestors, there was no emphasis on performing proxy sealings.[167] The change gave Latter-day Saints a new emphasis on family history. "We want the Latter-day Saints from this time to trace their genealogies as far as they can, and to be sealed to their fathers and mothers," he said. "Have children sealed to their parents, and run this chain through as far as you can get it."[168]

Before this revelation,[169] before President Woodruff's presentation in general conference, members of the Church were afraid of being sealed to people who did not have the priesthood and were afraid of breaking the eternal connections, but President Woodruff alleviated that fear. He

Pioneer Celebration 1897, Salt Lake Tabernacle; photo by C. R. Savage; Ronald Fox Collection

35

plainly stated that among those who died without knowledge of the truth and who then heard it preached in the afterlife, "There will be very few, if any, who will not accept the Gospel." President Woodruff said those who have suffered in spirit prison since ancient times have "doubtless gladly embraced the Gospel, and if so they will be saved in the kingdom of God."

And even more directly to members of the Church, he said, "The fathers of this people will embrace the Gospel. It is my duty to honor my father who begot me in the flesh. It is your duty to do the same."[170]

It was a broad message of the expansive grace of God, the primacy of family, and a broadened burden of seeking after the dead. It was only a few months later, on November 13, 1894, that the Utah Genealogical Society was organized.

When Woodruff inaugurated the work for the Signers of the Declaration of Independence, part of the legacy of their visit was the deep desire they expressed to have work done for them—all of it. In 1894, President Woodruff culminated the doctrine of sealing people together in a vast optimistic vision of the power of God to save and seal His children in eternal family bonds.

Chapter 9

WILFORD WOODRUFF'S LAST TESTIMONY

The last time President Woodruff ever spoke to the whole Church was on April 10, 1898, in the 2:00 p.m. session of general conference. He spoke for fifteen minutes and chose once again to mention the appearance of the Signers of the Declaration of Independence. This time he emphasized how the Signers' request for temple ordinances showed they were "the best spirits the God of heaven could find on the face of the earth. They were choice spirits, not wicked men." Along with George Washington, the Signers were inspired by the Lord and were "noble spirits before God."

He talked about how every father and mother had the responsibility to do temple work—to "redeem their dead." "Do not neglect it," he said. "You will have sorrow if you do."[171]

Over the next few months, his health declined, and he traveled to California in August to recuperate. A doctor in San Francisco accidently used a cracked catheter when treating his bladder and cut him in the process. Though he seemed to be recovering, he wasn't.[172]

On September 1, 1898, his kidneys and bladder failed, and he fell into a coma. At 6:40 a.m. the next morning, President Woodruff died. "He slept peacefully all night, and passed away without movement," Cannon wrote in a telegram.[173]

In the reunions and greetings on the other side of the veil, one can imagine Woodruff embracing those whose souls he brought to Christ in mortality. Though he saved many people through countless different missions he fulfilled in life, it was, perhaps, within the temple that his greatest impact on the Church took place.[174]

He testified and worked to bring his fellow beings unto the Savior and unto His ordinances and kingdom. Woodruff saw little dividing line between this life and the afterlife. In that grand reunion and among those redeemed souls, it would have been fitting to see fifty-plus men who had visited him decades earlier in a gleaming white temple among the red rocks of Southern Utah.

"Any man will [have sorrow] who neglects the redemption of his dead

Wilford Woodruff;
photo by Charles Ellis Johnson;
scan of original glass negative by Ronald Fox;
courtesy of Moon's Rare Books

37

that he has power to officiate for here," President Woodruff said before he departed. "When you get to the other side of the veil, if you have entered into these Temples and redeemed you[r] progenitors by the ordinances of the House of God, you will hold the keys of their redemption from eternity to eternity. Do not neglect this! God bless you. Amen."[175]

Chapter 10
"INDEPENDENCE FOREVER"

The Signers of the Declaration of Independence won freedom. To do this, they had to come together, both as a group of signers and as countrymen. This meant they had to put aside jealousies and arguments and a host of other aspects that divided them.

In other words, they had to do with each other what England refused to do with the colonies.

Many of the 1776 delegates to the Continental Congress thought they could solve the difficulties with Britain. They thought the problems, from the colonial perspective, didn't seem impossible to overcome.

But still others saw broader trends.

England was rapidly beginning to regard America as a competitor on the world's economic stage. They also saw it as an opportunity to raise money and impose taxes.

Americans were infuriated. Not because of the taxes but because of the principle. If England needed money, fine. Let that question be hashed out, and then let the colonies decide how to raise the revenue. But Parliament wanted to bypass traditional methods and impose the taxes directly, which was unacceptable. To be taxed without representation struck at basic liberty.

If Britain could do that, it could do anything.

And it did. Step-by-step, England sought to enforce its will, and step-by-step, it pushed the colonies together until the only option left was independence.

Because taxes were involved, it was easy to think this was all about money, but it wasn't. The easiest solution would have been to pay. It would have been the cheapest method for maintaining safety.

But the fifty-six men who signed the Declaration of Independence instead enacted the most dangerous method. It was risky. It was almost madness.

In writing the Declaration, Thomas Jefferson demonstrated his eloquence through his ability to bring out the thoughts and feelings of many people. They were his expressions but not his ideas alone. The principles of the Declaration of Independence belonged to all humanity.

Each Signer had nobility. Each had weakness. They were indeed some of the best men of their age and some were even the best men of the ages.

The short biographies that follow are as varied as the men they review. These vignettes make no attempt to make the Signers more than what they were. They do not try to hide their faults, because their greatness often flourished in spite of their faults. This does not tear them down but,

Independence Hall, 1915;
Ronald Fox Collection

Thomas Jefferson; painting by Gilbert Stuart; National Portrait Gallery, Washington, D.C.

to the contrary, shows what true greatness is—the extraordinary rising from the ordinary.

When John Adams was asked to come up with a toast for a celebration of the fiftieth anniversary of the Declaration of Independence, he said two simple words, "Independence Forever!" When asked if that was all, he had nothing to add.

Each of these lives speaks those words to us today. Regardless of their mistakes, pettiness, and blindness to acts that could make today's Americans shake their heads, the Signers of the Declaration of Independence understood something deep, profound, and true: Independence Forever!

* * *

The biographies are in alphabetical order—with the exception of beginning with Samuel Adams. Having the two Adamses together gives a nice overview of the whole panorama of the struggle for liberty.

Notwithstanding Samuel Adams's importance in the events that shaped the nation's independence, and with the exception of his own biography, references in the book to "Adams" invariably mean John Adams.

Signatures on the Declaration of Independence; Stone engraving; National Archives Washington, D. C.

40

Chapter 11
SAMUEL ADAMS
Massachusetts

Massachusetts royally appointed governor, Thomas Gage, knew Samuel Adams was always on the verge of being poor. He also knew Adams was the mastermind of the opposition to British rule in America. Talk of arresting Adams and bringing him back to London to be tried and hanged was not an idle possibility.

In June 1774, Gage, who was also the general over British troops in the colonies, sent a colonel named Fenton to bribe Adams to stop his political machinations, his inflammatory speeches, and his traitorous articles, petitions, and pamphlets.

If Adams agreed to behave, he would get 2,000 guineas a year and a title of nobility in America. If he refused.... Well, it was much better not to.[176]

Adams had Col. Fenton swear to give his reply to Gage word for word: "Sir, I trust I have long since made my peace with the king of kings. No personal consideration shall induce me to abandon the righteous cause of my country. Tell Governor Gage it is the advice of Samuel Adams to him no longer to insult the feelings of an exasperated people."[177]

* * *

Samuel Adams was born on September 27, 1722, in Boston.[178] His mother had a dozen children, but only three, including Samuel, lived to see their fourth birthday.[179] He was named after his father, who was a wealthy merchant, a brewer, and a respected leader in the Whig party.[180] Samuel entered Harvard when he was fourteen years old, the typical age at the time, to study theology, but his interests eventually shifted to politics.[181]

A few years later, he had his first taste of the long and irrepressible reach of Britain's Parliament when the lawmaking body passed an act that divested a land bank Adam's father had started. This act was a great blow to his father's wealth, and many felt it went against the colonists' freedom.[182]

After graduating from Harvard in 1740, Adams continued studying there, culminating in his 1743 master's thesis: "Whether It Be Lawful to Resist the Supreme Magistrate, if the Commonwealth Cannot Be Otherwise Preserved."[183] Already he saw the issues that defined his life's work.

But Adams's attempts to make money never seemed to go well.

His father helped him find apprentice work at Thomas Cushing's counting house. Cushing was a fellow merchant and friend of Adams's father and had to report to him that Adams wasn't cut out to be a clerk.[184] So his father loaned Adams 1,000 pounds to start his own business. Immediately, Adams loaned half of the money to a friend, who never paid it back, and before long, the rest of the money was gone as well.[185] The economic conditions of Boston during the 1740s and 1750s didn't help.[186]

In January of 1748, Adams and his friends started a political newspaper, *The Public Advertiser*.[187] A few months later, Adams's father died at about fifty-nine years old.[188] His mother died the next year.[189] Although Adams's inheritance was large, he didn't manage it well, and with the ongoing legal battles over his father's failed land bank, it wasn't long before Adams brought the family brewery to bankruptcy.[190] On October 17, 1749, Adams married Elizabeth Checkley. They had one son and a daughter.[191] But even as a family man, he still managed his money poorly. He worked as a tax collector but was as lousy at that as he was at business—he was too soft on people who wouldn't pay.[192]

His wife, Elizabeth, died in 1757, and he married again in 1764 to Elizabeth Wells.[193] He was forty-two years old and eighteen years older than she.[194]

Even though Adams was a failure in business, he was extraordinary in politics and political writing.[195] His cousin John Adams said he was "a universal good character, unless it should be admitted that he is too attentive to the public, and not enough to himself and his family."[196]

* * *

After Adams's second marriage, his star rose fast as he gained power in the Massachusetts legislative body.

Britain wanted money from the colonies to help pay for its costly wars, but Adams and others objected to Britain's Parliament taxing them without proper representation.

He worried that moves like the Stamp Act in 1764 and the Sugar Act would establish an oppressive rule over the colonies. He was chosen in the Boston town meeting in May 1764 to write to their legislators to tell them what they should do about the oppressive Stamp Act. He questioned the right of Parliament to tax the colonies, and he suggested they call for all the colonies to come together in a congress to coordinate their opposition—leading to the Stamp Act Congress the next year.[197]

On May 16, 1766, word reached Boston that the Stamp Act had been repealed.[198] Adams knew that if men understood their rights, they would rise to defend them. "But Adams was not trying to change society," historian Mark Puls wrote. "He was attempting to preserve rights he believed the colonists already possessed."[199]

Then came similar taxes through the efforts of Charles Townshend, chancellor of the Exchequer.[200] Britain may have backed down at the opposition to the Stamp

Act taxes, but Parliament wanted to assert its power. The Townshend Acts called for raised taxes and more troops. The acts also ensured the loyalty of royal officials by paying them from England instead of through the colonial governments.[201]

On February 11, 1768, Adams wrote the Massachusetts Circular Letter that the legislature approved and sent to the other colonies' legislatures for action. It looked for a united response to the Townshend Acts.[202]

To Britain, all the boycotts, opposition, and articles denying the right of Parliament's power over the colonies was too much. Boston needed a strong hand against it to show the colonists who was boss. In one fell swoop, the royal governor dissolved the legislature.[203] In May 1768, the *Romney*, a fifty-gun British warship, arrived in Boston Harbor. It was not there as a token of Parliament's friendship.[204] At the same time, two regiments of British troops arrived in Boston to keep the peace[90] but instead fanned discontent toward the British.[206]

Boston was a powder keg. And it went off on March 5, 1770, when British troops opened fire on a small group of civilians who were taunting them and throwing snowballs.

The Boston Massacre was too much for the town and for Adams.[207] Adams confronted Acting-Governor Thomas Hutchinson over keeping the two regiments in town and demanded they both be moved out.[208] Hutchinson's reply was condescending.[209] He said he only had the authority to reduce the troops to one regiment. This infuriated Adams, who said if Hutchinson had the authority to remove one regiment, he had the authority to remove both. Hutchinson folded and ordered the troops out of town to a fort outside the city.[210]

In April 1770, the Townshend Acts were partially repealed (with the exception of a tax on tea).[211] Again, England backed down to Adams's rhetoric and political maneuvering. Hutchinson said, "I doubt whether there is a greater incendiary in the King's dominion or a man of greater malignity of heart."[212]

Adams recognized the problems of uniting the colonies: their royal governors often shut down the separate legislatures before they could communicate or act on problems that were not in favor of British policy. On November 2, 1772, Adams set up a committee of correspondence.[213] Towns would appoint committees that would keep each other informed on what was happening across the colonies. It was an organization outside the king's control, and it was a framework for revolution.[214]

Still anxious to press its power, Parliament passed the 1773 Tea Act. The tea taxes left in place from the Townshend Acts hadn't caused much grief in the colonies—people just bought cheaper, smuggled tea. However, the new Tea Act arranged various laws and regulations to enable the East India Company to offer its tea in the colonies at a price the smugglers couldn't match—even with the tax. It wasn't a matter of price to the colonists. They knew that if they bought the cheaper tea, they would be affirming taxation without representation.

A gauntlet had been thrown down. Adams recognized its political dangers and tried to stop the implementation of the act. When ships full of the cheaper tea arrived, the North End Caucus and the Boston committee of correspondence agreed that they would not allow taxed tea to be unloaded in Boston Harbor.[215] But the royal government appointees wouldn't allow the tea to be sent back to England. It was a standoff with a deadline—it had to be unloaded, according to officials, by December 17, 1773.

On December 16, 1773, Governor Hutchinson refused to send the tea back to England.[216] In a town meeting that lasted from 10:00 a.m. to 6:00 p.m., neither side made progress. Then Adams concluded the meeting with what some historians think was a prearranged signal. He said simply, "This meeting can do nothing more to save the country." Several men appeared dressed like Mohawk Indians, then went to the wharf and destroyed the tea by throwing it into Boston Harbor.[217] The British warships within firing range could do nothing because if they fired, they would damage the ships or kill bystanders on the dock.

Parliament was not pleased and passed the Coercive Acts that closed Boston Harbor at the end of March 1774.[218]

Adams knew the colonies needed to unite to decide how to respond to this and other crises and attacks on their liberties. He knew there needed to be a Continental Congress—a body that could represent the common interests of the colonies—but if the Massachusetts legislature gave any hint that it was going to approve of and appoint representatives to such a gathering, Gage would shut the legislature down.

Adams instead introduced a resolution calling for the Congress on June 17, 1774. Upon the announcement, a loyalist ran out to warn Governor Gage, and Adams had the doors locked, then put the key in his pocket. Gage's secretary came back quickly with the order to dissolve the legislature . . . but he couldn't get into the room. The secretary read the order outside the door, and the legislature dissolved as ordered but not until it had approved the resolution and chosen delegates—including Samuel Adams.[219]

* * *

Adams wore a new suit friends provided when he went to the 1774 Continental Congress in Philadelphia[220] to face a group of delegates from diverse colonies who had a spirit of distrust—particularly of the Massachusetts delegates. Adams worked behind the scenes to move things along, developing friendships with delegates from other states to help establish the revolutionary movement as something that wasn't just a Boston dream but an American dream. To dispel distrust against Massachusetts' Puritan faith, Adams proposed having an Episcopalian minister lead Congress's prayers.[221]

One loyalist said of Adams, "He eats little, drinks little, sleeps little, thinks much, and is most decisive and indefatigable in pursuit of his objects."[222]

More and more, Adams became Britain's chief scapegoat. It felt that if it were not for Adams, none of these rebellious assertions of rights would have happened.

Governor (and British Commander) Gage sent his army to capture weapons and gunpowder supplies at Lexington and Concord during the night of April 18, 1775. And perhaps even more importantly, Gage wanted to capture Adams and fellow revolutionary John Hancock, who were hiding out at the home of Reverend Jonas Clark at Lexington.[223] Paul Revere, who often carried messages for Adams, warned the two leaders, who narrowly escaped.[224]

The British did not succeed in their operation as they had hoped. After a tense standoff on Lexington Green between the British Redcoats and the hastily gathered local militia, someone fired a shot. The British decimated the colonists and continued their march to Concord, but as word spread and more colonists gathered, the British made a retreat that turned to a rout. This became the first battle of the American Revolutionary War, and, surprisingly, the British were not the victors. Adams knew what the battle meant. He later said a declaration of independence should have been made immediately.[225] To him, the day was "glorious."[226]

Two months later, in an effort to stop the bloodshed, Gage offered a pardon to all the colonists who would lay down their arms—except for Samuel Adams and John Hancock, "whose offences are of too flagitious a nature to admit of any other consideration about that of condign punishments."[227]

Adams got his declaration of independence a year later when he voted for independence on July 2, 1776. The written explanation, the Declaration of Independence, was approved two days later on July 4. Then, with most of the delegates, he signed the famous and elaborate calligraphy version of the Declaration on August 2.[228] It was everything he had worked for.

Adams played little part in Congress after 1775.[229] He was, at heart, a local politician—though he saw the broader currents of power and politics.[230] But even in Massachusetts, John Hancock eventually surpassed him politically.[231] Adams served on the committee that drafted the Articles of Confederation, and he signed them.[232]

* * *

In 1781, before America had won the Revolutionary War, Adams ended his career in Congress and instead became a Massachusetts state senator and Massachusetts senate president.[233] He refused to attend the Constitutional Convention in 1787 and opposed the Constitution until it had the promise of a Bill of Rights.[234]

Adams made an unsuccessful attempt at becoming a member of the first U.S. Congress under the new Constitution but lost because of his Anti-Federalist tendencies.[235] He did, however, serve as lieutenant governor of Massachusetts under John Hancock from 1789 to 1793. After Hancock died, Adams served as governor from 1794 to 1797.[236]

Adams retired from public life in 1797.[237]

"Sam Adams," John Adams wrote, "a grief and distress to his family, a weeping, helpless object of compassion for years."[238] But after Adams died penniless in

Boston on Sunday, October 2, 1803,[239] John Adams took a broader look at his cousin's contributions. "Without the character of Samuel Adams, the true history of the American Revolution can never be written. For fifty years his pen, his tongue, his activity, were constantly exerted for his country without fee or reward."[240]

Adams once wrote to Samuel P. Savage about his hopes for the future liberty of the country. He said, "I now begin to promise myself the Pleasure of seeing the Liberties of our Country established on a solid Foundation. It will then be my most earnest Wish to be released from all public Cares, and sit down with my Family and a little Circle of *faithful* Friends in the Cottage of Obscurity. There we will give Thanks to the God of Heaven for the great Things he has done for America, and fervently pray that she may be virtuous, without which she cannot long enjoy the Blessings of Freedom."[241]

Chapter 12
JOHN ADAMS
Massachusetts

John Adams, a Signer of the Declaration of Independence, left Congress in the chill of February 1778 and made his way in utmost secrecy as a diplomat to help craft an alliance between the new United States and France.[242]

He rowed out to the U.S. frigate *Boston* with his ten-year-old son, John Quincy, and later said the voyage was symbolic of his life.[243] Snow and wind slowed the ship's progress toward France. Three British warships gave chase—only to lose their quarry when a terrific winter storm struck the Atlantic, blowing Adams's ship 100 miles off course and leaving the *Boston* with a mast split by lightning.[244] Nearing France, the ship encountered a heavily armed British merchant ship, and Adams was ordered below but came back up on deck with his musket to join the fight. He narrowly missed death when a cannon shot splintered a wooden spar just above his head, but in the end, the British merchant ship was captured, and Adams came into friendly French waters.[245] Before he landed, he was treated to a dinner aboard a French warship, where he learned that an alliance had already been signed between the two countries.[246]

* * *

John Adams was born in Braintree, Massachusetts (now called Quincy), on October 30, 1735.[247] His father, also named John, was a farmer and cobbler,[248] as well as a graduate of Harvard, where he sent his namesake when the boy was sixteen. Adams graduated from Harvard[249] and was promptly hired as a schoolmaster in Worcester, Massachusetts. It wasn't a pleasant experience. He described his pupils as "a large number of little runtlings, just capable of lisping A, B, C, and troubling the master."[250]

He considered becoming a minister[251] but decided instead to move into the home of James Putnam, an attorney in town, to begin the study of law.[252] He was admitted to the bar in Boston and began his practice in his old hometown of Braintree, Massachusetts.[253]

Adams was short and stout, even doughy, physically. Emotionally, he was transparent. He was unable to conceal his feelings and brought self-examination to the level of obsessive art. Historian Thomas Fleming said Adams "needed someone with whom he could share his perpetual inner agitation."[254]

That person was Abigail Smith, a clergyman's daughter, whom he married on October 15, 1764.[255] "Without Abigail to listen to his explosions of self-pity, one shudders at what might have happened to John Adams," Fleming said.[256] Abigail helped assure Adams that he was a good person and that others should appreciate him more.

The next year, events began to push Adams toward political action, and he wrote against the Stamp Act in the *Boston Gazette*.[257] In 1766, he moved his practice to Boston, where he gained some notoriety for defending John Hancock against the British, who had charged Hancock with smuggling.[258]

Then, on March 5, 1770, the Boston Massacre took place. Adams and his friend Josiah Quincy defended the soldiers in court while Robert Treat Paine, who also later signed the Declaration of Independence, led the prosecution.[259] The verdict was mixed, but, importantly for Adams, defending the unpopular British soldiers didn't hurt his reputation but may, in fact, have bolstered it.[260] He was elected to Massachusetts' legislature but fell ill and went back home to Braintree.[261] Adams then worked on the committee of correspondence his older cousin Samuel Adams set up.

In December 1773, Boston residents vocalized their opposition to yet another tax the angry British Parliament had imposed—the tax on tea.

Britain's punitive action led colonists to a call for all the colonies to send representatives to a Continental Congress in 1774. Adams was one of those chosen to meet in Philadelphia.

* * *

Congress convened September 5, 1774,[262] and Adams met George Washington, Patrick Henry, and other lovers of liberty. But caution was the mood in Congress. The body called for a boycott of British goods and appealed to the king to relax Britain's harsh grip. Adams was convinced such petitions were great for uniting the colonies but "would be but waste water in England."[263]

Then came the battles of Lexington and Concord on April 19, 1775, and everything changed. The war had come.

Less than a month later, on May 10, 1775, Congress again gathered in Philadelphia. By June, they had formed a Continental Army. Adams nominated George Washington as head of the army, and Samuel Adams seconded the motion. The next day, Washington's appointment was unanimously approved.

While some in Congress still held out hope that the conflict could be resolved peacefully, Adams felt differently. "I saw from the Beginning that the Controversy was of such a Nature that it never would be settled," he wrote to his wife, Abigail. "And every day convinces me more and more."[264]

Adams keenly felt his separation from his family. It was no exaggeration, however, that his work in Congress was essential. Nobody worked harder.[265] Through 1777, Adams would serve as a member of ninety different committees and would chair twenty-five of them.[266]

Yet he longed to be home and wrote his wife:

Among all the Disappointments, and Perplexities, which have fallen to my share in Life, nothing has contributed so much to support my Mind, as the choice Blessing of a Wife.... This has been the cheering Consolation of my Heart, in my most solitary, gloomy and disconsolate Hours. In this remote Situation, I am deprived in a great Measure of this Comfort. Yet I read, and read again your charming Letters, and they serve me, in some faint degree as a substitute for the Company and Conversation of the Writer.

I want to take a Walk with you in the Garden—to go over to the Common—the Plain—the Meadow. I want to take Charles in one Hand and Tom in the other, and Walk with you, Nabby on your Right Hand and John upon my left, to view the Corn Fields, the orchards, &c. Alass poor Imagination! how faintly and imperfectly do you supply the Want of original and Reality![267]

Adams's patience was rewarded when, on June 7, 1776, Richard Henry Lee of Virginia proposed a resolution "that these United Colonies are, and of right ought to be, free and independent States."

Adams seconded.[268]

The delegates from several colonies did not have permission from their legislatures to vote for such a resolution, so the vote was postponed until July 1. In the meantime, however, a committee was created to draft a declaration of independence, of which Adams was a part.[269]

Jefferson provided the words for the Declaration, and though Adams made some changes, his role was to get the Declaration passed.[270] He worked tirelessly and gave multiple arguments in Congress—pushing for his dream of independence in public and in private.

"John Adams was our Colossus on the floor," Jefferson said in 1824. "He was not graceful, nor elegant, nor remarkably fluent; but he came out occasionally with a power of thought & expression, that moved us from our seats."[271]

On July 2, Congress voted in favor of independence. The next day, July 3, Adams wrote to his wife, Abigail. "Yesterday the greatest Question was decided, which ever was debated in America, and a greater perhaps, never was or will be decided among Men. A Resolution was passed without one dissenting Colony 'that these united Colonies, are, and of right ought to be free and independent States.'"

Adams had no illusions that it would be easy.

"It is the Will of Heaven," he wrote, "that the two Countries should be sundered forever. It may be the Will of Heaven that America shall suffer Calamities still more wasting and Distresses yet more dreadful. If this is to be the Case, it will have this good Effect, at least: it will inspire Us with many Virtues, which We have not, and correct many Errors,

Follies, and Vices, which threaten to disturb, dishonour, and destroy Us.... But I must submit all my Hopes and Fears, to an overruling Providence, in which, unfashionable as the Faith may be, I firmly believe."[272]

His excitement was such that he wrote another letter to his wife the same day and predicted that that date would never be forgotten: "The Second Day of July 1776, will be the most memorable Epocha, in the History of America.... It ought to be commemorated, as the Day of Deliverance by solemn Acts of Devotion to God Almighty. It ought to be solemnized with Pomp and Parade, with Shews, Games, Sports, Guns, Bells, Bonfires and Illuminations from one End of this Continent to the other from this Time forward forever more."[273]

Adams miscalculated when people would celebrate—the day Jefferson's Declaration of Independence was adopted—but his excitement was still highly warranted.

* * *

On the heels of the Declaration, it didn't seem to be going well for the fledgling states. General Washington's loss at the battle of Long Island in August 1776 gave the British the upper hand—at least they thought so. It probably wasn't a big surprise when Lord Richard Howe sent a message to Philadelphia asking for a peace discussion.[274]

Adams went with Benjamin Franklin and Edward Rutledge to Howe's headquarters on Staten Island in New York, where Howe asked in what capacity he was to receive the gentlemen of Congress. Adams replied, "In any capacity his Lordship pleased except in that of BRITISH SUBJECTS."[275]

Basically, Howe's offer was for the colonists to submit to the king and Parliament's laws, but, needless to say, the three patriots rejected the offer.

Adams intended on leaving Congress in November 1777 to shore up his financial situation by reviving his legal practice.[276] Before the month was over, though, Congress appointed him as a diplomat to join Benjamin Franklin and Arthur Lee in France, with the goal of negotiating an alliance.[277]

After Adams's harrowing voyage on the *Boston* to France and learning the alliance was already a done deal, he still had to conduct diplomacy. But tensions rose between Adams, Franklin, and Lee because their duties overlapped and their styles of diplomacy conflicted. It also didn't help Adams's vanity when he was often asked if he was "*le fameux* Adams,"[278] meaning his "famous" cousin Samuel Adams.

Congress solved the conflicts and righted the intrigue among its delegates by putting Franklin in charge as minister to France and Lee as minister to Spain. They gave Adams nothing. He returned to Massachusetts in August 1779, where he helped write the state's constitution.[279]

He didn't stay long.

The British decided they wanted to negotiate for peace. Congress appointed Adams to work for the treaty and sent him to France, where the talks were to take place. Adams left in October with his sons John Quincy and Charles in tow. The ship unfortunately began to leak and put into Spain, but after a long journey by land, Adams arrived in Paris in February 1780.

Once again, the reason he was sent evaporated. The British, by that time, had changed their minds and felt they could crush Washington.

Adams didn't come home, however. He took the place of American Henry Laurens, who had been captured by the British, in negotiating a loan from the Netherlands. It took two years, and by October 1782, the Netherlands recognized the United States and loaned the new country the funds needed to carry on the war with England.

The alliance and money from the Dutch, along with military reversals, such as the surrender of the British at Yorktown and Virginia, convinced Britain to come again to the peace negotiation table. Adams joined the other peace commissioners—Benjamin Franklin, John Jay, and Henry Laurens—in Paris. A provisional treaty was signed on November 30, 1782. The final agreement, the Treaty of Paris, ended the Revolutionary War on September 3, 1783.[280]

Several French dubbed Adams the "Washington of negotiation." Adams wrote in his official journal how a "few of these compliments would kill Franklin if they should come to his ears."[281]

After the peace treaty, Adams went to England for his health and visited Parliament, where he had the satisfaction of hearing King George III recognize the independence of the United States of America. In 1784, Adams negotiated another loan with the Netherlands and his wife joined him in Paris. The next year, he was appointed minister to Great Britain.

Meanwhile, back in the United States, the great debates and compromises that created the U.S. Constitution were taking place. Adams weighed in on the question by writing *Defense of the Constitutions of Government of the United States of America*. His book was accepted in Europe but offended some in America who saw it as a tract to raise an aristocracy in the new country.[282]

The Adamses returned to America in June 1788.

* * *

In 1789, George Washington won unanimous support of the states' electors to become the country's first president under the Constitution. Adams won the split roster of vice presidential candidates, with only thirty-four of sixty-nine electoral votes cast. He was sworn in on April 21, 1789 as the country's first vice president.

It didn't take him long to voice his opinion of this new post. "My country has in its wisdom contrived for me the most insignificant office that ever the invention of man contrived or his imagination conceived."[283] Even so, Adams, in his role as tiebreaker in the Senate, cast more deciding votes than any vice president since.[284]

In 1792, the country was becoming divided between the Federalist Party, which Alexander Hamilton led, and the Anti-Federalist or Republican Party (not the same as the modern Republican Party), which Jefferson headed. Nobody would dare oppose George Washington for president, so the battle between the two parties played out in the contest for vice president. Washington was reelected unanimously as president, and Adams battled as a Federalist against Governor George Clinton of New York, the Republican choice. Adams won seventy-seven to fifty electoral votes.[285]

Four years later, after Washington announced he was not going to run again for president, the Federalists and Republicans put up their candidates. Adams ran against the Republican Jefferson, and the campaign was ugly. Supporters of both Adams and Jefferson went at it in the newspapers. Adams was accused of wanting to set up a monarchy. Jefferson was accused of being an atheist.[286]

When the dust settled, Adams received seventy-one electoral votes and Jefferson sixty-eight. The Constitution stated the person with the most electoral votes became president and the person with the next largest amount became vice president. In the first two elections, nobody opposed Washington for president, and Adams received the next largest amount of votes. This time, however, the result wasn't as pleasant. Adams became president, and his rival, Jefferson, became vice president.

* * *

Abigail was unable to attend the inauguration. Adams wrote to her describing how serene and calm Washington seemed. He wrote that it was almost as if Washington were saying, "Ay! I am fairly out and you fairly in! See which of us will be the happiest!"[287]

Adams immediately got caught in the middle of war between England and revolutionary France, which had killed its king. The Federalists were opposed to France. The Republicans were pro-France. Adams tried to avoid war and didn't please either side.

Then tensions increased when French minister Talleyrand said France would approve of a treaty with the United States if they would bribe him. France also demanded a $10 million loan.[288] Adams balked at such brazen actions, yet he still strove to avoid war and succeeded.

In the midst of the problems at home and abroad, Adams approved of the infamous Alien and Sedition Acts. The alien portion of the acts allowed the president to imprison or deport any foreigner. The sedition part made any criticism of the government, Congress, or the president punishable as a crime. Several Republican critics of Adams and his policies were sent to jail. But the punishment of critics did not increase Adams's popularity, nor did it decrease criticism.

The election of 1800 was even more bitter than the previous campaign, with pro-war hawks in the Federalist Party, such as Alexander Hamilton, disavowing Adams. Adams lost by eight electoral votes to Jefferson and his running mate, Aaron Burr. Burr and Jefferson tied in electoral votes, leaving the decision to the House of Representatives, which chose Jefferson over Burr.[289]

* * *

Adams was furious at how Jefferson's party criticized and treated him and refused to even attend the inauguration on March 4, 1801.[290] He returned to his home in Braintree (now Quincy), Massachusetts, and spent most of the rest of his life there. He did live to see the political rise of his son, John Quincy Adams, who became president in 1825.

For years, Adams and Jefferson did not communicate. It took the intervention of a common friend (and fellow Signer), Dr. Benjamin Rush, to help reconcile them. The bitter enemies became close friends once again.

But Adams's closest friend and soul mate, his Abigail, died of typhoid fever on October 18, 1818—three days after their fifty-fourth wedding anniversary.[291]

Five months before he died, Adams wrote to Jefferson about how he did not fear death: "I contemplate it without terror or dismay." He affirmed his faith that it was not the end but a transformation.[292]

Adams died on July 4, 1826, around 6:00 p.m. It was the fiftieth anniversary of the passage of the Declaration of Independence. Near the end, he whispered, "Thomas Jefferson still survives."[293]

But Jefferson didn't.

His friend, turned enemy, turned friend again, had died around 1:00 p.m.—only a few hours earlier.[294]

Adams was ninety years old when he died. Only Charles Carroll remained as the last surviving Signer.[295]

A few days before he died, Adams was asked what toast he would like to be given in his behalf during Quincy, Massachusetts', celebrations of the fiftieth anniversary of the Declaration of Independence. "I will give you," Adams replied, "Independence forever!"

They asked him if he would like to add anything else. He replied, "Not a word."[296]

Chapter 13
JOSIAH BARTLETT
New Hampshire

Josiah Bartlett lay dying. The fever was as insistent as the doctor, who, following medical practice of the day, said Bartlett should drink nothing. The doctor declared his situation fatal. Bartlett, however, refused the advice, drank liquids, and recovered.[297]

Just because people thought a certain thing didn't mean they were right. Bartlett took this attitude toward his own medical practice . . . and toward the decrees King George III enacted on the country he ran.

* * *

Bartlett was born on November 21, 1729, in Amesbury, Massachusetts. His father was a shoemaker. Bartlett started his study of medicine when he was in his teens and then married his cousin, Mary Barton, in 1754. Together they had a dozen children.[298]

Being a doctor was the first thing Bartlett did well. He had a practical sense of experimentation and developed a few treatments on his own, such as using Peruvian Bark (quinine) to treat a throat ailment.

His reputation sent him on to a career in politics in New Hampshire and then to the attention of the colony's royal governor, who appointed him justice of the peace, and, later, colonel of a regiment of militia. But Bartlett was no loyalist to Great Britain and the governor soon stripped him of his positions. By 1774, Bartlett was elected to the first Continental Congress but had to decline after his house mysteriously burned down (perhaps torched by Loyalists).

When he was set to go to the Continental Congress in 1776, he knew what the agenda would be. He wrote, "The time is now at hand when we shall see whether America has virtue enough to be free or not."[299]

Bartlett stood and gave his assent to the experiment in freedom. His voice was loud as he practically shouted his vote for independence, making the rafters shake. Because the voting order went from north to south and New Hampshire was at the top, Josiah Bartlett was the first in the Continental Congress to vote to sever ties with Great Britain. He was also the first to vote to adopt the Declaration of Independence. And if John Hancock hadn't been president of Congress, Bartlett would have been the first to sign the formal document as well.[300]

He later helped with the Articles of Confederation, the precursor to the Constitution and, in New Hampshire, rose to become the chief executive.

In the end, his first profession drew his interest, as he secured a charter for the New Hampshire Medical Society. Three of his sons and seven of his grandsons followed in his doctorly footsteps.

Chapter 14
CARTER BRAXTON
Virginia

It was up to Carter Braxton to stop the bloodshed.

On April 20, 1775, the day after the battles at Lexington and Concord, Virginia's Royal Governor, Lord John M. Dunmore, seized the colony's gunpowder at Williamsburg and put it on a British warship.[301] In response, Patrick Henry gathered militia and marched toward Williamsburg to get it back, to get payment, or else.

Dunmore called out the British marines to prepare to stop the militia, and Braxton stepped in as mediator. Braxton couldn't get Henry to back down, so he went to his father-in-law, Colonel Richard Corbin, who was the receiver-general of customs and a loyalist, and convinced Corbin to pay the colonists for the seized gunpowder. His efforts were successful, and Henry disbanded the militia.[302]

* * *

Braxton was born the son of a wealthy planter on September 10, 1736, in Newington, Virginia, but his mother died seven days later. In 1755, he graduated from the College of William and Mary in Williamsburg, and around this time, his father died, and he inherited an estate with five plantations and many slaves.[303]

At age nineteen, Braxton married Judith Robinson, who died less than two years later while giving birth to their second child. In his grief and restlessness, Braxton escaped to England in 1758, losing himself in the social scene in London and attending Cambridge University.

Two years later, he came back to Virginia, and things began to look up. In 1761, he married Elizabeth Corbin, who, because of her father's position, had loyalist leanings. Elizabeth would eventually give birth to sixteen children—six of whom died in infancy and young childhood.[304]

Braxton lived the life of a wealthy and well-connected Virginian and was always thinking up ways to increase his wealth. In 1763, for example, he tried unsuccessfully to convince some slave traders to let him invest in importing slaves from Africa for sale in Virginia.[305]

* * *

Braxton was elected and served as a member of the Virginia House of

Burgesses from 1761 to 1771 and from 1775 to 1776. In this body, he became acquainted with Washington, Jefferson, Richard Henry Lee, and Patrick Henry. With them, he opposed the British Parliament's excessive taxation and supported Boston as it reeled under the forceful closing of its harbor following the Boston Tea Party.

He mediated the dispute with Patrick Henry over the British seizing of gunpowder in the spring of 1775, but by June, tensions were increasing. Royal Governor Dunmore fled to a British warship and began marauding the Virginia Coast. At the end of 1775, Braxton was elected as a member of the Continental Congress in order to fill the vacancy Peyton Randolph's sudden death left open.

Braxton was a somewhat reluctant revolutionary. As in his mediation with Patrick Henry and the gunpowder, he always sought a solution that avoided violence. In April 1776, he wrote, "Independence is in truth a delusive bait which men inconsiderably catch at, without knowing the hook to which it is affixed."[306]

But his time in the Continental Congress changed his mind.

He hoped for a peaceful solution but was afraid the country would be harmed if Congress appeared to be divided over independence.[307] He voted for the Declaration of Independence on July 4 and then signed the official handwritten document on August 2.

However, nine days later, his term ended because Virginia's legislature decided to reduce the number of delegates to Congress.[308]

* * *

As the war began, normal trade routes to Britain were cut off. This caused devastating economic consequences for the colonies. Braxton saw an opportunity to open new trade with other countries, realizing its importance to both the new states' economies and his own personal fortunes. His investments failed, however, as one by one his ships were captured by the British or privateers. His debts overwhelmed him, and he was forced to sell his plantations, slaves, and other property. Finally, his estate was seized, and his life as a wealthy country gentleman was over. By 1786, he had moved to Richmond, Virginia.

Braxton's skills in politics, however, did not lag, and he served in the Virginia Council of State or the legislature until his death. In his capacity, Braxton gave his support to Jefferson's Bill for Establishing Religious Freedom in Virginia, which was later a model for the First Amendment of the Constitution.[309]

Braxton died in Richmond, Virginia, on October 10, 1797, of a "paralytic stroke." He was sixty-one.[310]

Chapter 15

CHARLES CARROLL OF CARROLLTON

Maryland

*I*n 1773, after the Boston Tea Party, another ship arrived with a load of tea—this time in Annapolis, Maryland. As occurred in Boston, Marylanders didn't allow the ship to unload the tea. Angry crowds gathered outside the ship owner's home, and he feared for his life. A member of the committee enforcing the tea boycott, Charles Carroll, suggested burning the tea would be enough to honor the boycott and satisfy the citizens who were still angry over how Boston was treated. But Carroll underestimated that anger. The people wanted more.

Merely burning the tea would not be enough. The ship owner apologized and set his ship on fire in front of a large crowd. With sails set, flags flying, and no crew onboard, the ship and its shipment of tea burned down to the water. The angry Marylanders were appeased, and another symbolic message had been sent to Britain.[311]

* * *

Charles Carroll was born in Annapolis, Maryland, on September 19, 1737. His mother was Elizabeth Brooke, the common-law wife of Charles Carroll Senior.[312]

Carroll was first taught by Jesuits at another estate, and then sometime between eight and eleven years of age, Carroll went to France with his father to continue his education. He stayed for six years at a school run by English Jesuits, and his cousins Adams and Daniel Carroll also attended the school.[313] Carroll spent six years in studies at Rheims, Bourges, and Paris, and in 1757, he began another six years of study at Middle Temple in London, *the* place to learn law.[314] While Carroll was in Europe, his father took the necessary steps to make Carroll a legal heir by officially marrying Carroll's mother. She died four years before Carroll returned to America, so he never saw her again.[315]

By the time Carroll returned to Annapolis in 1765 at the age of twenty-eight, he was very much a European aristocrat in manner and abilities and helped run his family's operations, which included hundreds of slaves and an ironworks.[316] His father

58

gave him the 10,000-acre estate called the "Manor of Carrollton," and from that time on, he was known as Charles Carroll of Carrollton to distinguish himself from his father, who was called Charles Carroll of Annapolis. He was married in June 1768 to Mary "Molly" Darnall. Carroll also had a son and called him Charles Carroll.[317]

* * *

Maryland's anti-Catholic laws prevented Carroll from holding any political office, but this didn't mean he couldn't voice political opinions—he gained popularity as he argued in letters to the newspapers against overreaching royal authority.

Carroll recognized that the ultimate resolution of the problems between the colonies and Britain would be through military conflict. A member of Britain's parliament wrote to Carroll that 6,000 British soldiers could put down any opposition. Carroll replied that that may be true to an extent, but "if we are beaten on the plains, we will retreat to our mountains and defy them. . . . Necessity will force us to exertion; until, tired of combating, in vain, against a spirit which victory after victory cannot subdue, your armies will evacuate our soil, and your country retire, an immense loser, from the contest.—No, sire.—We have made up our minds to abide the issue of the approaching struggle, and though much blood may be spilt, we have no doubt of ultimate success."[318]

The Revolution had no political prohibitions against Catholics and used Carroll in various capacities. In February 1776, the Continental Congress appointed Carroll, who was not a member of Congress, to go to Canada to encourage Canadians to join them in the struggle against Britain. Carroll went with Benjamin Franklin, Samuel Chase, and his cousin John Carroll, but American military incursions against the British in Canada (they had taken Montreal and had Quebec City under siege) turned Canadian opinion against them.

When Carroll returned in June 1776, he found that Congress was debating independence but that Maryland's delegates were under instructions to oppose it. Carroll would have none of this and hurried back to Annapolis, where he lobbied the provincial convention to allow the delegates to unite with the other colonies for independence. He was successful. On July 2, Maryland's delegates voted for independence, and on July 4, they approved the Declaration of Independence.

That very same day, Carroll was appointed to Congress. On August 2, when delegates were signing the official handwritten copy of the Declaration, John Hancock asked Carroll if he wanted to sign it even though he hadn't been there when it was adopted. "Most willingly," Carroll said, "to this record of glory."[319] As he signed the document, another delegate recognized the wealth Carroll was risking and quipped, "There goes a few million."[320]

Carroll was the only Roman Catholic among the Signers.

* * *

Carroll served in Congress until 1778, but when he was elected again in 1780, he declined to serve. Instead, he served in Maryland's state senate. When he helped draft the Maryland state constitution, he was particularly interested that it included provisions on the freedom of religion.

In 1782, before the official end of the war, his wife, Molly, died.[321]

Carroll declined serving in the Constitutional Convention but supported the document and was elected as a United States Senator in 1787 and was reelected in 1791. He served on the committee that helped decide the final wording of the Bill of Rights amendments to the Constitution.

Carroll resigned his U.S. Senate seat on November 30, 1792, because a Maryland law was passed that disqualified state senators from serving in the state senate if they held seats in Congress. He left political life in 1801 and devoted himself to managing his estates, which comprised 80,000 acres stretching across Maryland, Pennsylvania, and New York.[322] In 1828, at the ripe age of ninety-one, he helped establish the Baltimore and Ohio Railroad Company.

Carroll died at age ninety-five on November 14, 1832, while wintering with his youngest daughter in Baltimore. He was the last surviving Signer of the Declaration of Independence.[323]

At his passing, the federal government closed down for a day in his honor.[324]

Chapter 16
SAMUEL CHASE
Maryland

Samuel Chase was proud of whipping up the people against Britain. And he was good at it too. He opposed the Stamp Act of 1765 and later boasted, "I was one of those who committed to the flames, in effigy, the stamp distributor of this province, and who openly disputed the parliamentary right to tax the colonies.... Others of you meanly grumbled in your corners, not daring to speak out your sentiments."[325]

One political opponent described him as a "busy, restless incendiary, a ringleader of mobs, a foul-mouthed and inflaming son of discord and faction, a common disturber of the public tranquility, and a promoter of the lawless excesses of the multitude."[326] This didn't bother him in the least because he considered his opponents "despicable tools of power."[327] And how did he feel about King George? Chase said, "I despise, I hate, and wish to destroy him, and all such Tyrants."[328]

* * *

Chase's mother died giving birth to him in Princess Anne, Maryland, on April 17, 1741. He was the only son of Episcopal clergyman Thomas Chase.

He was a fast learner. He studied law at eighteen, was admitted to the bar at twenty, married Anne Baldwin the next year, and two years later, at twenty-three, was elected to the General Assembly of Maryland, where he served through its various incarnations until 1784. He fought against actions he did not think were fair, even helping pass laws to reduce wages for Episcopal clergymen, something his father may not have appreciated.

* * *

When Chase arrived at the Continental Congress in 1774, he wasn't pleased with those who sought a peaceful resolution with Britain. Adams noted in his diary on September 15, 1775, that Chase was "violent and boisterous" and that he was "tedious upon frivolous Points."[329] Months later, in February 1776, Adams seemed to have warmed more to Chase and wrote to James Warren that Chase was "very active, eloquent, spirited, and capable."[330]

In fall 1775, Chase discovered that another delegate, John Joachim Zubly, from Georgia, had been feeding information to the royal governor of Georgia. Chase dramatically denounced Zubly on the floor of Congress, and Zubly fled to Georgia and the protection of the governor. Chase won the admiration of his fellow delegates.

In 1776, Chase traveled to Canada with Charles Carroll of Carrollton, John Carroll, and Benjamin Franklin in a failed attempt to win Canadians to the side of the Colonists. When they arrived back in Philadelphia, Maryland's delegation was under instructions to not vote for independence. He went back to the state with Charles Carroll and worked day and night to whip up support for independence, giving impassioned speeches to people around the state. The pressure on the Maryland convention worked, and Chase arrived back in Philadelphia in time to vote for independence on July 2 and 4 and then sign the Declaration of Independence on August 2.

Chase's wife died in 1776.

He left Congress in 1778 after Alexander Hamilton disclosed that Chase was using insider information he gained in Congress to corner the market on the sale of flour to the army. Rush described it as an act that "exhibited marks of a mind tainted with that spirit of speculation which at that time pervaded nearly all ranks of citizens of the United States."[331]

* * *

In 1783, Maryland sent Chase on assignment to England to recover stock belonging to the state that was worth between $650,000 and $800,000. He didn't get the money, but he did find love. While there, he married Hannah "Kitty" Giles of Kentbury, England, on March 3, 1784.[332]

In 1787, Chase declined to attend the Constitutional Convention and, in line with his Anti-Federalist views, opposed the new Constitution. His political star began to rise again in judicial circles as he served as a judge in the Baltimore criminal court in 1788 and in the General Court of Maryland in 1791.

In time, Chase did a 180-degree turn on his Anti-Federalist opinions and joined the Federalist Party. This did wonders—at first—for his career when President George Washington appointed him to be Associate Justice of the Supreme Court in 1796.

Then Federalist Adams became president, and Chase did not win any friends in Jefferson's Democratic-Republican Party for his enthusiastic upholding of the Alien and Sedition Acts, which were used to punish people who spoke against President Adams.

After Jefferson became president in 1803, the tide turned against Chase. The Democratic-Republican Party now controlled the U.S. House of Representatives, and it impeached Chase. It thought he had been unfair. In the trial in the Senate, a majority found him guilty, but luckily for Chase, a two-thirds plurality was required for conviction, so he was acquitted and stayed in his post.

Chase's later years were plagued with gout. In 1808, Joseph Story, a visitor, said Chase "abounds with good humor. He loves to croak and grumble, and in the same breath he amuses you extremely by his anecdotes and pleasantry."[333] Chase was corpulent enough for one person to write that he was "one of the largest men I ever saw."[334]

As he was dying in Baltimore on June 19, 1811, Chase appeared calm and resigned. Earlier, he had taken the bread and wine of the sacrament of the Lord's Supper and said he was at peace with all mankind.[335] He was seventy years old.

Chapter 17
ABRAHAM CLARK
New Jersey

Abraham Clark was furious with Washington. In 1777, General Washington offered amnesty for any loyalist who took an oath of allegiance to the United States. Clark thought this went beyond Washington's authority, and he went so far as to label it "tyranny." But even Clark was careful enough to place the blame on people who were influencing Washington more than on Washington himself. "Though I believe him honest," Clark wrote, "I think him fallible."[336]

* * *

Clark was considered witty and satirical,[337] with a strong distaste for those who abused their power and/or considered themselves part of an elite. He was born on February 15, 1726, and grew up as a frail child who did more reading than farm work. He liked mathematics and used that knowledge to become a surveyor.

Dealing with disagreements between neighbors led to his interest in the law. He never officially became a lawyer, but he gave advice freely and became known as the "Poor Man's Counselor."[338] From there, his popularity rose. He became sheriff of Essex County, New Jersey, and soon ended up in the New Jersey Colonial Legislature.

* * *

About the same time New Jersey arrested the loyalist governor William Franklin (Benjamin Franklin's son), Clark was chosen to represent the state in the Continental Congress to replace an earlier delegate who opposed independence.

Clark arrived in Philadelphia on July 1, 1776. He was just in time to hear the debate on independence, and the next day, he cast his vote for independence and approved the adoption of the Declaration of Independence on July 4.

Clark was wary, along with others, of Washington's power during the war. In a 1777 letter, Jonathan Dickinson complained about the state of affairs of the war, saying he believed Clark's opinion that "we may talk of the Enemy's Cruelty as we will, but we have no greater Cruelty to complain of than the Management of our Army."[339] For Clark, the army was not an abstract. Two of his sons were captured during the Revolutionary War, and one was held in horrible conditions on the infamous prison ship *Jersey* in New York.[340]

Clark left Congress in 1784 and served in his legislature until 1787. He was selected to represent New Jersey at the Constitutional Convention, but sickness prevented him from going. This did not stop him from voicing his opinion, however, and he opposed the ratification of the Constitution at first because it did not have a Bill of Rights attached.[341] He served two terms in the House of Representatives under the new Constitution, always working to eliminate privilege and the creation of an elite class.

In 1794, he called for all trade to be cut off from Britain until it paid damages for American ships seized in the war and until it removed their troops from frontier forts as it agreed to do in the Treaty of Paris in 1783. If his resolution passed, it would tie the Washington administration's hands in negotiations with Britain. Clark's resolution was approved in the House but defeated in the Senate by Vice President Adams's tie-breaking vote.

When Congress adjourned that June, Clark retired from public life at the age of sixty-eight. Three months later, on September 15, 1794, Clark suffered sunstroke in Rahway, New Jersey, and died.

His gravestone reads:

"Firm and decided as a patriot,
Zealous and faithful as a friend to the public,
He loved his country,
And adhered to her cause
In the darkest hours of her struggles
Against oppression."[342]

Chapter 18
GEORGE CLYMER
Pennsylvania

George Clymer put his money where his mouth was when it came to the revolution against Britain. He was one of the wealthiest men in Philadelphia, yet he exchanged his hard cash for Continental currency. He persuaded other wealthy people to do the same.[343] It was a risky financial decision even if the colonies were successful, and if the Revolution failed, he would lose everything.

* * *

Clymer was born in Philadelphia on March 16, 1739, and the first time he lost everything, he was only a child. His mother Deborah died when he was eleven months old. His father died when Clymer was seven.

Clymer's uncle, William Coleman, raised him. Coleman was a wealthy Philadelphian merchant, not to mention a friend of Benjamin Franklin. Clymer was a full partner in his uncle's firm by the time his uncle died, and he merged his business with Reese Meredith's to form the firm of Meredith and Clymer. He then merged with Meredith's family by marrying Meredith's daughter Elizabeth in 1765.

Clymer did not like British taxation policies, so it wasn't a surprise that in a 1773 town meeting, those present made him the chairman of a committee to persuade fellow merchants to refuse to handle tea the British taxed.[344]

Clymer was involved with Pennsylvania's Committee of Safety, the unofficial opposition government, and then on July 29, 1775, he was appointed one of the Continental Congress's first treasurers. His job was to help raise money to support Washington's army in Boston.

When the vote for independence came in 1776, several of Philadelphia's delegates voted against it. These delegates were promptly replaced with more fervent patriots—like Clymer, who became a delegate on July 20. Although he was too late to vote for independence, he said it was his "dearest wish" to sign the Declaration of Independence. He did so on August 2.[345]

When British troops were close enough to threaten Philadelphia in December 1776, Congress fled to Baltimore but left Clymer, Robert Morris, and George Walton behind to conduct business. It was an exhausting four months for Clymer. After a few of Washington's victories, Congress returned to Philadelphia in March 1777, and Clymer took a leave of absence for his health.

In July 1777, Congress sent Clymer to investigate the condition of the army and the abuses in the commissary department. Washington said that if conditions didn't improve, the commissary department would have to be disbanded. He told Clymer that "our soldiers have scarcely tasted any kind of vegetables" for a long time. Clymer urged Congress to improve food delivery to the army.[346]

When the British captured Philadelphia a few months later, Loyalists pointed out Clymer's house outside the city. It was then trashed and looted. Clymer didn't go back to Congress at that time. Instead, he was sent to Fort Pitt (now called Pittsburgh) to investigate Indian uprisings that turned out to be British instigations. Congress ordered Lachlan McIntosh to take his troops and restore order, but McIntosh failed.

In 1780, Clymer was back in Congress. He worked with Robert Morris to create the Bank of North America—the first national bank. He also toured the South to solicit funds to finance the war and tried to get them to pay what was due to the federal government.

The war was all but over when Clymer left Congress in 1772. He wanted his sons to attend Princeton in New Jersey and wanted the family to stay together, so he moved the whole family to Princeton.

* * *

After moving, Clymer served in Pennsylvania's House of Representatives. He worked to keep the national Bank of North America going and also promoted prison reform. In 1787, he was honored to be a delegate in the Constitutional Convention—one of only six Signers of the Declaration of Independence to do so. In the convention, he opposed using the word *slaves* in the Constitution because he thought it sullied the document.[347] When he was elected to the first Congress, he didn't want the Bill of Rights or other future amendments to be inserted into the text of the Constitution. He wanted the unaltered text to "remain a monument to justify those who made it."[348] He got his wish, and all amendments are appended onto the end of the document.

After Clymer left Congress and went to Pennsylvania, Washington put him in charge of collecting taxes on alcohol. The Federalists thought it was the best tax to get the nation out of debt. The Anti-Federalists, however, thought alcohol taxes reflected the taxes Britain had imposed before the war. Many rural people agreed and agreed violently, leading to what was called the Whiskey Rebellion. As the person collecting the alcohol taxes, Clymer was a hated figure among those who opposed the tax, but President Washington called out the militia to put down the rebellion. One of Clymer's sons was in that militia and was killed in action against the rebels.

In 1795, still reeling from the loss of his son, Clymer took his wife with him on a trip to Georgia to try to negotiate peace between the Creek Indian confederacy and the settlers. He felt the settlers were the primary cause of the tension because they had driven the Indians off their lands without even so much as an attempt at compensation.

The negotiation was the end of his public life. In his later years, Clymer was president of the Philadelphia Bank and other civic organizations. He died in Morrisville, Pennsylvania, on January 23, 1813, at the age of seventy-three, having lived to see his fondest dream of independence grow into a nation under a Constitution of freedom he helped create.

Chapter 19
WILLIAM ELLERY
Rhode Island

William Ellery knew the consequences could be serious. It was August 1776, when most members of the Continental Congress were gathered to sign the Declaration of Independence. "I was determined to see how they all looked, as they signed what might be their death warrant," he later recalled. "I placed myself beside the secretary, Charles Thomson, and eyed each closely as he affixed his name to the document. Undaunted resolution was displayed in every countenance."[349]

* * *

Ellery was born on December 22, 1727, in Newport, Rhode Island. He was, at one time, a naval officer and never lost his interest in maritime affairs. Like many of the Signers, he studied law. He filled the vacancy in the Continental Congress brought about by the death of Samuel Ward and served from May 14, 1776, to 1785. Before he went to Congress, Rhode Island's legislature declared itself free of British rule.

In Congress, Ellery was known for his spontaneous dry wit . . . and for his distaste for exercise. He never walked when a ride was available.

After witnessing his fellow delegates sign the "death warrant," the Declaration of Independence, he also signed it on August 2, 1776.

During the war, the British invaded Rhode Island and occupied Ellery's town of Newport for almost three years. They burned his home and destroyed other property he owned. After the war, at nearly sixty years old, Ellery had to start over.

Counterfeit colonial money spread in 1778, so food suppliers were more apt to sell to the British, who bought with English pounds, than to the needy American Army at Valley Forge. "The love of country and public virtues are annihilated," an exasperated Ellery said. "If Diogenes were alive and were to search America with candles, would he find an honest man?"[350]

While Ellery was serving in Congress, one of his children died. He wrote of his grief to a friend and then commented, "He that loveth father or mother, he that loveth son or daughter more than liberty, is not worthy of her."[351]

He supported Rufus King's legislation in 1785 to forbid slavery in any states to be formed in the Northwest Territory—Ohio, Indiana, Illinois, Michigan, Minnesota, and Wisconsin. But his primary work in Congress was on committees concerned with building up the American navy.[352]

* * *

After Ellery retired from Congress in 1785, he stayed closer to home with his family and books, and Washington appointed him collector of customs for the city of Newport, which he did for three decades.

On the day he died, February 15, 1820, the doctor stopped by. He had trouble reading Ellery's pulse, but it soon strengthened. "Oh yes, doctor," Ellery said with typical humor, "I have a charming pulse." But then he turned serious, "But it is idle to talk to me in this way. I am going off the stage of life, and it is a great blessing that I go free from sickness, pain, and sorrow."[353]

Later that day, he died. His daughter found him sitting upright in bed, his chin on a book of Cicero as if he had just fallen asleep. Ellery's aversion for exercise didn't prevent him from reaching age ninety-two. Of all the Signers, only Charles Carroll of Carrollton reached a greater age before dying.

Chapter 20
WILLIAM FLOYD
New York

In 1774, after coming home from the Continental Congress, William Floyd learned that the British had ships in Gardiner's Bay off Long Island, New York, and were planning on invading to get supplies. Floyd, who was a major general in the militia, led his men to the beach to meet the invaders. No shots were fired, and the British withdrew their plans.[354]

* * *

William Floyd was born in Brookhaven, Long Island, New York, on December 17, 1734, into a family of prosperous farmers.[355] His education was limited but practical because when his father died, Floyd, at eighteen years old, took over the large estate.[356]

By the time of the Revolution, Floyd was a wealthy man. During his stints in the Continental Congress (1774–1776 and 1779–1783), he didn't participate much in the debates, but he was consistent in his support of the Revolution. In 1776, he abstained, with other New York delegates, from voting for independence, but after New York gave its approval, Floyd signed the Declaration of Independence on August 2.

While Floyd was at Congress in 1776, the British invaded Long Island and seized Floyd's estate. His family fled to Middletown, Connecticut, which left him with no home and no source of income for the duration of the war—almost seven years.[357] While his family lived in exile, his home was used as a barracks for the British.[359] Whenever he could, Floyd would leave his duties in Philadelphia to visit with his wife and children in Connecticut. His wife, Hannah, would never see her Long Island home again. She died May 16, 1781, and was buried in Middletown.[359]

James Madison lived at the same boardinghouse as Floyd and his family during the war. Madison was notoriously shy, but over time, and with the encouragement of Jefferson, he fell in love with Floyd's daughter, Kitty. They were engaged in 1783—Madison was thirty-two, and Kitty was sixteen—but after the war, Kitty broke off the engagement and married William Clarkson.

* * *

In 1784, fifty-year-old Floyd married thirty-seven-year-old Joanna Strong.[360] That same year, he began acquiring land on the western frontier of New York on the Mohawk River, where he worked for several summers.

Floyd was elected to the first United States Congress in 1789, but he served only one term. He dabbled in politics, trying for lieutenant governor in 1795 and serving as an elector in 1800 and as a delegate to New York's Constitutional Convention in 1801.[361]

But he had the pioneering bug. At the age of sixty-eight, in 1803, he left his Long Island estate in his son's hands and moved with his wife and other children to his new lands on the Mohawk River. He even built an almost identical home on the new property.[362] In fighting for the Declaration of Independence, Floyd lost his home but gained a nation. Now he was living the quintessential pioneering American dream.

Floyd's health was strong for eighteen years, but then he fell ill. After four days of sickness, he folded his arms calmly and closed his eyes and died in Westernville, New York, on August 4, 1821, at age eighty-six.[363]

Chapter 21
BENJAMIN FRANKLIN
Pennsylvania

Less than a month before Benjamin Franklin voted to accept the Declaration of Independence on July 4, 1776, his son, William, was arrested as a traitor. The personal price Franklin paid to help forge a new and united nation was division in his family and the loss of his closest companion and friend, his own flesh and blood, his son.

Benjamin Franklin has become a symbol of the possible—an embodiment of the American spirit of ingenuity, boldness, and freedom. His résumé would include the occupations of printer, humorist, author, businessman, fireman, philanthropist, scientist, inventor, philosopher, celebrity, musician, educator, politician, diplomat, Signer of the Declaration of Independence, and signer of the Constitution of the United States of America.

* * *

Benjamin Franklin was born on January 17, 1706, and was the youngest son in a family that would include seventeen children.[364] His father was a candle and soap maker in Boston, Massachusetts. Franklin's formal education was cut short when he was ten because he was put to work in the family business. A few years later, at twelve, Franklin agreed to work as an apprentice for eight years in his half-brother James's print shop.

Franklin's life course, influence, and eventual wealth were thereafter tied to printing. He educated himself with books, both bought and borrowed, and began writing essays for his brother's newspaper, the *New England Courant*. He knew James wouldn't print essays from an upstart sixteen-year-old, so Franklin created a fake character, Mrs. Silence Dogood, who submitted a series of witty satirical letters by slipping them under the printing shop door. Nobody suspected Franklin was the outrageous gossiper.

But his secret "Dogood" outlet for his observations on Boston's hypocrisy and pretention wasn't enough for the youngster. He often argued with his half-brother and legal master, James. James answered Franklin's impudence with beatings. Eventually, Franklin had enough of the rough treatment, sold what he had, and took passage on a ship to New York. He couldn't find any work, so he traveled to Philadelphia, where he landed a job as an assistant for a printer named Samuel Keimer.

He also caught the eye of his future wife, Deborah Read.

Franklin's skills and intelligence came to the attention of Sir William Keith, the royal governor of Philadelphia, who knew Franklin's sister Mary's husband.[365] Keith encouraged Franklin to start his own print shop with promises of lucrative government printing contracts, then sent Franklin back to Boston with a letter of introduction to try to get Franklin's father to front the money for the expensive press and other equipment. It had been months since Franklin had broken his apprenticeship with James, and the family was relieved to see him again, though his father couldn't (or wouldn't) provide the money.

When Franklin returned to Philadelphia, Keith said he would provide the funds and told Franklin to sail to London to make the purchases. Franklin made the trip in 1724—arriving in Britain on Christmas Eve—but Keith never provided the letters of credit. Franklin was stuck penniless in London.

Before he sailed to England, he and Deborah were practically engaged, but once they were separated, they soon drifted apart emotionally too. Franklin found a job in a British print shop and continued his independent life. He became friends on the voyage to England with a wealthy Philadelphian merchant, Thomas Denham. Denham convinced Franklin to come back with him to Philadelphia to work in his business.[366]

When Franklin arrived back in Philadelphia on October 11, 1726, he discovered Deborah had married a man named John Rogers a year earlier.[367] Then his dreams of becoming a merchant disappeared when his friend Denham died. Franklin ended up back where he had started, an assistant printer for Keimer. He began to save his money to someday start his own shop.

* * *

In 1728, Franklin went into a printing partnership with Hugh Meredith. Before long, they purchased the *Pennsylvania Gazette*.

Franklin was becoming an established figure in the community, and when he discovered that a woman (who was never identified) gave birth to his illegitimate son, Franklin took responsibility and sought help from Deborah Read, whose husband had abandoned her. Franklin wanted her to become his wife and raise the child as her own. This left her in a difficult situation. Rogers had confessed he was already married in England, which made Deborah's marriage to him a sham. He'd also fled to the West Indies, so when rumors came back that Rogers had died, Deborah felt she was free to marry Franklin, but the legalities and realities of the time meant it had to be a common-law marriage without "official" recognition.[368]

In September 1730, Benjamin and Deborah began living as husband and wife and raising little William Franklin.[369] The match worked well. Deborah had a sense for frugality and kept the business books. Franklin's business grew as he became the official printer of paper money for Pennsylvania.

In December 1732, he began publishing *Poor Richard's Almanac*. The almanac was a nearly universal bestseller. It contained directions about the weather and astronomical data like other almanacs, but it also included wit and wisdom, such as these famous Franklin epigrams:

"God helps them that help themselves."

"A penny saved is a penny earned."

"Early to bed and early to rise, makes a man healthy, wealthy, and wise."

"Keep your eyes wide open before marriage and half shut afterwards."

* * *

Franklin entered politics and became the clerk of the Pennsylvania General Assembly in 1736. He organized the first fire department in America that year.[370] The next year, he obtained the lucrative position of postmaster of Philadelphia. By the 1740s, he was wealthy enough to basically retire from business and live off his wealth and income from the business and other political salaries. His interests turned to science.

In 1746, a merchant in London, Peter Collison, sent an "electric tube" to Franklin. The tube was used to create static electricity, which fascinated Franklin and culminated in his famous kite experiment in the summer of 1752.[371]

Franklin suspected lightning was the same force as electricity. Joseph Priestly, a close friend of Franklin's, wrote about how Franklin decided he could use a kite to try to collect electricity from the sky the same way he collected static electricity into Leyden jars—an early form of a capacitor. "Preparing, therefore, a large silk handkerchief and two cross-sticks of a proper length, on which to extend it, he took the opportunity of the first approaching thunderstorm to take a walk in the field, in which there was a shed convenient for his purpose," Priestly wrote. "But dreading the ridicule which too commonly attends unsuccessful attempts in science, he communicated his intended experiment to nobody but his son [who was twenty-one years old at the time], who assisted him in raising the kite."

The goal was not to have lightning strike the kite (he knew that would be fatal) but to collect what he hypothesized was electricity in the clouds and air. William flew the kite and brought the end of the string into the doorway of a small shed. He then brought his hand up to a key tied at the end of the string, and a spark snapped to his knuckle—proving his theory.[372]

From his discovery, Franklin invented the lightning rod but refused to patent it. He gave it as a free gift to the world to save property and lives.[373] Franklin did, however, gain world renown from his experiments and invention. For example, he received multiple honorary degrees from institutions such as Yale and Harvard in 1753. In 1756, he was inducted into the Royal Society of Science in London.

And his reputation couldn't have hurt in him getting the prestigious post of deputy postmaster general of the British North American Colonies.

*　*　*

At the outbreak of the French and Indian War in 1754, Franklin was called as a delegate to the Albany Congress, held in Albany, New York, in which seven colonies in the north met to decide how to defend themselves against the French. The forty-eight-year-old Franklin proposed a "Plan of Union" with, he said, a government "administered by a president-general, appointed and supported by the Crown, and a grand council, to be chosen by the representatives of the people of the several colonies, met in their respective assemblies."[374] Franklin's son, William, was his close companion during the congressional meeting and acted as his aide.

The Albany Congress approved Franklin's plan, but the individual colonies did not.

Franklin printed one of the first American editorial cartoons at the time—a snake cut in pieces with each piece labeled as one of colonies in danger. Above the snake was the caption, "Join or Die!"

*　*　*

In 1757, Pennsylvania chose Franklin to be its agent in London. He brought William with him, but Deborah was terrified of crossing the ocean and would not accompany him. Having her stay home helped secure the family's financial interests, but it also solidified a growing emotional distance between them.[375]

Three decades had passed since Franklin had returned from his first unsuccessful trip to London. Now the successful Franklin went back—this time not as a young man on a fool's errand but as the agent of Pennsylvania's legislature to settle a tax dispute. The Proprietors, the descendants of the founder of Pennsylvania, William Penn, opposed any defense taxes unless it exempted them. Franklin was able to broker a compromise and began to turn Parliament against the Proprietors.

While in England, in 1758, Franklin took time to investigate his family history. He discovered he was the youngest son of the youngest son for five generations in a row.[376] Then William had a son out of wedlock, whose name was William Temple, and Franklin helped find a suitable home to take care of this unexpected grandchild.

As the French and Indian War ended, the French offered a settlement to Britain of either the island of Guadeloupe in the West Indies or Canada. Franklin wrote a pamphlet in 1760 encouraging Britain to choose Canada. Franklin also saw the coronation of King George III in 1760.

In 1762, Franklin returned to the colonies. He was fifty-six years old. William also returned and, through the influence of his father, was made royal governor of New Jersey the next year.

Franklin didn't stay home long. The Pennsylvania legislature became increasingly frustrated by the power the Proprietors exercised over the colony, and in 1764, they sent him back to England to try to strip the Proprietors of their power and set up the colony as a crown colony. Other events, however, overshadowed his mission and challenged Franklin's loyalty to the British Empire.

* * *

In February 1764, Parliament was debating the adoption of the Stamp Act, and Franklin spoke out against it, though it was approved anyway. Franklin shrugged his shoulders and, as a printer, ordered stamps to be sent to his business in Philadelphia.[377] His popularity back in America, at least briefly, evaporated when the public thought Franklin had argued *for* the Stamp Act. His wife wrote to tell him she obtained some guns so she would feel safer in their house from angry colonists in the "City of Brotherly Love." News from America's "Stamp Act Congress" also helped Franklin understand how poorly the Stamp Act was received at home. So he moved quickly into action to try to convince the British that the Stamp Act was a bad idea.

On February 3, 1766, the sixty-year-old Franklin was peppered with 174 questions by Parliament as it grilled him for hours about the possible repeal of the Stamp Act. When at last the Stamp Act was repealed, Franklin was a hero again.[378]

But that wasn't the end of tensions between Britain and its American colonies.

Franklin struggled to convince the British that their course of action was foolish. The dance of diplomacy required ingratiation to leaders while appearing independent to his constituency back in the colonies. He complained that he would be "suspected, in England of being too much an American, and in America, of being too much of an Englishman."[379]

Then, in 1773, letters from Massachusetts' royal governor, Thomas Hutchinson, fell into Franklin's hands and showed the governor's arrogance and animosity toward his own people, asking for troops and curtailment of American liberty. Franklin sent the letters to America to be secretly shown to various important people. Samuel Adams, however, released the letters to the public. Americans were outraged at Hutchinson.[380]

Franklin publically admitted his role in the release of the letters and had the task of presenting Massachusetts' petition to remove Hutchinson from his post. On top of this, the news of the Boston Tea Party on December 16, 1773, arrived in England. Franklin was summoned before the king's Privy Council because of his role in the Hutchinson letter embarrassment, and the king's attorney general insulted and accused Franklin, humiliating him as the audience laughed and applauded. The ever-eloquent Franklin didn't say a word.[381]

* * *

For years Deborah wrote and begged for her husband to come home. Franklin wanted her to come with him to England, but she refused. She was getting older and was often ill. Franklin would promise to come home—but crisis after crisis would keep him in England year after year. By 1773, Deborah's health was failing. She often wept about how she would never see Franklin again.[382]

And she didn't.

Deborah suffered a series of strokes and declined rapidly. In 1774, Franklin's sixty-nine-year-old wife suffered a major stroke, which Franklin didn't know about until after she died on December 19, 1774. They had not seen each other for nine years.

* * *

Franklin lingered in England for a few more months after his trial and even offered to pay for the destroyed tea in Boston out of his own pocket as a conciliatory gesture. Instead, the furious British sent warships and troops to close Boston's harbor. Franklin saw the writing on the wall and sailed back to Philadelphia on March 21, 1775. He brought William's sixteen-year-old son back home with him.

While Franklin was at sea, on April 19, the battles of Lexington and Concord took place. The Revolutionary War had come to the colonies. In Philadelphia, Franklin wasted no time. He was quickly chosen as a delegate to the Continental Congress, and he joined the Pennsylvania Committee of Safety, which acted independently of the royal government. Congress even gave him his postmaster title again.

On July 21, 1775, he submitted a Plan of Union to Congress, an outline that later became a guide to creating the Articles of Confederation, the first federal government of the United States.[383]

* * *

A greater challenge faced Franklin, however, when he met with his son, William, and urged him to resign as royal governor. Franklin knew the halls of power in England—after all, he had helped William get his appointment in the first place—and he knew a break was inevitable. He wanted his son to, once again, be at his side, working for the same cause. William could be a leader in the new nation. He could carry on the Franklin dynasty with William Temple following in his footsteps.

This time, William told Franklin, in effect, to go fly his own kite.[384] He refused to resign his governorship—committing himself, instead, to the cause of King George III. The relationship between the aged Patriot and the young Loyalist was destroyed for life.[385]

Franklin's actions destroyed his relationship with his son but solidified his reputation among Patriots such as Abigail Adams. "I thought I could read in his countenance the Virtues of his Heart," she gushed on November 5, 1775, after meeting him, "among which patriotism shined in its full Lustre—and with that is blended every virtue of a Christian, for a true patriot must be a religious Man."[386]

In the fateful year of 1776, Franklin served as president of Pennsylvania's Constitutional Convention and pushed through a single house of legislators and a plural executive branch—an executive council headed by a president instead of a governor. Franklin was now seventy years old. In the Continental Congress, he was on the committee to write the Declaration of Independence with Adams, Robert R. Livingston, Roger Sherman, and Jefferson.

Jefferson wrote the first draft, and Franklin made a few changes to it. One of his more memorable edits was changing Jefferson's, "We hold these truths to be sacred & undeniable," to, "We hold these truths to be self-evident."[387]

Franklin voted for the Declaration of Independence on July 4 and, with the bulk of the Congress, signed it on August 2, 1776. John Hancock, the president of Congress, said at the signing, "We must be unanimous; there must be no pulling different ways; we must all hang together."

"Yes," Franklin replied, "we must indeed all hang together, or most assuredly we shall all hang separately."[388]

Franklin did band together with those who fought for freedom and dedicated all his liquid funds to Congress for the war effort—between 3,000 and 4,000 pounds.[389]

Late in 1776, Congress selected Franklin to go to France as a diplomatic commissioner. America desperately needed help if it was to stand up to the might of Britain.

Franklin's son had been imprisoned by this time and refused parole, for which he was taken into custody by the revolutionary government of New Jersey in June. Franklin worried that William Temple was beginning to take his father's side, so Franklin took him and his daughter Sally's son, Benjamin Bache, with him to France.

* * *

Franklin understood the value of proper publicity and presented himself to the French as a rustic American from Quaker Pennsylvania. He dressed plainly in a simple gray suit and wore a fur cap instead of a white powdered wig.[390] The French loved it, but they sent no help and signed no treaty.

Then came news of the battle of Saratoga in October 1777. The defeat of British General John Burgoyne proved the Americans actually had a chance. A few months later, on February 6, 1778, Franklin placed his signature on a treaty of alliance with France.[391]

After American success at the battle of Yorktown, Franklin, along with Adams, John Jay, and Henry Laurens, began working toward a peace treaty with Great

Britain. Franklin was a member of the American delegation to sign the Treaty of Paris, ending the Revolutionary War on September 3, 1783.

In 1785, Jefferson came to France as Franklin's replacement as American minister. "There appeared to me more respect and veneration attached to the character of Dr. Franklin, in France, than to that of any other person in the same country, foreigner or native," Jefferson wrote.[392]

* * *

In 1784, William, who was released from prison in an exchange and fled to England, wrote to his father to "revive" the relationship that had in earlier days given both father and son such joy. Franklin wrote back that "nothing has ever hurt me so much and affected me with such keen sensations, as to find myself deserted in my old age by my only son; and not only deserted but to find him taking up arms against me, in a cause where in my good name, fortune and life were at stake."[393] He did not accept his son's efforts at reconciliation.

Franklin left France on July 12, 1785, with his grandsons.[394] He spent some time in England, where he met with William to discuss money and the American land William still had title to. By the end of the meeting, William's connections to America were severed. Franklin convinced him to sign over his American lands to William Temple, and Franklin and William would never meet or correspond again.[395]

* * *

On the way home, Franklin continued scientific investigations and inventions and was the first person to chart the Gulf Stream.[396] On September 14, 1785, Franklin arrived back in the United States for good. The seventy-nine-year-old was greeted as a hero and promptly made president of the executive council of Pennsylvania.

He had lost or given up his son, but now with his daughter's children gathered around, he found some comfort. "I am now in the bosom of my family," he said, "and find four new little prattlers, who cling about the knees of their grandpapa, and afford me great pleasure. I am surrounded by my friends, and have an affectionate, good daughter and son-in-law to take care of me."[397]

* * *

Then came another call for his intervention. Franklin became the oldest delegate at the Constitutional Convention. He, of all the delegates, had seen the most history. He'd seen wars and assemblies and delegations and negotiations his whole life. He knew the experiment in freedom was on the verge of collapse.

Franklin had his own pet ideas about what made a good government. He loved the single house for a legislature and the plural executive, for example. Yet even though his ideas were given due respect in the convention, they were not adopted. He wasn't surprised and, instead, used it to good effect, modeling graceful defeat and encouraging real compromise.[398]

His final speech on September 17, 1787, read aloud for him by another delegate, to encourage his fellows to sign the Constitution, was one of the most important speeches in American history. He admitted there were parts in the document he didn't approve of but then added that he might someday approve of them. Opinions change, and for that reason, he said, "I am to doubt my own judgment."[399] He told the members to support the document and not speak about their objections to it, saying they should "doubt a little of [their] own infallibility" and put their signatures on it.[400]

When Franklin approached the document, he wept as he signed it.

His speech was widely published to garner support for the Constitution's eventual ratification.

A year after signing the Constitution, he retired as president of Pennsylvania.

* * *

Franklin's gout and a bladder stone kept him in pain and at home. He continued to be as active as possible, however. For example, Franklin was president of the Society for Promoting the Abolition of Slavery.[401] His last public act, in 1790, was signing a petition to Congress to abolish slavery.[402]

Only a few weeks before Franklin died, Adams wrote jokingly (with a touch of envy) to Rush about Franklin's place in history: "The History of our Revolution will be one continued Lie from one end to the other. The essence of the whole will be that Dr. Franklin's electrical Rod, smote the earth and out sprung General Washington. That Franklin electrified him with his rod—and thence forward these two conducted all the Policy, Negotiations, Legislatures and War."[403]

Benjamin Franklin died at 11:00 p.m. on April 17, 1790, at the age of eighty-four. His grandsons Benjamin and William Temple and other family and friends were at his bedside. About 20,000 came out for his funeral.[404]

"Death is as necessary to the constitution as sleep; we shall rise refreshed in the morning," Franklin once said to a friend. "The course of nature must soon put a period to my present mode of existence. This I shall submit to with the less regret, as, having seen, during a long life, a good deal of this world, I felt a growing curiosity to become acquainted with some other, and can cheerfully, with filial confidence, resign my spirit to the conduct of that great and good Parent of mankind who created it, and who has so graciously protected and preserved me from my birth to the present hour."[405]

James Madison said this of Franklin: "Whilst the last members were signing [the Constitution], Doctor Franklin, looking towards the President's chair, at the back of which a rising sun happened to be painted, observed to a few members near him, that painters had found it difficult to distinguish in their art, a rising, from a setting, sun. 'I have,' said he, 'often and often, in the course of the session, and the vicissitudes of my hopes and fears as to its issue, looked at that behind the President, without being able to tell whether it was rising or setting; but now at length, I have the happiness to know, that it is a rising, and not a setting sun.'"[406]

Chapter 22
ELBRIDGE GERRY
Massachusetts

The British troops marched past the inn in Menotomy, Massachusetts, on their way to Lexington and Concord. It was the night of April 18, 1775, and Elbridge Gerry, dressed in a nightshirt, watched through the window.[407] Some soldiers broke away from the troops and headed toward the inn. Gerry was a member of the Massachusetts provisional congress in opposition to the British and was at the village because of a council of safety meeting. He fled out of the inn and hid in a cornfield.

Historians have called Gerry a "maverick"[408] who would too often "flip-flop."[409] His enemies acknowledged him as a man of ability and integrity.[410] Adams, however, called him in 1776, "a faithful Friend, and an ardent persevering Lover of his Country."[411]

* * *

Gerry was born in Marblehead, Massachusetts, on July 17, 1744. He was a successful merchantman involved in the family business of exporting dried cod to the West Indies and Europe when he became interested in politics. He was a skinny man and spoke with a stammer, but his poor speaking skills never stopped him from voicing his opinion as a delegate from Massachusetts in the Continental Congress.

After the Continental Congress approved the Declaration of Independence, the rotund Benjamin Harrison joked with Gerry about what would happen when they were all captured by the British: "I shall have a great advantage over you, Mr. Gerry, when we are all hung for what we are now doing. From the size and weight of my body I shall die in a few minutes, but from the lightness of your body you will dance in the air an hour or two before you are dead."[412]

Adams summed up Gerry's work in 1776: "If every Man here was a Gerry, the Liberties of America would be safe against the Gates of Earth and Hell."[413]

Gerry also worked at the 1787 Constitutional Convention, arguing for many points, both important and unimportant. In the end, however, he chose not to sign the document. One of his reasons was that he didn't think the vice president should be the head of the Senate.

His opposition didn't last. By April 1789, the New York *Daily Advertiser* said he had "become the avowed friend of the Constitution."

* * *

His friend, President Adams, sent him, along with Charles Cotesworthy Pinckney and John Marshall, to make peace with an increasingly belligerent France. French Foreign Minister Talleyrand sought bribes from the United States through intermediaries who were given letters as codenames. The XYZ Affair enraged Americans, but Gerry stayed in France. Back home, he was seen either as a peacemaker or a lackey—or even as a traitor.[414]

After France, Gerry ran for governor of Massachusetts several times before succeeding in 1810, 1811, and 1812. During his last term, his party redrew the voting district lines to limit the opposing party to only one district. One of the resulting districts was so distorted that it looked like a lizard—giving rise to a term still used today: *Gerrymander*.[415]

The next year he was defeated, but that freed him to run as vice president for James Madison's second term as president. He was inaugurated as vice president on March 4, 1813. A year and eight months later, Gerry was on his way to preside over the Senate, a duty he'd once argued against, when he suddenly fell ill and died. He was seventy years old and penniless and was buried at public expense. Adams said Gerry "devoted himself, his fortune and his family in the Service of his Country."[416]

Chapter 23

BUTTON GWINNETT
Georgia

It was while he was serving in the Continental Congress that Button Gwinnett almost landed his dream job. Sure, declaring independence was a big deal—he represented Georgia well—but he really wanted to take charge of the Continental brigade in Georgia as a brigadier general.

Instead, his archrival, Lachlan McIntosh, outmaneuvered him to snag the appointment.

Gwinnett, and his temper,[417] wouldn't let it rest. It would be a fatal mistake.

* * *

Gwinnett was born a minister's son in 1735 in Down Hatherley, Gloucestershire, England. Gwinnett became a merchant, working in Bristol and Wolverhampton.[418] He married Ann Bourne when he was twenty-two, and within the next five to eight years, they had left for the American colonies, eventually settling in Georgia.[419]

By 1765, he was just prosperous enough to buy St. Catherine's Island, near Sunbury, Georgia, and began to set up a plantation. This put him in deep debt and signaled the beginning of lifelong financial troubles. But around the same time, he began a life, albeit a short life, in politics. He served from 1769 to 1771 in Georgia's colonial assembly, then took an absence to work on his business concerns. In May 1776, he was chosen as a delegate to the Continental Congress and voted for the Declaration of Independence on July 4, signing it with most of the delegates on August 2. Because his signature is at the top of the Georgia delegation on the left side of the page, it looks like he was the second person to sign the Declaration. Instead, he was actually one of the last to sign that day[420] (others signed it months or even years later). He would, however, be one of the first of the Signers to die.

* * *

By February 1777, Gwinnett was back in Georgia and wrote the first draft of Georgia's new constitution. When the governor, Archibald Bulloch, died, Gwinnett was appointed to finish the few months left in Bulloch's term.

This also meant he was Georgia's commander in chief over his rival, McIntosh.

Gwinnett took over the planning of an expedition from McIntosh that

85

aimed to secure Georgia's border with British-controlled Florida. His executive duties prevented him from leading the expedition, but even then, he wouldn't let McIntosh lead and put a lower-lever officer in charge.

The expedition was a dismal fiasco.

As a result, Gwinnett failed to win the election to the post he had filled in for from only March to May 1777. At least in the messy inquiry about the Florida expedition Gwinnett was cleared of malfeasance.

Except in McIntosh's mind.

McIntosh, who was probably also upset that Gwinnett had had McIntosh's brother arrested for treason, lashed out at Gwinnett, calling him a scoundrel.[421] Gwinnett responded with a challenge to a duel.

On May 16, 1777, in Thunderbolt, Georgia, McIntosh and Gwinnett squared off against each other. One witness, George Wells, said McIntosh and Gwinnett stood only about ten feet apart. "Both pistols went off nearly at the same time when Mr. Gwinnett fell, being shot above the knee and said his thigh was broke," Wells testified.[422] McIntosh had also been hit in the thigh but not as badly. He asked Gwinnett if he had had enough or if he wanted another shot. All agreed one shot was enough, and McIntosh and Gwinnett shook hands.

McIntosh recovered from his wound, but Gwinnett did not. Eleven days later, he was dead.[423]

Gwinnett's accomplishments were great—signing the Declaration of Independence and helping establish Georgia's constitution—but the value he placed on other accomplishments and his own honor did him in.

Ironically, his early demise plays into one of the main reasons he is remembered among the Signers today. If not for the duel, Gwinnett would probably have continued in politics and public life and would have signed many more letters and documents. Instead, only about fifty examples of his signature are known to exist. If a collector wanted a complete set of the Signers of the Declaration of Independence, the hardest task would be finding a Button.

Chapter 24
LYMAN HALL
Georgia

Lyman Hall was frustrated. He lived in St. John's Parish in Georgia—a concentration of New Englanders who had moved south. Although his community was full of red-hot revolutionaries, the rest of the sparsely populated Georgia was, at best, indifferent.[424]

By 1775, the people in the area were so disappointed at the lack of revolutionary fervor in their fellow Georgians that they tried setting up some representation in the movement by attempting to join South Carolina. But South Carolina said no. With the refusal, the parish acted on its own.[425] It elected Lyman Hall as St. John's Parish's delegate to the Continental Congress.

* * *

Hall was born in Wallingford, Connecticut, on April 12, 1724.[426] His life went along without event—for a while. He went to Yale and studied to be a Congregationalist preacher with his uncle Samuel Hall, and by 1749, he was a preacher in Fairfield, Connecticut.

That didn't go well. He was soon fired—partly, perhaps, because of clashing theological views and partly for unspecified "immorality." He confessed his guilt and was reinstated as a preacher, going here and there on temporary assignments wherever a pulpit was empty. But his heart wasn't in it anymore.[427]

Instead, he studied medicine. He married Abigail Burr on May 20, 1752, and started his practice. Abigail died the next year. Three months later, in October 1753, Hall married again, this time to Mary Osborn.[428] He then moved south, first to Dorchester, South Carolina, then to the rich and large New England colony at the seaport of Sunbury, Georgia, in St. John's Parish. It was a good place to move for a doctor—a nearby swamp gave him plenty of patients with malarial fevers.[429]

And there was plenty of revolutionary fever as well.

* * *

When Hall went to the Continental Congress in May 1775, he was an anomaly. He wasn't really representing a colony, yet Congress didn't want to reject the only revolutionary supporters in Georgia, so they admitted him as a nonvoting delegate. Adams described Hall as "intelligent and spirited."[430]

By summer, events such as the battles at Concord and Lexington had swayed the hearts of Georgians, and they sent official delegates, confirming Hall as one of their number.[431] One of those delegates, however, was a secret loyalist named John Joachim Zubly. He lasted only a few months in Congress before Chase denounced him as a traitor in September 1775.[432]

Hall was present for the debates over independence in July 1776 and signed the Declaration of Independence on August 2.

During the war, when the British controlled the coasts of Georgia, they ruined Hall's home. His family, however, was safe in the north. When the British withdrew in 1782, Hall was in Georgia. He was elected to the legislature, which then made him governor of Georgia in 1783.

* * *

One of the things he worked on as governor, besides rebuilding after the war, was to get land set aside for a state-chartered college. The next year, Franklin College was charted (it is now the University of Georgia).[433] After this, he worked as a local judge and moved a lot. He acted as the executor of Gwinnett's estate after the fellow Georgia Signer of the Declaration of Independence was killed in a duel.[434]

Hall died on October 19, 1790, at the age of sixty-six.[435] He may have failed as a preacher, but he found success during life as a living sermon of patriotism.

Chapter 25
JOHN HANCOCK
Massachusetts

John Hancock isn't remembered for his philanthropy.

As the richest man in Boston, Massachusetts, Hancock often gave money to rebuild homes destroyed by fire. He donated food and waived rent for the poor. He donated to many different churches, paying for seats, Bibles, window glass, pulpits, and bells. He bought Boston its street lamps and funded its first concert hall.[436]

His largesse continued in the cause of revolution. He bought shiploads of gunpowder, ammunition, and arms.[437]

But more than for this charity, Hancock is remembered for his bold and flourished signature. For years before the names of all the Signers of the Declaration of Independence were generally made public, Hancock's name was printed with large and conspicuous capital letters at the bottom of copies of the Declaration. As president of the Continental Congress, his name was synonymous with the cause of liberty. To the British, he ranked with Samuel Adams as the man they most wanted to hang for treason.

* * *

John Hancock was born in Braintree (now Quincy), Massachusetts, on January 23, 1737.[438] He was a childhood friend of John Adams, who was a year and a half older.[439] When Hancock's father died, Hancock's mother moved with him and his younger brother and sister to live with his grandfather, a minister in Lexington, Massachusetts. His uncle Thomas Hancock was a successful but childless merchant in Boston, so he and his wife took Hancock to raise as their own son, making the boy heir to the merchant riches of the House of Hancock.[440]

Hancock graduated from Harvard in 1754 at the age of seventeen and worked in his uncle's business. Adams later described Hancock's time there: "And what a school was this! Four large ships constantly plying between Boston and London, and other business in proportion. This was in 1755. He became an example to all the young men of the town. Wholly devoted to business, he was as regular and punctual at his store as the sun in his course."[441]

In 1760, Hancock sailed to England on business for the House of

Hancock. While there, He saw the funeral of King George II and just barely missed the coronation of King George III.[442]

When he returned, he was made a full partner with his uncle on January 1, 1763. The partnership didn't last long, however. Hancock's uncle died on August 1, 1764, leaving the twenty-seven-year-old a fortune and making him the wealthiest merchant in New England.[443]

With wealth came importance, and with importance came political position. He became a selectman of Boston (town council), and in 1766, he joined Samuel Adams, Thomas Cushing, and James Otis in the Provincial Congress of Massachusetts as representatives from Boston. They were all members of the Whig Party and opposed what they saw as unwarranted British extension of authority, such as the Stamp Act.

* * *

Hancock's ship *Liberty* arrived in Boston Harbor on May 9, 1768, at sunset. Rather than inspect it at night, the customs officials waited until the next morning. Although customs officials kept watch through the night, when they inspected the hold the next day, the ship was mostly empty, with only a quarter of the ship holding casks of Madeira wine. Hancock paid the duties on the wine.[444]

A month later, the *Liberty* was ready to sail again when a British warship, the *Romney*, arrived in port. A customs agent then changed his story and claimed he was held captive on Hancock's ship while most of the cargo was illegally unloaded in the night. It is possible that Hancock smuggled some of his cargo to avoid taxes. It is also possible that the British decided to clamp down on a rising voice against their rule. It may also be that the customs agent just saw a good opportunity to make a lot of money since informers received a third of confiscated property.

The ship was declared British property, and marines were dispatched to bring Hancock's ship next to the *Romney*'s guns. A riot ensued as dockworkers threw stones at the marines before turning their attention to custom officials and their homes. Then, when the *Liberty* was out of range, they dragged a customs boat ashore and burned it on Boston Commons.

Hancock stayed out of the fray and probably watched the flames from his mansion. He became a symbol of resistance and victimhood at the hands of British overreaching.[445] John Adams, as Hancock's attorney, defended Hancock until the smuggling charges against him were dropped.

Meanwhile, the British had grown weary of Boston's resistance and treasonous rhetoric and sent troops to be a visual reminder of who was in charge. At Samuel's Caucus Club, they were discussing ways to get the British out of Boston when Hancock showed his resolve. "Burn Boston, and make John Hancock a beggar, if the public good requires it."[446]

* * *

The Boston Massacre in 1770, ignited by the tensions of keeping so many British soldiers in the city, led Samuel, Hancock, and others to demand the British's removal. The royal governor backed down and removed the troops from the city.

Tensions seemed to relax, and in 1772, Hancock even accepted an appointment to be in charge of acting Royal Governor Thomas Hutchinson's honor guard. But the British wouldn't retreat from what they saw as Parliament's supreme authority to tax the colonies without representation, which led to the tax arrangement that hurt colonial tea merchants, such as Hancock, and to the boycott of British tea. The impasse came to a head on December 16, 1773, and a huge crowd gathered at Boston's South Meeting House to decide what to do.

The governor sent orders to Hancock to use his honor guard troops to disperse the huge crowd, but instead, Hancock had his troops guard the ships to prevent them from unloading.[447] When it was announced at the meeting that Governor Hutchinson again refused to let the tea ships leave without unloading their cargo, the meeting ended abruptly. One person said he heard Hancock yell, "Let every man do what is right in his own eyes."[448]

Boston Harbor became a teapot that night as Bostonians systematically dumped the tea ship's expensive cargo into the water.

* * *

The resistance became too much for the British, who clamped down on Boston and shut the port. On April 18, 1775, the new governor and commander, Thomas Gage, sent British troops to capture Samuel and Hancock in Lexington and seize arms in Concord. Paul Revere arrived in time to warn the men of the danger. They fled but were still close enough to Lexington to hear the first shots of the war fired on Lexington Green.

* * *

Hancock was one of Massachusetts' delegates to the Continental Congress. A few weeks after it began in 1775, Hancock was elected to replace Peyton Randolph as president. He served as president of Congress from May 1775 to October 1777.

Even as president, he hoped to be commander in chief of the Colonial Army. Adams, however, thought Hancock's fickle health and lack of experience made him a bad choice. The great need to unite the colonies and choose a general from the south proved the struggle was not just a New England problem.[449]

When John Adams arose in Congress on June 14, 1775, and proposed appointing a general, Hancock listened "with visible pleasure." But when John Adams nominated George Washington and Samuel Adams jumped up to second the nomination, Hancock was not happy. "When I came to describe Washington for the commander," John Adams later wrote, "I never remarked a more sudden and striking change of countenance. Mortification and resentment were expressed as forcibly as his face could exhibit them."[450]

A few months later, on August 28, 1775, Hancock married Dorothy Quincy at Fairfield, Connecticut.[451]

When the vote for independence was put forward on July 2, 1776, Congress met as a Committee of the Whole—meaning the committee's chairman, Benjamin Harrison, presided. However, Hancock presided when the Declaration was approved on July 4, 1776. Hancock, as president of Congress, and Charles Thomson, the secretary of the Congress, were the only two to sign the document that day. It was whisked off and printed in time to be sent off to provincial congresses, committees of safety, and other patriots. On the printed broadsheet at the bottom, it said, "Signed by Order and in Behalf of the Congress, John Hancock, President."

On August 2, Hancock signed the official handwritten version of the Declaration of Independence with huge letters. Legend says he made his signature large so King George could read it without his spectacles.[452]

Hancock resigned as president in October 1777 because of his battle with gout. He continued as delegate, however, and signed the Articles of Confederation in 1778.

* * *

In 1778, Hancock finally received a real military command as senior major general of the Massachusetts militia. He was in charge of about 6,000 troops from New England and was part of the plan to recapture Newport, Rhode Island, from the British.[453] The French allies, however, did not provide the planned sea power support, forcing the Americans to retreat.

If Hancock kept any animosity for Washington being appointed general instead of himself, it must have dissipated. He named his son Thomas George Washington Hancock, but his son lived only nine years. Bad blood with Samuel, however, lasted more than a decade, according to John Adams.[454]

For the most part, Hancock retreated from national politics and rose in state politics. He took part in the Massachusetts constitutional convention in 1780 and became the first governor of the state of Massachusetts. He served as governor for five years until he was elected to be president of the Continental Congress. Again, illness intervened, and he did not serve, resigning on May 29, 1786. He was again elected governor of Massachusetts and served to the end of his life. Samuel was also active in state politics and served as Hancock's lieutenant governor starting in 1788.

* * *

Hancock did not participate in the Constitutional Convention, but he was essential in the Massachusetts ratification convention. He was, as usual, elected president of the proceedings. His friends flattered him that if Virginia didn't ratify the Constitution, he would be the natural choice for president of the country (George Washington being from Virginia). Hancock pushed for the Constitution's ratification. But Virginia ratified it as well. Once again, George Washington bested him as he became the obvious choice for president.[455]

The vice presidency was probably John Hancock's for the taking—if he had wanted it. Madison wrote that he heard that Hancock told his wife, "She had once been the first in America, & he would never make her the second."[456] Hancock had indeed once been the chief executive of the United States of America—and some argue that he should be seen as its first president. He was, after all, president of the only national government—the Continental Congress—when it declared independence.

Hancock died in Quincy, Massachusetts, on October 8, 1793, at the age of fifty-six. Thousands paid tribute during his funeral. Lieutenant Governor Samuel Adams walked in front of the coffin during the procession. Vice President John Adams walked behind.

"When will the Character of Hancock be understood?" John Adams wrote in 1812. "Never. I could melt into Tears when I hear his Name. . . . If Benevolence, Charity Generosity were ever personified in North America, they were in John Hancock."[457]

John Adams knew Hancock's signature was just another act of his philanthropy—a gift for the ages.

Chapter 26
BENJAMIN HARRISON
Virginia

Benjamin Harrison was called the "Falstaff of Congress" because of his considerable size (he was six feet four inches tall and weighed about 250 pounds) and his love of wine, food, and good humor.[458] The only time his fellow delegates remembered him getting angry was when Samuel Adams cancelled a ball.

* * *

Harrison was born in Berkeley mansion at the family plantation in Charles City County, Virginia, in 1726.[459] He was named after his father, who was named after his father, and so on. He attended the College of William and Mary in Williamsburg, Virginia, but never officially graduated because of a dispute or misunderstanding with officials. But he didn't need to graduate to take over the family business. Tragedy provided that responsibility when his father and two sisters were killed in Berkeley mansion by a lightning strike.[460]

Harrison did well—owning eight plantations with thousands of acres on the James River, many slaves, and factories. He even built his own shipyards.[461] He married his second cousin Elizabeth Bassett in 1748[462] and was soon an ensconced member of the Virginia Colonial House of Burgesses.

* * *

In 1764, he was on a committee to draft a protest of the Stamp Act, but he was conservative enough that he didn't support Patrick Henry's calls for civil disobedience to the act.[463] By 1774, he was a delegate to the Continental Congress. The next year, he lived in the same Philadelphian home as Washington and Randolph. After Washington left and Randolph died, Harrison lived so grandly and hosted so many delegates that he accumulated a debt that took the rest of his life to pay off.

Adams called him "an indolent, luxurious, heavy gentlemen, of no use in Congress or committee, but a great embarrassment to both."[464] This assessment probably had more to do with Harrison's conservative caution than anything else. Rush said Harrison was "a useful member of Congress, sincerely devoted to the welfare of his country."[465] Jefferson thought Harrison's short speeches were the "most successful remarks ever heard in congress."[466] Adams even had to admit that Harrison "contributed many pleasantries that steadied rough sessions."[467]

For example, when some were considering choosing Hancock as president of the Continental Congress, Hancock seemed too humble to Harrison. Harrison grabbed Hancock—whom Britain desperately wanted to bring across the ocean to try for treason—and placed him in the president's chair. "We shall show Mother Britain how little we care for her," Harrison said.[168]

His greatest honor at the Continental Congress was serving as chairman of the Committee of the Whole House. This put him in the position of chairing the deliberations that led to the adoption of the Declaration of Independence. Under Hancock, he presided over Lee's resolution on June 10, 1776, to declare independence and then over the vote for independence on July 2, 1776.

* * *

After serving in Congress, Harrison went back to Virginia and served in its legislature. During the war years, Virginia's legislature fled from town to town to avoid capture. He also served as governor of Virginia from 1782 to 1784. The war was hard on his fortunes. He wrote in 1789 about how "the distresses brought on me by the ravages and plunderings of the British, have reduced me so low" and that his service in Congress "marked me out as a peculiar object of British vengeance; and which they did not fail to execute in the most outrageous manner, when the fortune of war put my whole estate in their power."[469]

At the state convention to ratify the new Constitution in 1788, Harrison opposed it because he thought basic rights should be incorporated in the text. But like other people who opposed the Constitution, he later supported it—with the Bill of Rights amendments.[470]

In April 1791, Harrison was reelected once more to the state legislature, and when it looked as if once it met he would again be made governor, he held a celebration at his home but fell ill and died not long after on April 24, 1791.

His son, William Henry Harrison, became ninth president of the United States, and his great-grandson, yet another Benjamin Harrison, became the twenty-third president.[471]

Chapter 27
JOHN HART
New Jersey

When he was a local justice of the peace, John Hart earned the nickname "Honest John."[472] Ironically, most biographies of Hart exaggerate how he hid from the British and even get his birthplace wrong.

* * *

John Hart was born in late autumn 1713 on the family farm in Hopewell Township, New Jersey. His education was modest, but he worked hard and built up the 400-acre family farm. Over time, he had a gristmill, a fulling mill, and a sawmill.[473] He married Deborah Scudder in 1740, and they had thirteen children.[474]

In 1747, even though he was a Presbyterian, Hart donated land to the Baptists so they could build a church. After that, the area was often called Baptist Meeting House.[475] Hart's generosity and work as a judge landed him in the Provincial Assembly of New Jersey in 1761. He opposed the Stamp Act, and over time, he found himself on the Committee of Safety, the unofficial patriotic government.

* * *

In 1776, the New Jersey delegates in the Continental Congress were opposed to independence, so they were dumped, and the provincial congress chose new delegates, including Hart. He arrived just a few days before the votes for independence and was able to vote for and later sign the Declaration of Independence. Rush described Hart as "a plain, honest, well meaning Jersey farmer, with but little education, but with good sense and virtue enough to pursue the true interests of his country."[476]

In August, under New Jersey's new state constitution, Hart was elected to the first New Jersey State General Assembly and was made speaker. He went home to see his sick wife on October 5, then returned to the assembly but was called home again. His wife died on October 8, and the assembly shut down for about a month because it was unable to work without the speaker.[477]

By November, the British were in New Jersey. In December, they were close to Hart's home. He sent his two young children, eleven-year-old

Deborah and fourteen-year-old Daniel (his oldest child was born thirty-four years earlier)[478] to stay with friends. The sixty-three-year-old widower then fled to a cave for a few days while the British plundered his farm.[479]

Other histories often erroneously have him on the lam for more than a year only to come home to learn his wife had died, his home had been destroyed, and his children had gone missing. Then he died from sorrow. In reality, less than a month after going into hiding, after Washington's victory at Trenton, the British retreated from the area and Hart returned.

Hart continued in state politics. In June 1778, he played host to Washington and 12,000 troops who camped in his fields. But he didn't live to see the end of the war. John Hart died on his estate at Hopewell on May 11, 1779, at the age of sixty-eight from a case of gravel (what today we call kidney stones).[480]

Hart's grave is in the cemetery of the Baptist Church he donated years earlier. Even Honest John's gravestone gives the wrong year of death: 1780 instead of 1779.

Chapter 28

JOSEPH HEWES
North Carolina

Joseph Hewes, as chairman of the Continental Congress's naval committee, tried his best to get his friend John Paul Jones a commission as a captain on a ship. Adams, however, wasn't about to give any more high-ranking jobs to anybody from the South after Virginian Washington was made the commander of the army.[481]

The best Hewes could do was to get his buddy the job of first lieutenant on the *Alfred*—the colonial navy's first ship, which sailed in February 1776.[482] It wasn't a captain's position, but Jones would end up doing fine. Hewes believed in the fight against Britain and the necessity of ships like the *Alfred*, but, ironically, he was also one of the last holdouts on choosing actual independence.

* * *

Joseph Hewes was born on January 23, 1730, in Kingston, New Jersey, and was the son of well-to-do, pious Quakers.[483] He was apprenticed to a Philadelphia merchant as a clerk and then started his own business and moved to Edenton, North Carolina, in 1756. Edenton was a bustling seaport town, and Hewes did well as a merchant, not to mention having his own fleet of ships for trade with Britain.[484] He also brought in his nephew Nathaniel Allen Jr. as his partner.

Hewes raised his political prospects when he fell in love with Isabelle Johnston. Unfortunately, just a few days before their marriage, she died suddenly.[485] His relations with her well-connected family, however, continued as if he had become the Johnston's son-in-law. Success in business made Hewes viable for politics, and he entered the Colonial House of Commons in 1766.

In 1774, he was sent as a delegate to the Continental Congress in Philadelphia. Even though his business relied on trade with Great Britain, he agreed with his fellow delegates to stop trading with the country if the British didn't recognize the colonists' rights. At the time, he reflected on the possible fate of those in Congress should the British capture them. He wrote, "Were I to suffer in the cause of American liberty, should I not be translated immediately to heaven as Enoch was of old?"[486]

Hewes broke philosophically from the Quakers in 1775 when they spoke out against the Continental Congress.[487] His expertise with his own ships made him ideal to chair the committee responsible for fitting out the first U.S. Navy warships. At some point, he even rented some of his ships to Congress.[488]

Hewes was a strong supporter of rebellion but not quite independence, so he was not enthused about the Halifax Resolves—instructions from the North Carolina provincial assembly that if independence were proposed, North Carolina's delegates should vote for it. "We do not want to be independent," he wrote to someone in England. "We want no revolution. But every American to a man is determined to die or be free."[489]

Hewes changed his mind about independence after a speech in July 1776. Adams recalled, "Mr. Hewes, who had hitherto constantly voted against it, started suddenly upright, and lifting up both his hands to Heaven, as if he had been in a trance, cried out, 'It is done! and I will abide by it.'"[490]

Adams said Hewes's outburst put a look of "terror and horror" on those who had previously counted on Hewes's opposition to independence.[491] Adams gave much of the credit for the unanimity of the states to Hewes's change of heart.[492]

Hewes was defeated for reelection in 1777 and didn't get back to the Continental Congress until 1779.[493] He arrived back in Philadelphia in July 1779 and would never return home.

He said once, "My country is entitled to my services, and I shall not shrink from her cause, even though it should cost me my life."[494]

On November 10, 1779, he died of illness in Philadelphia. He was forty-nine years old and had never married.

Congress wore black mourning armbands for a month.[495]

Chapter 29

THOMAS HEYWARD JR.
South Carolina

Thomas Heyward Jr. joined the South Carolina militia in 1779 and was a captain of artillery when he was wounded during the successful defense of Port Royal Island. The British meant business, however, and laid siege to Charleston. Along the way, the British looted Heyward's large estate, even taking many slaves and selling them to work on sugar plantations in Jamaica.[496]

When Charleston finally surrendered on May 12, 1780, Heyward and his fellow Signer of the Declaration of Independence, Edward Rutledge, were rounded up with many others and sent to prison in St. Augustine, Florida.[497]

* * *

Heyward was born in St. Luke's Parish, South Carolina, on July 28, 1746. He was the eldest son of tobacco planter Daniel Heyward. He got stuck with "junior" to distinguish himself from his uncle Thomas.[498] He was shipped off to study law at Middle Temple at Cambridge University in London, England, and five years later, on May 25, 1770, at the age of twenty-three, he was admitted to the bar. After the obligatory European tour, he was back in South Carolina and starting his practice. Heyward rose quickly. He had a large estate north of Savannah, began in politics, and married Elizabeth Matthews on April 20, 1773.[499]

From the South Carolina General Assembly, Heyward was sent as a delegate to the Continental Congress and arrived in time for the debate on independence, followed by the signing of the Declaration of Independence. He stuck around long enough to also sign the Articles of Confederation in 1778.

* * *

In addition to acting as a circuit judge and serving in the State House of Representatives, Heyward signed up with the militia when the British captured him in 1780. As a prisoner in Florida, he was more under house arrest than in chains. The prisoners—who had to give their parole or promise not to escape—could walk around the town, and they lived in a large house with a garden and orange grove. Besides the loss of freedom to leave and rejoin the fight or their families, the worst trial was the smelly water they had to drink.[500]

After about a year, in July 1781, they received news that they were going to be exchanged for British prisoners. A July 4 banquet was held that included, according to some sources, a rousing rendition of "God Save the King." The prisoners' version, however, had more revolutionary-appropriate lyrics that Heyward may have written for the occasion:

God save the Thirteen States!
Long rule the United States!
God save our States!
Make us victorious,
Happy and glorious;
No tyrants over us;
God save our States![501]

On the way to freedom in Philadelphia, Heyward almost died when he fell overboard. He clung on to the rudder until they were able to pull him back aboard. His wife, Elizabeth, was there in Philadelphia to meet him when he arrived. Their reunion lasted about a year. She died August 16, 1782, a few days after giving birth to a boy they named Thomas. The baby lived two months.[502]

When the British finally left Charleston, Heyward returned home. He married his second wife, Elizabeth Savage, on May 4, 1786, and mostly retired from public life. Heyward died on April 17, 1809, in St. Luke's Parish, South Carolina, at the same family estate where he was born. That estate, however, was now part of an independent nation, "victorious, happy, and glorious," which Heyward had helped create and defend.

Chapter 30
WILLIAM HOOPER
North Carolina

*I*t was a revolt about unfair taxation, and William Hooper was against it. The "Regulator" uprising in North Carolina pitted rural colonists against the corrupt taxing authorities. Hooper was deputy attorney general of the colony and advised the royal governor, William Tryon, to put down the uprising with the militia. Hooper was there when the militia finally crushed the rebellion at the battle of Alamance in 1771.[503] Five years later, Hooper would start a little rebellion himself when he signed a certain document in Philadelphia.

* * *

Hooper was born in Massachusetts in 1742. His career path was to follow his father into the Episcopal priesthood.[504]

It didn't happen. Instead, he studied law with James Otis, a political radical. Otis was a leading attorney in Boston and, at the time, was fighting a legal battle with the British abuse of writs of assistance or search warrants. Tax agents were using the writs to harass Boston merchants they suspected of smuggling, and Otis was at the center of calling the British on the citizens' rights carpet, which probably influenced young Hooper.

Hooper moved to Wilmington, North Carolina, in 1767, was married that year to Anne Clark, and started his legal and political rise. His father, however, wanted him to return to Boston because he was worried about Hooper's health.[505]

After the Regulator uprising, Hooper parted political company with Tryon. He wrote to a friend in 1774: "The Colonies are striding fast to independence, and ere long will build an empire upon the ruins of Great Britain; will adopt its Constitution, purged of its impurities, and from an experience of its defects, will guard against those evils which have wasted its vigor."[506]

One of the things that pushed Hooper toward independence was the Loyalists proposing a plan to prevent creditors from putting liens on the property of people who were not residents of North Carolina. This was specifically designed to protect North Carolinians from getting money out of landowners who lived in England. Hooper condemned this favoritism in a series of newspaper articles he signed under the pseudonym "Hampden."[507]

* * *

Hooper served in the Continental Congress from 1774 to 1777. In Congress, Adams identified him as one of the better orators.[508] While in Congress, in 1775, Hooper wrote to people in Jamaica to explain the political situation and complained that the British ignored petitions for justice and saw them as signs of rebellion. Britain instead sent armies. "It has plunged us in all the horrors and calamities of civil war: it has caused the treasure and blood of Britons . . . to be spilt and wasted in the execrable design of spreading slavery over British America: it will not, however, accomplish its aim: in the worst of contingencies, a choice will still be left, which it can never prevent us from making."[509]

That choice was independence. Hooper arrived in Philadelphia in 1776 in time to vote in favor of the Declaration of Independence on July 4 and to sign his name in August.

In 1777, Hooper had to return home to help his family because when the British invaded North Carolina, they burned his home in Wilmington. He had to rely on the charity of friends as he avoided capture and was separated from his wife and children. By the time the war was over, he had lost everything but his family.[510]

Hooper's moderate and charitable position toward Loyalists[511] didn't help his political career either (he couldn't even get elected to the state's convention to ratify the Constitution). In 1786, Congress sent him to help solve a boundary dispute between New York and Massachusetts but ended up solving it without his help.

Hooper never regained his place of prominence—or his health. He died in Hillsboro, North Carolina, on October 14, 1790, the day before his daughter's planned wedding.[512] He was forty-eight years old and left a legacy of integrity and sacrifice.

Chapter 31
STEPHEN HOPKINS
Rhode Island

Like several of the Signers of the Declaration of Independence, Stephen Hopkins, of Rhode Island, owned slaves. Unlike most, he freed his slaves during his lifetime.

In 1773, Hopkins became an abolitionist, and in 1774, he successfully pushed for the Rhode Island legislature to pass a bill that forbade importing slaves to the colony. It may have been the first anti-slavery legislation in America.[513]

* * *

Stephen Hopkins was born in Providence, Rhode Island, at the place later called Scituate, on March 7, 1707.[514] His education was basic, but his proficiency in math opened up surveyor's work. He married Sarah Scott on October 29, 1726, and started out with a 160-acre farm.[515]

Before long, Hopkins was town clerk and was elected to the colonial legislature. It was almost as if he were collecting political positions rather than going from one to another. By 1736, he was a legislator, town clerk, president of the town council, and justice of the peace. A few years later, he was speaker of the Rhode Island legislature. A year after that, he was chief justice of the Court of Common Pleas.

Hopkins expanded his interests further by entering the merchant marine business with his brother Esek in 1740. Two years later, he sold his farm and moved to Providence to work more on the business—owning and having ships built.[516] In Providence, he maintained his public career—and even helped found the Providence public library.[517]

Hopkins's wife, Sarah, died in 1753. The next year, he was a delegate to the Albany Convention, where Franklin proposed a plan to unite the colonies—something the British government rejected.

Hopkins married his second wife, the widow Ann Smith, in 1755 and was the colonial governor of Rhode Island—a position he held on and off until 1767.

* * *

Independence was still twenty years away when Hopkins opposed the Stamp Act. His career continued as a judge and as the first chancellor of Rhode Island College in 1764, which was later named Brown University.

By the end of 1764, Hopkins wrote "The Rights of Colonies Examined," a pamphlet attacking the Stamp Act and the Sugar Act. He argued that direct taxation of a nonconsenting people was tyrannical.[518] 1764 was also the year Esek was captain of the slave ship *Sally*. The *Sally* left Africa with 196 slaves on board. Through sickness, suicides, and even a violent attempt to take over the ship, 109 of those Africans died on the journey. It may have been this horrific journey his brother faced that influenced Hopkins to free his slaves in 1773.[519]

By the time Hopkins was chosen as a delegate of Rhode Island for the first Continental Congress in 1774, he was sixty-seven years old. Only Franklin was older.[520] Hopkins's life experience gave him wisdom to see to the heart of the conflict with Britain. He told Congress, "Powder and ball will decide this question. The gun and bayonet alone will finish the contest in which we are engaged, and any of you who cannot bring your minds to this mode of adjusting this question had better retire in time."[521]

But he was not all grimness and was known to imbibe a bit. Adams said, "Hopkins never drank to excess, but all he drank was immediately not only converted into wit, sense, knowledge, and good humor, but inspired us with similar qualities."[522]

By May 1776, Rhode Island had severed its ties to King George III.

Hopkins worked on the naval committee, and Esek was appointed the first commander in chief of the continental navy. When the colonies declared independence and it was time to sign the Declaration of Independence in August, Hopkins's hand shook so badly he had to hold his right wrist with his left hand to write. He commented as he signed his signature, "My hand trembles, but my heart does not."[523]

Hopkins retired from public life in 1780. He lived to see the Revolution's success, and after an extended illness, he died in Providence on July 13, 1785. He was seventy-eight.[524]

Chapter 32
FRANCIS HOPKINSON
New Jersey

Francis Hopkinson was the Jay Leno or Stephen Colbert of his time. He wrote humorous poems ridiculing politicians and kings, and his most popular work was the song "The Battle of the Kegs" about an attempt to sink British ships at Philadelphia during the Revolutionary War by floating explosive-filled-barrels down the Delaware River.[525] The British responded to the mines by shooting at anything that floated. Hopkinson couldn't resist mocking the British as they bravely battled the infernal barrels. One verse of the song (sung to the tune of "Yankee Doodle") follows:

Such feats did they perform that day
Against those wicked kegs, sir,
That years to come, if they get home,
They'll make their boasts and brags, sir.[526]

* * *

Hopkinson was born in Philadelphia in the fall of 1737. His father was a lawyer educated at Oxford in England and was a friend of Franklin. Hopkinson was fourteen when his father died. He was in the first class to graduate from the College of Philadelphia (later the University of Pennsylvania) in 1757. His interests and skills ran the gamut. He wrote poems, satires, songs, and music. He painted and drew cartoons. He played the organ and, like Franklin, was an inventor.[527]

But a man had to eat, so he studied law and was admitted to the bar in 1761. He was then appointed collector of customs in Salem, New Jersey. When he was twenty-eight, he went to England to visit his uncle, the bishop of Worcester, and spent fourteen months there, even dining with the prime minister, Lord Frederick North (an even more distant relative).[528] He was hoping for a better government appointment but had no luck. He did, however, visit with his father's old friend Franklin and also Penn and the artist Benjamin West.

When Hopkinson got back, he married Ann Borden on September 1, 1768. They lived in Bordentown, New Jersey, which was named after her father.[529]

* * *

In 1774, Hopkinson wrote a satire called "A Pretty Story." It portrayed the British king as the owner of a large farm who meddled with his children who had moved to a distant farm.[530] "His forte was humour and satire, in both of which he was not surpassed by Lucian, Swift, or Rabelais. These extraordinary powers were consecrated to the advancement of the interests of patriotism, virtue, and science," Rush said.[531]

Hopkinson's advancement of patriotism stepped up after the New Jersey legislature imprisoned the royal governor, William Franklin (Benjamin Franklin's son). Hopkinson was chosen as part of the new delegation to the Continental Congress. He didn't serve long, only June 22 to November 30, 1776, but a lot happened in that time period—including the signing of the Declaration of Independence.

Adams wrote his wife, Abigail, about Hopkinson: "He is one of your pretty, little, curious, ingenious men.... His head is not bigger than a large apple.... I have not met with anything in natural history more amusing and entertaining than his personal appearance—yet he is genteel and well-bred, and is very social."[532] Rush also commented on Hopkinson's small size."His features were small, but extremely animated. His speech was quick, and all his motions seemed to partake of the unceasing activity and versatility of the powers of his mind."[533]

One thing Hopkinson applied the powers of his mind to was the design of the American flag. Others may claim that honor, but Hopkinson left a paper trail. It is pretty certain that he at least designed some version of an American flag, if not the familiar one, because he sent a bill to Congress for the flag design. His price was "a Quarter cask of the Public Wine." Congress refused to pay, however, saying the work fell under his duties.[534]

He continued writing satire, including the hilarious "Battle of the Kegs" in 1778. He served as judge of the admiralty of Pennsylvania for a decade, beginning in 1779.

In 1779, Hessians, the German mercenaries employed by the British, plundered his house at Bordentown. After the war, Hopkinson was mysteriously delivered one of his books that had been stolen. Inside was a new inscription by the commander of the Hessians, Captain Johann Ewald. Ewald wrote, "This man was one of the greatest Rebels, nevertheless, if we dare to conclude from the library and mechanical and mathematical instruments, he must have been a very learned Man also."[535]

* * *

Satire again flowed from Hopkinson's pen in defense of the new Constitution in 1787. In "The Roof," he likened the Anti-Federalists to someone who preferred a leaky roof over one built by an expert.[536]

After the Constitution was ratified, Hopkinson organized the Grand Federal Procession on July 4, 1788, that took place in Philadelphia. Five thousand people came to watch the parade, which included a thirty-six-foot-high "Grand Federal Edifice" float featuring a Greek temple on a cart pulled by ten white horses.[537]

Washington appointed Hopkinson as a federal circuit judge for eastern Pennsylvania in 1789. He opened his court on November 10, 1789—the first operating court under the Constitution. That same year, he helped organize the Protestant Episcopal Church.[538]

Another first for Hopkinson, of which he was proud, was the composition of the music for the first original American song put down on paper, "My Days Have Been So Wondrous Free."[539]

Hopkinson's life was cut short on May 9, 1791, at the age of fifty-three, when he suddenly lost consciousness—possibly from a stroke—and died within two hours.[540] His humor and artistic talents found their outlet in freedom and a flag that continues to fly.

Chapter 33
SAMUEL HUNTINGTON
Connecticut

When Samuel Huntington was apprenticed to a cooper to learn how to make barrels, it probably seemed a step up from being a plowboy. But he wasn't satisfied, so when he finished his apprenticeship at age twenty-two, he studied law on his own and was admitted to the bar in 1758.[541] Huntington rose quickly in the legal ranks, becoming a judge of the superior court in 1774.

The only thing that ever seemed to hold him back was ill health.

* * *

Huntington served in the Continental Congress in 1776 and signed the Declaration of Independence. Three years later, he replaced John Jay as president of Congress. The Articles of Confederation went into effect in 1781 after the last state, Maryland, ratified them, making Huntington the first president of the United States Congress under the Articles of Confederation. But he had to step down because of overwork and ill health later that year. He was reelected in 1782 but didn't go back to Congress for his last year in 1783.

After he left Congress, he served in every important Connecticut state office, from chief justice of the superior court to governor in 1786.[542] He was liked well enough to be reelected as governor every year for a decade.

Huntington supported the new Constitution in 1787 and even received two electoral votes in the first presidential election in 1789. (Everyone knew Washington would win, but the vice president's position was still up for grabs.)[543]

Huntington and his wife, Martha Devotion, had no children but adopted two of Huntington's brother Joseph's children.[544] One person who lived with Huntington's family for twenty-four years said they never saw Huntington angry, that he never spoke a word to wound anyone's feelings, and that he never spoke negatively about people behind their backs.[545]

In 1795, while still governor of Connecticut, Huntington fell seriously ill—losing control of his body and mind. He died in his home in Norwich, Connecticut, on January 5, 1796, at the age of sixty-five.

Chapter 34
THOMAS JEFFERSON
Virginia

Virginia Governor Jefferson had had his fill of leadership by 1781 and was anxious for his term to expire and for someone else to take charge. During much of the Revolutionary War, Britain concentrated its invasions on other parts of the emerging nation, but in May, Lord Cornwallis invaded the unprepared Virginia. The traitor Benedict Arnold attacked the state's capital, Richmond. Jefferson and the legislature fled to what they thought was the isolated safety of Charlottesville.

When Cornwallis learned where Virginia's rebel government was conducting business, he planned a bold attack.

On June 3, Cornwallis sent British Lieutenant Colonel Banastre Tarleton, with a small group of cavalry, to surprise the legislature and governor. Tarleton moved fast through the undefended countryside. There was nothing to stop him from capturing the writer of the Declaration of Independence at his home in Monticello.

* * *

Thomas Jefferson was born on April 13, 1743, in Albemarle County, Virginia, at his father, Peter Jefferson's, plantation, Shadwell.[546]

In 1757, Jefferson was fourteen and the oldest of his nine siblings—so when his father died, he inherited more than 2,000 acres and thirty slaves.[547] A few years later, he entered the College of William and Mary in Williamsburg, Virginia. Jefferson graduated in 1762 and began to study law under George Wythe, who would one day sign the Declaration of Independence that his student wrote.

When Jefferson was twenty-two years old, he was deeply impressed as he heard Patrick Henry speak against the Stamp Act. "He appeared to me to speak as Homer wrote," Jefferson later wrote.[548]

Jefferson became a lawyer in 1767 and practiced law for seven years in Williamsburg. It was during those years that Jefferson entered politics. He was elected to the House of Burgesses, Virginia's royal legislature, in 1769, but he avoided debate and made a reputation for himself in writing well.

In 1770, he began building his magnificent Monticello home near Charlottesville, and two years later, he married Martha Wayles Skelton, a widow. Jefferson and his talented but frail wife would have six children, though only two daughters survived to adulthood. The first, Martha "Patsy," lived to 1836.

As events pushed forward toward independence in 1773, Jefferson met with Richard Lee, Francis Lightfoot Lee, Patrick Henry, and Dabney Carr to write resolutions to form a committee of correspondence. Carr, Jefferson's brother-in-law, died a month later, and Jefferson's sister, with her six children, came to live at Monticello.[549] A few weeks later, Jefferson's father-in-law, John Wayles, died. Jefferson's wife's inheritance of 11,000 acres and 142 slaves made the couple rich.[550] With his newfound wealth, Jefferson abandoned his law practice to his cousin Edmund Randolph in 1774.

Jefferson also continued working in the House of Burgesses and, in May 1774, approved of a resolution calling for fasting and prayer for the king and Parliament to lift the closing of Boston Harbor. Instead, the royal governor of Virginia shut down the legislature.

This led the legislature to join the call for a general gathering of representatives from the various colonies—a Continental Congress.[551]

* * *

Jefferson didn't attend the first Congress in 1774. The next year, he went to Philadelphia as a replacement delegate after the president of the Congress, Randolph, came back to Virginia. As he had been in the House of Burgesses, Jefferson was silent on the floor but eloquent in committees and with the written word.[552]

Jefferson traveled back and forth between Congress and Monticello for business and tragedy. His baby girl, Jane, died in August 1775, and his mother died in March 1776. He was back in Congress by May 14, 1776.

"During the whole Time I sat with him in Congress, I never heard him utter three Sentences together," Adams wrote in his autobiography. But Jefferson had another skill. "Mr. Jefferson had the Reputation of a masterly Pen."[553]

Less than a month after Jefferson returned to Congress, on June 7, 1776, fellow Virginian Richard made a formal call for independence. The motion was tabled for several weeks to give time for delegates to confer with their legislatures. In the meantime, a committee was chosen to prepare an expression of the reasons for independence. If Richard's resolution passed, they wanted to be ready.

The logical choice of people to write the motion would have been the person who called for it, Richard. But he had to return home. Adams also could have been the main author, but he was shrewd enough to know that a Southern voice could help unify the delegates. "I had a great Opinion of the Elegance of his pen and none at all of my own," Adams wrote of Jefferson.[554]

A week after Richard's motion, thirty-three-year-old Jefferson was selected to chair the committee. Also joining him was Adams from Massachusetts, Franklin from Pennsylvania; Sherman, from Connecticut; and Robert R. Livingston, from New York.

"The committee of 5 met . . . [and] they unanimously pressed on myself alone to undertake the draught," Jefferson recalled forty-seven years later.

> I consented; I drew it; but before I reported it to the committee, I communicated it <u>separately</u> to Dr. Franklin and Mr. Adams requesting their corrections; because they were the two members of whose judgments and amendments I wished most to have the benefit before presenting it to the Committee. . . . Their alterations were two or three only, and merely verbal. I then wrote a fair copy, reported it to the Committee, and from them, unaltered to Congress. . . . Whether I had gathered my ideas from reading or reflection I do not know. I know only that I turned to neither book or pamphlet while writing it. I did not consider it as any part of my charge to invent new ideas altogether and to offer no sentiment which had ever been expressed before.[555]

Jefferson wrote the Declaration at his apartment on the second floor of a home on Market Street and Seventh Street. He used a portable writing desk he had invented—a sort of eighteenth-century laptop.

On July 2, Richard's independence resolutions were approved, and the debate over the wording of the Declaration of Independence began. Jefferson chafed as Congress debated various passages of his draft.

They cut criticism of the people of England.

Jefferson's clauses criticizing the slave trade were removed.

Notwithstanding the changes, Jefferson joined the delegates in signing the Declaration on August 2, 1776.[556] He did not initially win any fame for his authorship—he wouldn't be publicly known as the author of the Declaration of Independence until 1784.[557]

* * *

Before long, Jefferson found himself the only Virginia representative still present in Congress. His wife begged him to come home, but he couldn't find any other Virginia delegate willing to return to Congress to relieve him. Eventually, on September 1, 1776, he just left—leaving Virginia without a vote.[558]

While in Williamsburg, he received the request from Congress to go to France. It was the chance of a lifetime for Jefferson. But trips abroad were not counted in days or weeks but in months and years. His wife's health took precedence, and he turned down the request.[559] Instead, Jefferson threw himself into making a state out of Virginia. He worked in Virginia's House of Delegates, the lower house of the new state's legislature.[560] He wrote bills on subjects ranging from limiting the death penalty to establishing free public schools.

His crowning achievement in Virginia was writing the statute for religious freedom. The document stated, among other things that "all men shall be free to profess and by argument to maintain their opinions in matters of religion, and that the same shall in no wise diminish, enlarge or affect their civil capacities."[561]

During the time of his political work in Virginia, he and his wife had more children. In May 1777, Jefferson and Martha had a son. He lived only a little more than two weeks. A year later, in August 1778, they had a daughter, Mary "Polly." In 1780, Lucy Elizabeth was born, but she died in the spring of 1781.

Jefferson's political star seemed to rise higher when, in June 1779, Virginia's legislature selected him to succeed Henry as governor of Virginia.

* * *

Governor Jefferson only faced problems. The economy was tanking. He couldn't get the militia into shape. Then, in 1781, Lord Cornwallis and Arnold invaded Virginia. Later, on June 3, Cornwallis sent Tarleton to capture Jefferson and the Virginia legislature at Charlottesville.

It was around 10:00 p.m. when Tarleton and his men approached the Cuckoo Tavern about forty miles from Monticello. They had been making good time and decided to rest the horses and soldiers for the final leg of their journey. If all went well, they would surprise the governor and legislature and, in one swoop, capture Virginia's entire government.

But things didn't go well for the British.

A captain in the Virginia militia, Jack Jouett, saw Tarleton's approaching troops and realized at once what it meant. He jumped on his horse and galloped west. Jouett knew the countryside and left the main road, and legend says his trip through the thick woods, trees, and bushes left his face scarred. In the last hour of his ride, the moon set. He arrived at Monticello at about 4:30 a.m. After informing Jefferson, Jouett continued his ride to warn the rest of the legislators in town.

Thinking they had plenty of time, Jefferson calmly ate breakfast, then sent his guests and his family away. He stayed behind, supervising the hiding of valuables and the securing of important documents. When a neighbor warned that the troops were at the foot of the mountain, Jefferson jumped on his horse and fled through the woods.

Tarleton's troops missed capturing him by just minutes.

Henry and others later accused Jefferson of abandoning his position as governor—even though his term had officially expired on June 2, two days before he'd fled. The accusations left Jefferson frustrated.

* * *

About a year later, on May 8, 1782, Martha gave birth to their final child, also named Lucy Elizabeth.[562] Martha, her health always fragile, did not recover.

In her decline, she wrote a quote from a favorite book on a piece of paper:

"Time wastes too fast: every letter
I trace tells me with what rapidity
Life follows my pen. The days and hours
Of it are flying over our heads
Like clouds of windy day, never to return
More everything presses on—"

Jefferson finished writing the quote in his own hand:
"—and every
Time I kiss thy hand to bid adieu,
Every sentence which follows it, are preludes to
that eternal separation
Which we are shortly to make!"[563]

On September 6, 1782, Martha died.[564] It was a month before her thirty-fourth birthday. As she lay dying, she made Jefferson promise to never marry again. She had suffered under her father's second wife and feared the same thing for her own children.[565] On her grave monument, Jefferson caused to be written how she was "torn from him by death."[566]

Her death was devastating for Jefferson. Randolph described Jefferson's mourning as "violent." People said he would faint whenever he saw his children.[567] "This miserable kind of existence is really too burthensome to be borne," Jefferson wrote about a month after his wife died. The responsibility of taking care of his children kept him going, but all he saw was "gloom unbrightened with one cheerful expectation."[568]

Two years later, he observed, "I have had many causes of gratitude to heaven, but I have also experienced its rigors."[569]

* * *

Jefferson finally began to emerge from his grief and accepted Congress's appointment for him to join Franklin in Paris to help negotiate peace. He left Monticello and arrived in Baltimore, where he was to take a ship to France. Before he went, however, reports said a treaty had already been struck. He returned to Monticello, once again missing his chance to travel abroad.[570]

In 1783, he was back in Congress again.

The next year, however, Jefferson finally went to Europe to work with Franklin and Jefferson's old friend, Adams, in negotiating various treaties. He brought Martha "Patsy," his twelve-year-old daughter, with him. His younger daughters, Mary "Polly" and Lucy "Lu," stayed with their aunt Elizabeth Epps.

In January of 1785, a letter told him his baby daughter Lu had died from sickness. The loss kept him out of commission all winter.[571] In spring, Ambassador Franklin returned home, and Jefferson took his place. Adams went to Britain. When people asked him if he was Franklin's replacement, Jefferson would reply, "No one can replace him. I am his successor."[572]

While in France, Jefferson saw the first rumblings of the French Revolution and was kept abreast of the Constitutional Convention back in America by Madison.

Jefferson liked the proposed Constitution, except it did not have any guarantee of basic rights. He advocated not ratifying it until a promise was given that a Bill of Rights would be added to the document.

* * *

When Jefferson came home in October 1789, he was surprised when Washington, the first president of the United States under the newly ratified Constitution, asked him to be secretary of state. After a few months, Jefferson accepted—albeit reluctantly.[573]

Alexander Hamilton was Washington's secretary of the treasury. In 1790, Hamilton tried to get the federal government to take over the states' individual war debts, but Jefferson opposed this, seeing it as a backhanded way to decrease the states' autonomy. Out of this and other conflicts grew the beginnings of the two-party system in America. Hamilton's party became known as the Federalist Party and Jefferson's group as the Democratic-Republicans.[574]

In 1793, Jefferson watched the French Revolution and the execution of France's royalty from afar. With France and Great Britain at war, Jefferson wanted neutrality—although he wanted the United States to supply the French.

By July 1793, Jefferson had had his fill of politics. He stayed in Washington's cabinet until December and then returned to Monticello, once again withdrawing from society. In December 1796, Jefferson told Adams, "I have no ambition to govern men. It is a painful and thankless office."[575]

By 1797, he had changed his mind.

* * *

When Washington declared he was not going to seek a third term, Jefferson found himself running against Adams for the 1797 presidential election.

Adams won the presidency with seventy-one electoral votes. Jefferson, because of the way the elections were set up in the Constitution, won the vice president's office with sixty-eight electoral votes.[576] At the end of Adams's turbulent presidency, Jefferson ran against his former friend again. The campaign was brutal.

Hamilton considered Jefferson "an *Atheist in Religion* and a *Fanatic* in politics."[577] Adams would later say, to charges that Jefferson was irreligious, that it had nothing to do with the public and that Jefferson was a good patriot, citizen, and father.[578]

Disagreements between Hamilton and Adams split the Federalist vote, leaving Adams with sixty-five electoral votes. Jefferson and Burr, Jefferson's running mate, both won seventy-three electoral votes. This sort of thing was not supposed to happen. The tie went to the House of Representatives, where the Federalists tried to make the voting last as long as possible. On the thirty-sixth ballot, Jefferson won over Burr, who became vice president.

Two strange elections in a row eventually led to the twelfth amendment to the Constitution, which changed the way the president and vice president were elected.[579]

Jefferson's popularity soared when he struck a deal with Napoleon Bonaparte to buy the territory of Louisiana from the French, doubling the size of the United States for a mere $15 million. He also sent Meriwether Lewis and William Clark on their epic journey of discovery across the West.

In 1804, Jefferson was easily reelected, but his happiness dissolved when his youngest daughter, Mary "Polly," died in April.[580]

Jefferson continued to try to balance neutrality and interests as Britain and France were at war. At the end of his presidency, he withdrew from political life for good. He supported his secretary of state, Madison, for president and in 1809 returned to Monticello. "Never did a prisoner released from his chains feel such relief," he later wrote.[581]

* * *

Even though his political days were over, Jefferson did not really retire. He was particularly fond of his "child," the University of Virginia, which he had founded in nearby Charlottesville, Virginia, in 1825. He did everything from deciding the coursework to designing the buildings and hiring the teachers.[582]

Jefferson renewed his friendship with Adams through Rush's efforts. Jefferson and Adams had become bitter enemies during both of their presidencies. Rush successfully encouraged the two Founding Fathers to write to each other. "I rejoice in the correspondence which has taken place between you and your old friend Mr. Jefferson. I consider you and him as the North and South Poles of the American Revolution," Rush wrote to Adams.[583]

Jefferson spent his final years on the edge of economic ruin. He even sold his library to Congress to pay debts. His books became the seed that started the Library of Congress.[584]

In 1826, his health began to fail.

As the fiftieth anniversary of the signing of the Declaration of Independence approached, Jefferson was fading fast. He struggled to last until the Fourth of July. He died around 12:50 p.m. Adams died later that evening.

* * *

Jefferson left a poem of farewell to his surviving child, Martha. Part of it said,
"I go to my fathers, I welcome the shore
Which crowns all my hopes and buries my cares. . . .
Two seraphs [his wife and daughter Mary "Polly"] await me long shrouded in death
I will bear them your love on my last parting breath."[585]

Six months later, almost everything and everyone he had owned were sold at auction. His home was stripped. Although he had given some slaves their freedom, 130 slaves were put up for sale. Monticello itself was eventually sold for $7,000. But even all that was not enough to pay Jefferson's debt. His namesake grandson, Thomas Jefferson Randolph, spent two decades working to pay off those debts out of honor to his grandfather.[586]

* * *

Although much has been written about Jefferson and his slaves, this short biography doesn't go into detail about the topic. This is simply because the issues raised are so complicated and show so many apparently contradictory sides of Jefferson's character that it deserves greater attention than this short work can provide. The possibility of his having children with his slave Sarah "Sally" Hemings is also not discussed for the same reason. DNA evidence points toward a Jefferson male as being the father of at least one of Hemings's children—most likely Jefferson himself or his brother Randolph Jefferson. In many books, articles, movies, and popular media, the romantic story appeal of having the "father of freedom" in a long-term relationship with a slave often trumps the actual but frustratingly inconclusive scientific and historical record. The sad fact remains, however, that even if Jefferson did not have children with Hemings, he owned her and legally or practically could have done as he pleased. Suffice it to say that Jefferson, like other Signers, kept slaves—such is his tragic legacy. His extraordinary legacy, however, inspired later generations to complete the triumphant implications of the Declaration of Independence: All people are created equal. His strivings to push principles beyond their borders (and even his own social and intellectual borders) still challenge the enemies of liberty abroad, at home, and in the hearts of all people.

Chapter 35

FRANCIS LIGHTFOOT LEE
Virginia

Mark Twain said that Francis Lightfoot Lee's "life-work was so inconspicuous, that his name would be wholly forgotten, but for one thing—he signed the Declaration of Independence."[587] It is true that Lee's loquacious brother Richard Henry Lee overshadowed him, but Lee was considered by contemporaries to be even more enthusiastically patriotic.

* * *

Lee was born on October 14, 1734, at "Stratford" in Westmoreland County, Virginia—the same birthplace as a later and more famous Lee; however, that later Lee, General Robert E. Lee, would work to break up some of what the earlier Lee accomplished.

Lee was the fourth oldest of six brothers, but unlike his other brothers, Lee was not educated abroad. He was taught by tutors at the family estate.[588] After his father, Thomas, died in 1750, Lee's portion of the inheritance included a large estate, and a few years later, he was in the Virginia House of Burgesses. He never met a protest against England's rule that he didn't like, beginning with the protest against the Stamp Act in 1766; he signed the Westmoreland Resolves in opposition of it.[589]

He didn't get married until age thirty-eight, when he married his first cousin Rebecca Tayloe. She was the daughter of another wealthy plantation owner.

When the second Continental Congress was called in 1775, he joined his brother Richard as a delegate, replacing Richard's friend Patrick Henry. Unlike his brother, though, he wasn't a good speaker.[590] His strengths were in the committees. Lee served until 1779 and was often selected as the chairman of the Committee of the Whole.[591] He wasn't afraid to oppose his more outspoken brother.[592] Rush said, "He was brother to Richard Henry Lee, but possessed I thought a more acute and correct mind."[593]

His brother Richard introduced the resolution for independence but wasn't there for the vote in July 1776. Lee was there, however, and voted for independence on July 2 and approved the Declaration of Independence on July 4. He signed it, along with the majority, on August 2.

* * *

Another brother, Arthur Lee, got both Lee and Richard in trouble. Arthur was sent to France as a commissioner, along with Silas Deane and Franklin, to negotiate for war supplies and political support.[594] Arthur accused Deane of pocketing money meant for the purchase of weapons, but later history showed that Deane was innocent, though both of Arthur's brothers supported his version of the events in Congress. In the end, Franklin, who had more influence than Arthur, had Arthur recalled instead of Deane.

This whole turn of events did not make Richard popular, and he was snubbed for reelection.

Lee resigned from Congress out of protest, as did other like-minded supporters (their resignations were refused). All was eventually forgiven, and both Lee brothers were soon side by side in Congress again.[595]

Lee was on the committee that drafted the Articles of Confederation in 1778, but he had had enough of national politics and turned to serving a few years in Virginia's state house and senate. After he left the state senate, and after the war was over, Lee spent the rest of his life as a wealthy plantation owner and tinkered with various agricultural experiments.[596]

It was a cold winter in 1796 when Lee and his wife, Rebecca, fell ill (perhaps from a virus or tuberculosis) and developed pleurisy, a painful inflammation of the lungs. His wife died on January 7, 1797. Four days later, Lee breathed his last, painful breath. He was sixty-two.[597]

Twain may have considered him "inconspicuous," but his consistent voice for independence was essential to the Revolution.

Chapter 36
RICHARD HENRY LEE
Virginia

Richard Henry Lee was elected to the Virginia House of Burgesses in 1758. He was twenty-six years old and came from a wealthy, slave-holding family, yet he argued that slavery should be abolished. He said colonies without slaves prospered and that if the colony was ever attacked, the slaves would never support their owners. He also said it was against the principles of humanity and love.[598]

That was his first bold and surprising speech as an elected official. It would not be his last.

* * *

Lee was born on January 20, 1732, at "Stratford" in Westmoreland County, Virginia, about a month before Washington was born nearby. It was also a few years before another Signer, his brother Francis, was born.

When Lee became a teenager, it was his turn to attend Wakefield Academy in Yorkshire, England. His older brothers warned him his English classmates would bully him because he was from the colonies, so Lee didn't wait to prepare himself. He trained for the future fight by learning how to box from a slave.[599]

While he was in England, his father, Thomas, died. Nineteen-year-old Lee came back to Virginia to manage his inheritance of the family land and slaves. In 1755, he led a group of colonial militia to volunteer services to British General Edward Braddock in an attack against the French, but the general didn't want to use the militia. Lee was embittered by this rebuff.[600]

After a stint as justice of the peace in 1757, Lee married Anne Ayett on December 3, 1757.[601] He was elected to the House of Burgesses and served in it until 1775. At first he wasn't bothered by Britain's 1765 Stamp Act—and even applied to help administer it. But Henry and others convinced him otherwise. Lee's fervor for independence was growing.[602]

His wife, Anne, died in December 1768, leaving behind four children. The next year, Lee married the widow Anne Gaskins Pinckard.[603]

In May 1774, Lee joined fellow members of the House of Burgesses, including Henry and Jefferson, in protesting the British's closure of Boston Harbor. The royal governor grew weary of rebellious attitudes and dissolved the Virginia House of Burgesses for lack of loyalty. Lee called for a general congress of the colonies to be formed. He got his wish and was part of the first Continental Congress in 1774.

*   *   *

Lee discovered he was ahead of most of the other delegates on challenging Britain.[604] Rush was impressed with Lee's speaking ability. "I never knew so great an orator whose speeches were so short.... He conceived his subject so clearly, and presented it so immediately to his hearers, that there appeared nothing more to be said about it."[605] Part of Lee's flair was attributed to how he held a black silk scarf in one hand to conceal the loss of four fingers from a hunting accident eight years earlier. The scarf added flourish to his gestures.[606]

In 1775, Lee was happier with the mood of his fellow delegates. He wrote an address to the people of Great Britain that showed his view. "On the sword, therefore, we are compelled to rely for protection. Should victory declare in your favor ... Of this at least we are assured, that our struggle will be glorious, our success certain; since even in death we shall find that freedom which in life you forbid us to enjoy."[607]

As the next year's Congress gathered, Lee was energized by Virginia's assembly authorizing delegates to push for independence. He was more than happy to comply. On June 7, 1776, he introduced his famous resolution: "Resolved: That these United Colonies are, and of right ought to be, free and independent States." He then argued for the adoption of the resolution. "Why, then, sir, why do we longer delay? Why still deliberate? Let this happy day give birth to an American republic."[608]

But the votes were not quite there, so the resolution was postponed in hopes of reconciling with Britain. It was brought up for a vote on July 2, but Lee would miss the vote.

In case the resolution passed, Congress wanted a suitable document to proclaim it. So a committee was appointed to draft a document—a declaration of independence. There was no doubt who would be the leading voice on the committee. As the person who introduced the resolution, Lee would be the primary mover.

But he received word that his wife was seriously ill, and because he had already lost one wife, he left to be at this wife's side.[609] Jefferson, another redheaded Virginian, replaced Lee on the committee.[610]

Lee was not there for the successful vote on his resolution for independence. He was not there when the Declaration of Independence was adopted on July 4. And he missed the signing on August 2. But he signed it when he finally returned to Congress on September 4, 1776.[611]

He was pleased with the document and said it was "so good, that no Cookery can spoil the Dish for the palates of Freemen."[612]

Although Lee missed writing the Declaration, he wrote the first national Thanksgiving Day proclamation on October 31, 1777.

* * *

During most of the war, Lee stayed in Virginia and served in the state legislature. He also served as a militia colonel and even had a few skirmishes with British troops who were ranging through Virginia's countryside. At one point, his horse was shot out from under him.[613]

After the war, he was in Congress again and was even elected president of Congress. He declined serving in the Constitutional Convention in 1787 and opposed it because he didn't think it was democratic enough. Like other Signers, he wanted a Bill of Rights.[614]

Madison, often called the "Father of the Constitution," ran for the Senate under the newly approved Constitution, but he lost to Lee, who pushed for amendments in Congress to secure rights to the people. Lee saw the Bill of Rights passed but had to resign from the Senate because of gout.[615]

He died two years later at his home, "Chantilly" in Westmoreland County, Virginia, on June 19, 1794. He was sixty-two. As he wrote to the British in 1775, "Our struggle will be glorious, our success certain; since even in death we shall find that freedom which in life you forbid us to enjoy."[616] He declared freedom and saw its success.

Chapter 37
FRANCIS LEWIS
New York

Francis Lewis knew he'd struck it rich when he won a contract to provide clothes for the British Army in 1753. The French and Indian War had broken out, and three years later, the New York merchant found himself at Fort Oswego on Lake Ontario. Unfortunately, the French captured the fort and Lewis. He was also unfortunately one of several prisoners handed over to the French's Native American allies.[617]

Fortunately, he knew Welsh.

At least, that is the legendary aspect of Lewis's biography. Allegedly, the Indian chief heard him speak Welsh and understood enough of it to decide Lewis's life should be spared.[618] Of course, there was no similarity between the languages—but there were persistent tales among colonists of Prince Madoc of Wales, who was supposed to have discovered America in 1170—well before that upstart Columbus set sail. Madoc taught the Indians his native Welsh language, and it was incorporated into their tongue,[619] so this would explain why the Indian chief let Lewis live.

Allegedly.

More likely, some family member decided to brush up Lewis's story to line it up with a common belief of the time. Or perhaps the chief really was impressed with the spectacle of a man speaking a language unlike any he had heard before. In any case, Lewis was not killed and was taken prisoner to France, where he stayed for about seven years.[620]

When he got back after the war, Britain awarded him 5,000 acres of land. And he was back in business.[621]

* * *

Francis Lewis was born in Llandaff, Wales, on March 21, 1713. His father was an Episcopal clergyman. When Lewis was about four or five years old, he was orphaned and then passed from relative to relative. His uncle put him through school at Westminster in London, and then Lewis worked in the counting house of a London merchant. He learned the business well and came to America in the mid-1730s. He took his inheritance and invested it in building his own merchant business in New York and Pennsylvania, and in 1745, he married his partner's sister, Elizabeth Annesley.[622]

Because he was a trader, he traveled the world. He was even shipwrecked twice on Ireland's coast. After his adventures in the French and Indian War, Lewis became more concerned about how the land of his birth was lording over his adopted home. He became one of the Sons of Liberty. About the same time he retired from business, he joined the 1765 Stamp Act Congress in New York City to try to convince Parliament to repeal the act.

* * *

Lewis served in the Continental Congress from 1775 to 1779, working on the marine, foreign affairs, and commerce committees.[623] Like the other New York delegates, he was there on July 4, 1776, when the Declaration of Independence was adopted—but he didn't vote for it. The New York delegation was not authorized by its legislature to vote for independence yet. The New York legislature, however, did approve independence in time for Lewis to sign the document on August 2.[624]

Many of the delegates feared reprisal for their bold act. Few felt it as directly and swiftly as Lewis.

On September 19, 1776, a British warship fired on his Long Island home while he was at Congress. A shell landed near where his wife, Elizabeth, was standing. When a servant told her to run, she replied, "Another shot is not likely to hit the same spot."[625] British soldiers also came into the home and ransacked it. One was angry when he found out that the buckles he had grabbed off Elizabeth's shoes were not valuable. "All is not gold that glitters," she snarkily replied.[626]

She was about sixty years old, but this didn't stop the British from taking her prisoner and putting her into a cell in New York City without a bed or a change of clothing. One of her slaves sought her out and brought her clothes and food. For two months, she languished in horrid conditions. When news of her capture and treatment arrived in Philadelphia, Congress was incensed. Washington had two Loyalist women in Philadelphia put under house arrest and threatened to give them similar treatment if Elizabeth was not released.[627]

She was released, but the imprisonment had taken its toll, and she never returned to normal health. She died a few years later, and Lewis ended his career as a delegate.[628]

* * *

Lewis never rebuilt his destroyed Long Island home or his life. Instead, he stayed with his sons. His daughter had, against his wishes, married a British naval officer and moved to England;[629] his son, Morgan, took up the torch and became chief justice of New York and later, after his father had died, governor from 1804 to 1807.[630]

Lewis died in New York City on December 30, 1803, at eighty-nine years old.[631]

He was buried on Wall Street in New York City in the graveyard of Trinity Church, where he was a vestryman.[632]

Chapter 38
PHILIP LIVINGSTON
New York

Philip Livingston thought independence was "the most vain, empty, shallow and ridiculous project."[633] But he would change his mind.

* * *

Livingston was born on January 15, 1716, in Albany, New York, to one of the colony's largest landholding families, his grandfather having been granted about 250 square miles back in the 1680s.[634] Livingston's life followed the pattern of wealth, and he used his Yale College education to increase that wealth by following his brother Peter into the mercantile and importation business. Livingston married Christina Ten Broeck on April 14, 1740, and had five sons and three daughters.[635]

He became a large, portly man to match his affluence and influence. He became an alderman in New York City politics in a time when the city's population comprised almost 11,000 people[636] and helped found the New York City Library. He also helped found King's College (now Columbia University).[637]

From alderman, it was a short step in 1759 to represent New York City in the colonial assembly. He resented the taxing policies of Great Britain, and in 1764, he lit into New York's royal lieutenant governor, telling him, "We hope your honour will join with us in an endeavor to secure that great badge of English liberty, *of being taxed only with our own consent.*"[638]

Livingston had a lot of possessions that could be taxed. Just some of the items he was selling at his store in April 1768 show the extent of his business: He had Irish linens and other cloths. There were "patterns for breeches, tommies, Durants, and shakoons, fustians, Turkey stripes, burr dots, [and] silk damascus for summer vests." He had "paper by the ream, ... hats, ... brushes, ... marble hearths, ... sugar, tea kettles, ... cable, ... nails, ... twine for fishing nets, ... window glass, ... brandy, ... candles, ... cheese, ... choice beef and pork, ... rice, coffee in barrels, ... Jamaica nutmegs, ... bottles, ... buttons, shoe and knee buckles, ... snuff boxes, ... combs, ... needles, ... thimbles, ... oil, ... steel, ... [and] Teneriffe wine just imported."[639]

In 1768 the conservative patriots, or Whigs, gained control of the New York colonial legislature. Livingston was named speaker and pushed for the rights of the colonists versus Britain. The royal governor didn't like this, so he dissolved the assembly at the end of the year. The 1769 election, however, put the loyalist Tories into power. Livingston wasn't seated by the majority and spent a few years starting the New York City Chamber of Commerce and the city's first hospital.[640]

* * *

Livingston thought the Sons of Liberty were too radical.[641] But he was still radical enough himself to serve in the Continental Congress as a delegate from New York, starting with the first one in 1774. He served on a committee to create a document that spoke to the British king's subjects. He also worked on a boycott of British goods. He thought independence was dangerous. Adams complained that it was impossible to hold a conversation with Livingston on the topic of independence. Livingston thought it would lead to civil war.[642]

In the 1775 Congress, Livingston's brother William and a cousin named Robert R. Livingston joined him. William then left Congress for the military, but Robert was a like-minded New York delegate, whose fame came from being on the committee that drafted the Declaration of Independence.

Livingston missed the vote for independence, which didn't matter too much since New York delegates had to abstain anyway. But he did get there in time to sign the Declaration of Independence on August 2.[643] Ironically, his cousin Robert, who was on the drafting committee, never signed it.

* * *

Later that August, the Continental Army lost a major battle on Long Island and was pushed back to Brooklyn. Washington held a war conference in Livingston's home;[644] then, like the army, Livingston's family decided to evacuate as the British approached. The British seized Livingston's two homes, turning one into a hospital and another into a barracks.[645]

Livingston continued to serve in Congress and in local and state government. He was chosen as a state senator under the state's new constitution. In Congress, he served on the marine committee and the board of treasury.

As the sixth Continental Congress approached, Livingston's health was failing. On his way to congress, he visited his friends in Albany, New York, and gave them a final farewell. He did the same with his family, which was in Kingston because of the advance of the British.[646]

In May 1778, he arrived at Congress, even though he expected to die soon. The state of the war was critical, but the tide was beginning to turn to the Americans. The British had taken Philadelphia. Congress had fled to York, Pennsylvania. At this low time, and with his son Henry at his side, Livingston died of congestive heart failure (called dropsy at the time) on June 12, 1778, at the age of sixty-two.[647]

Chapter 39

THOMAS LYNCH JR.
South Carolina

Thomas Lynch Jr. was in trouble. His father, Thomas Lynch Sr., was a very important man—a respected South Carolinian planter and a powerful politician in the Continental Congress—and he wasn't happy that his son had accepted the position of captain in the First South Carolina Regiment in 1775.

Lynch's father wanted him to come to Philadelphia, where he might be able to get a higher commission in the Continental Army, but Lynch refused. He didn't think he had the experience needed for a higher commission—even if he had the connections.[648]

* * *

Lynch's connections began at birth on his father's plantation, Hopsewee, on the Santee River in South Carolina on August 5, 1749. His mother, Elizabeth Alston Lynch, died when Lynch was a child. Before Lynch was six years old, his father had remarried to Hannah Motte and had three daughters: Sabina, Esther, and Elizabeth.[649]

The family business was rice plantations—taking advantage of slaves' knowledge of rice cultivation.[650]

Lynch's father wanted the best for his son, including the best education, which meant sending him abroad. At twelve, Lynch went to Eton school in England. Then he graduated from Cambridge University and studied law at Middle Temple in London, all as part of his father's plans for his future.[651] In 1772, Lynch returned to America and told his father he didn't like law. His father didn't mind; he could alter his plans. He deeded Lynch Peachtree Plantation on the Santee River to run.[652]

Lynch soon married Elizabeth Shubrick. Her sister married another future Signer of the Declaration of Independence, Edward Rutledge.

* * *

Like his father, Lynch was drawn into the revolution and was a member of the first and second provincial Congresses of South Carolina, working on South Carolina's constitutional committee.

When he accepted the position of captain in the First South Carolina Regiment in July 1775, Lynch, with Charles Cotesworth Pinckney, recruited soldiers into the militia. Unfortunately, Lynch contracted malaria and never fully recovered.

Lynch's father had a stroke while he was serving in Congress in Philadelphia in 1776. Under normal circumstances, Lynch's position in the militia would have prevented him from going to his father, but his father's influence was enough to get Lynch appointed as an extra delegate. He went to Congress to act, in part, as his father's aide. They became the only father-and-son team to serve concurrently in the Continental Congress.[653] Adams wasn't terribly impressed with all the young representatives from South Carolina and called Lynch "uncouth and tedious." Rush, however, called him "sensible and well-spoken."[654]

South Carolina's delegates debated whether to support independence. After delaying the vote, the delegates cast South Carolina's vote to separate from Great Britain.

Lynch's father's health didn't improve enough for him to sign the Declaration of Independence along with his son on August 2. In deference to his position in the South Carolina delegation, however, a generous empty space was left on the document for him to sign. The space for Thomas Lynch Sr.—between South Carolina delegates Edward Rutledge and Thomas Heyward Jr.—remains to this day. That space is one of the most touching personal considerations on the document, symbolizing the many who strove for independence but never signed the document.[655]

Lynch, who turned twenty-seven three days after signing the Declaration, started home with his ailing father. In Annapolis, Maryland, however, Lynch's father suffered another stroke and died. Since Lynch was his father's only son, all his father's plantations, slaves, and wealth came to him—with all the attached responsibilities.[656] But the overarching problem remained Lynch's own health, and he retired from public life.

* * *

In the autumn of 1779, Lynch decided to travel to Europe to seek a cure for his illness, though the danger of capture was real because they were in the middle of war. He and his wife, Elizabeth, set sail to the West Indies, where they planned to get passage on a neutral country's ship to the south of France.

But Lynch's voyage for his health was a tragic one. They sailed to St. Eustatia (modern-day Statia, in the Netherlands Antilles) and then boarded another ship. Lynch, his wife, Elizabeth, and the ship were never heard from again. Many believed the ship was lost in a storm.[657]

At the age of thirty, Lynch wasn't the first Signer to die, but he was the youngest.

In Lynch's will, and following his father's wishes, he left his wealth to his sister Sabina's family with the stipulation that her son change his surname to Lynch to carry on the family name. John Lynch Bowman complied and changed his name to John Bowman Lynch. It didn't do any good, though, because John Bowman Lynch's three sons all died childless while fighting for the Confederacy.[658]

Chapter 40
THOMAS MCKEAN
Delaware

Thomas McKean, of Delaware, was open-mouthed stunned. The October 1765 Stamp Act Congress had produced a document outlining the colonies' objections to the taxes Britain imposed on them. It protested the hated Stamp Act, which required tax stamps on papers like legal writs and more, but when the time came on October 24 for the delegates to sign the protest document, the president of the Congress, Timothy Ruggles, of Massachusetts, said he wouldn't do it.

The Congress had gone well, and McKean was probably wondering how it would look if the president of the Stamp Act Congress wouldn't sign its own declaration. Ruggles refused to give a reason why. McKean pressed him until Ruggles finally said signing it was "against his conscience."

"*Conscience!*" the six-foot-tall McKean shouted back as he rose up from his seat. "Conscience! Conscience! Conscience!" He kept repeating the word, shouting it loudly and using different intonations, voices, and expressions each time. "Conscience! Conscience! Conscience!" His one-word-repeated speech infuriated Ruggles so much he challenged him to a duel. McKean accepted on the spot.[659]

Ruggles, however, calmed down, and he and his conscience slinked out of New York City before the sun came up the next day.[660]

* * *

Thomas McKean was born in New London, Pennsylvania, on March 19, 1734. He was the son of a farmer/tavern keeper.[661] At nine, he was sent to the Reverend Francis Allison's Academy in New London, and around the age of sixteen, he began studying law with a relative on his mother's side, David Finney, in New Castle, Delaware.[662] In the mid-1750s, he was admitted to the bar and began practicing law in the tri-colony area of Pennsylvania, Delaware, and New Jersey.[663] Oftentimes, the legal distinctions between these colonies were negligible.

McKean began his public service as deputy attorney general for Sussex County in Delaware in 1756 at age twenty-two. A few years later, he went to study law for a year at Middle Temple in London. When he arrived back at the colonies, his political career picked up when he was elected to the Delaware House of Assembly, where he served

129

even after he moved to Pennsylvania. He also married his first wife, the beautiful Mary Borden, on her nineteenth birthday in 1763—making him the brother-in-law of another future Signer of the Declaration of Independence, Francis Hopkinson.

After the Stamp Act Congress in 1765, McKean was appointed as justice of the peace for New Castle County in Delaware. He ordered his officers to ignore the Stamp Act's requirements to put tax stamps on every piece of paper.

After ten years of marriage and six children, McKean's wife died. In 1774, he married Sarah Armitage. He also served his first stint in the Continental Congress as a delegate from Delaware.

* * *

On July 1, 1776, McKean and George Read were the only two Delaware delegates in attendance to hear the debate on independence. McKean was for independence, and Read against, so Delaware's vote was split and wouldn't be counted. McKean realized that if Congress voted for independence, it was important to have as many colonies support it as possible. He sent an urgent message to his friend and Delaware delegate Caesar Rodney. Rodney was taking care of business in Dover, Delaware, when he got the message and rode day and night to Philadelphia. He arrived in time to vote in favor of independence on July 2 and to adopt the Declaration of Independence on July 4.[664]

Adams said McKean was one of three men in the Continental Congress who "appeared to me to see more clearly to the end of the business than any others of the whole body."[665]

A couple of days after the vote for independence, McKean, who was colonel of a militia regiment, marched to support the Continental Army in New Jersey. This meant he was gone from Congress when the official handwritten copy of the Declaration was signed by the majority on August 2. Some historians believe he signed the Declaration of Independence on or near January 18, 1777. Other historians believe it may have been as late as 1781.[666] McKean defended himself to some people in later years who questioned whether he had signed it (facsimile copies were more rare then). But he *did* sign it. In fact, by either the 1777 date or the 1781 date, he was the last person to sign it.

"Modesty should not rob any man of his just honour, when by that honour, his modesty cannot be offended," he wrote in a letter. "The fact is, that I was then a member of congress for the state of Delaware, was personally present in congress, and voted in favor of independence on the fourth of July, 1776, and signed the Declaration after it had been engrossed on parchment, where my name, in my own handwriting, still appears."[667]

* * *

In 1777, McKean was appointed as chief justice of Pennsylvania, a post he held for twenty-two years. Around that same time, the British captured Delaware's president (the state's title for their governor), John McKinly, and McKean stepped in to act as Delaware's president. So McKean was chief justice of Pennsylvania and president of Delaware at the same time. This garnered Britain's attention. "The consequence was," he wrote, "to be hunted like a fox by the enemy, and envied by those who ought to have been my friends. I was compelled to remove my family five times in a few months, and, at last, fixed them in a little log-house on the banks of the Susquehanna."[668]

He signed the Articles of Confederation in 1779, which became officially ratified in 1781. McKean was elected on June 10, 1781, to be the second president of the United States in Congress Assembled—the highest office in the land under the Articles of Confederation.[669]

While he was president, just before 2:00 a.m. on October 22, 1781, McKean received the news from Washington that Lord Cornwallis had surrendered at Yorktown.[670] The German watchman, who had led the messenger to McKean, continued on his way, according to a contemporary account, shouting out the time the British general was taken captive: "Basht dree o'glock, und Cornwal-lis isht da-ken!"[671]

The press didn't think it was legal for McKean to be both president of Congress and chief justice of Pennsylvania. So in November 1781, McKean stepped down as president of Congress and retained his position as chief justice of Pennsylvania. McKean was part of the convention in Pennsylvania to ratify the new Constitution on December 12, 1787. He finally ended his career in Pennsylvania's Supreme Court to become the state's governor in 1799 at the age of sixty-five. He fired all his enemies in state government jobs and appointed friends and family. This did not win over his political opponents, who, in 1807 and 1808, tried unsuccessfully to impeach him. It didn't matter too much because he retired from public life in 1808.

* * *

A few years later, he corresponded with Adams. He wrote, "Three years ago I shook hands with the world, and we said farewell to each other," he wrote. "Since my exemption from official and professional duties, I have enjoyed a tranquility, never . . . heretofore experienced; and my health and comforts are sufficient for a moderate man."[672]

His last public service came during the War of 1812 when, in 1814, he was elected chairman of a Philadelphia committee of defense. He argued against political division, saying, "There were then but two parties, our country and its invaders."[673]

McKean held public office for more than fifty years before, during, and after the Revolutionary War. Often, he held multiple offices simultaneously.

He died in Philadelphia on June 24, 1817, at the age of eighty-three. He was survived by only five other Signers of the Declaration of Independence.[674]

Chapter 41

ARTHUR MIDDLETON
South Carolina

Arthur Middleton earned his place in the Continental Congress in 1776 the old fashioned way: he inherited it. His father, Henry Middleton, was one of South Carolina's delegates to the Congress and, along with Washington and Carroll, was one of the wealthiest men in the colonies, with twenty plantations totaling 50,000 acres and 800 slaves.[675] Henry was even president of Congress for a short time.

But Henry fell ill and had to resign from Congress, and his son Arthur was elected to take his place.

* * *

Arthur Middleton was born on his father's huge estate near Charleston, South Carolina, on June 26, 1742. He attended school in England starting at twelve years old at Hackney, Westminster School, and then St. John's College, Cambridge University. He studied law at Middle Temple in London.[676] After his studies, he took a two-year grand tour of Europe. He came back to South Carolina in the mid-1760s and married Mary Izard in 1766. Then it was off for another European tour that lasted years. By 1773, they were back.

Two years later, he was on a secret committee to help prepare the defenses of the colony and then served on the Committee of Safety—the unofficial executive government of South Carolina.[677]

* * *

Middleton replaced his father at the Continental Congress just in time to sign the Declaration of Independence.

In 1778, the legislature of South Carolina adopted a new state constitution without getting approval from the people. The governor, John Rutledge, resigned in protest. Without asking him, the legislature then elected Middleton to replace Rutledge. Middleton refused the high office for the same reason Rutledge had resigned.

When the British conquered Charleston in 1780, Middleton was captured and sent to prison in St. Augustine, Florida. His estate was pillaged but not burned down. The British took two hundred of his slaves and sold them in the West Indies.[678] After months of imprisonment, Middleton was released through an exchange of prisoners and then immediately drafted again into Congress.

When the war ended, he was reunited with his family.

Middleton's passion came on a case-by-case basis. While he was out for a walk one day, a servant came running with a message that the main house on his estate was on fire. He was thinking of tearing it down and rebuilding anyway, so he simply said, "Let it burn" and continued on his walk. His wife had to direct saving the home herself.[679]

Middleton continued to serve here and there in state offices. In November 1786, he fell ill and then died on New Year's Day 1787.

Chapter 42
LEWIS MORRIS
New York

Life was pretty much set for Lewis Morris when he was born in Morrisania on April 8, 1726. His father was lord of Morrisania—a 2,000-acre agricultural manor in what is now the Bronx in New York City.[680] Morris was the heir and destined to be a lord himself under the British grant that established the manor.

Morris's mother, Katrintja, died when Morris was around five years old, and his father remarried to Sarah Gouverneur. One of Morris's more famous siblings was his younger half-brother Gouverneur Morris, who later signed the Constitution and was a U.S. senator.

Morris went to Yale College at sixteen and graduated in 1746. He married Mary Walton three years later, and over the years, they had ten children. In 1762, Morris's father died, and Morris became lord of Morrisania.[681]

* * *

Morris dabbled in politics and the law. He was judge of the Court of Admiralty and was briefly in the Colonial Assembly of New York until he was disqualified for nonresidence. On every side, Loyalists surrounded Morris, but he grew disenchanted with British rule and managed to be elected to the provincial convention in April 1775, which, in turn, elected him to the Continental Congress. Morris arrived the next month in Congress and worked with Washington to try to find ways to supply the army. In September, Morris went to the frontier in Pennsylvania to try to secure the loyalty of the Indians to the colonists.[682]

The next year, 1776, Morris became a brigadier general in the New York militia. He was serving in the militia when Congress voted on independence in July. The New York delegation that remained abstained from voting anyway.[683] But the New York provincial congress then voted to accept independence, albeit a tad tardy, on July 9. Morris arrived back in Congress in time to sign the Declaration of Independence on August 2.

For much of the rest of the summer, Morris was in the field with the militia.[684]

* * *

In June 1777, Morris left Congress to concentrate on his role in the military. His half-brother, Gouverneur, was elected to replace him.

134

The British took over Morrisania as Morris's family fled, and the soldiers vandalized the home, destroying thousands of trees and killing livestock for food. Some servants and slaves also ran away.[685] After the war, in 1783, Morris began to reestablish his agricultural estate and home at Morrisania.

When New York had to decide whether to adopt the new federal Constitution in 1788, Morris served in the state convention as an ardent federalist. Helping to pass the Constitution did not help him serve under it, however. He tried to become a U.S. senator in 1789, but because elections were by the states' legislatures at that time, and because the lower house was Anti-Federalist, they chose not to send a Federalist to represent them.

Morris retired from public life, for the most part—although he was on the board of regents for the University of New York.[686] He spent the last decade of his life quietly at Morrisania. His wife died in 1794, and Morris died four years later on January 22, 1798,[687] at the age of seventy-one—one of the few Signers who served in the military, and one of the many who risked all he owned.

Chapter 43
ROBERT MORRIS
Pennsylvania

Robert Morris, a wealthy and prominent merchant, was presiding over the annual dinner celebration of the Society of St. George. It was April 23, 1775, and the elite of Philadelphia had gathered to pay their respects to the patron saint of Britain—while enjoying the best food and drink the city had to offer. A motto on the wall reflected the spirit of those gathered: "Reconciliation." Then a messenger burst into the tavern with news. Four days earlier, the British had engaged in battles with colonists at Lexington and Concord in Massachusetts.

Pandemonium broke out as many Loyalists ran for the door, knocking over chairs and tables in their panic. Legend says that a stunned Morris was left alone in the room at the head table, his glass raised in a toast that was never finished. He knew what this meant. It was war.[688]

* * *

Robert Morris was born in Liverpool, England, on January 31, 1734.[689] There was no record of a marriage between his mother and father. Little is known of his mother, but his maternal grandmother raised him from childhood.[690] His father moved to America and did well in the tobacco trade in Maryland. When Morris was thirteen, his father sent for him to come to America and then promptly sent him off to Philadelphia for school. Morris wasn't impressed with his teacher and wrote his father, "I have learned, sir, all that he could teach me."[691]

In July 1750, Morris's father was killed in a freak accident while he was leaving a dinner party aboard a merchant ship that had just come into port. The ship fired a cannon in salute, and the paper wad from the cannon hit Morris's father in the shoulder; he died a short time later from blood poisoning. Morris became an orphan in a new country.

Charles Willing, one of the most successful merchants in Philadelphia, took Morris on as an apprentice clerk. After Willing died, Morris helped run the company with Willing's son Thomas. Thomas and Morris's partnership lasted for close to four decades. Thomas took the more political roles in society, such as serving as mayor of Philadelphia, and Morris managed the business,[692] though he did sign

136

the nonimportation agreement of 1765 during the Stamp Act protests. But politics didn't interest him. Yet.

When Morris finally got around to building a family life, he was thirty-five years old. His wife, Mary White, was nineteen when they were married on March 2, 1769.[693]

* * *

Everything changed after the battles of Lexington and Concord. "Ambition had no share in bringing me forward into public life nor has it any charms to keep me there," Morris wrote.[694]

Morris's first election was as a delegate to the Continental Congress in November 1775. The next year, he joined the majority of the Pennsylvania delegates, who opposed Lee's calls for independence. Morris thought it was premature, and his partner (and a delegate), Thomas, was also against independence.[695] Even so, Adams thought Morris was an excellent member of Congress. "I think he has a masterly understanding, an open temper and an honest heart," he wrote in a letter in April 1776.[696]

On July 1, Congress voted on independence and failed. Pennsylvania's vote was against it. Morris, Willing, John Dickinson, Charles Humphreys, and John Morton voted no. Wilson and Franklin voted yes.[697]

But Morris saw the writing on the wall. He wouldn't vote for independence, but he wouldn't stand in its way either. When the vote came up again on July 2, Morris and Dickinson walked out of the room. This enabled Franklin, Wilson, and (after a change of heart) Morton to override Humphreys's and Willing's votes. Pennsylvania's vote was in favor of independence. Morris also abstained on July 4 when the Declaration of Independence was passed.[698]

To Morris's own surprise, the Pennsylvania legislature reelected him to Congress later that month. On August 2, he signed the Declaration of Independence.

"There is no question that, of all the signers, Morris was the most reluctant," Charles Rappleye wrote in his excellent 2010 biography of Morris. "Yet the ensuing years would show that, having done so, none of his colleagues did more to bring it to fruition."[699] Rush said Morris was opposed to the time of independence but not the act. Morris later admitted to Congress that he had been mistaken about the proper time for independence and it should have been sooner.[700]

His motto was "the individual who declines the service of his country because its councils are not conformable to his ideas makes but a bad subject; a good one will follow if he cannot lead."[701]

But lead he would.

* * *

Late in 1776, the British invaded New Jersey. Congress fled to Baltimore but left Morris, George Clymer, and George Walton behind to conduct business, which meant aiding armies during that time of war. Washington needed supplies to conduct a counterattack. Morris knew what to do. He wrangled freshly shipped supplies from the docks—lead for bullets, gunpowder, arms, and clothing—and arranged to have them shipped to Washington's troops. The supplies arrived in time to enable Washington to perform his daring 1776 Christmas Eve attack and achieve victory across the Delaware River at Trenton, New Jersey. Victory and supplies were linked—and Morris was the man to thank.[702]

By March 1777, Congress was back, and the committee of three was disbanded. Morris shifted his attention to the committees of commerce and finance.[703]

In early 1779, Henry Laurens, the president of Congress at that time, accused Morris of profiting from the war by shipping his own merchandise under the guise of government shipping expeditions. A committee investigated the issue, and Laurens had to proclaim Morris's innocence before Congress.[704]

Morris continued throughout the war to secure funds for the fight by using his own finances as security. In fact, his credit was better than Congress's credit, and it came in handy in the summer of 1781 as Washington made plans to attack the British under Lord Cornwallis in Virginia.[705] Morris issued notes to purchase ammunition and other supplies. He even loaned his home to Washington to use as headquarters as he marched toward Yorktown and a victory that would bring the war to a close.[706]

Morris's largesse did not come without a personal price. As the superintendent of finance under the Articles of Confederation, he faced high inflation, worthless Continental currency, and a national government that had no way to raise money.[707] To that pressure was also added his own stretching credit. In October 1782, he wrote, "My credit has already been on the brink of ruin; if that goes, all is gone."[708] One of his solutions was to establish the Bank of North America to lend money to the United States.

He served in his thankless position over finances until 1784.

* * *

Morris's difficulties convinced him of the need for a stronger federal government. His dream came true with the calling of a Constitutional Convention in 1787. As a delegate, he nominated his friend Washington as the convention's president. After the Constitution had been ratified and Washington was elected as the nation's first president, Morris turned down Washington's offer to be the first secretary of the treasury.[709] Instead, he served in the Senate from 1789 to 1795.

When the capital of the country moved from New York City to Philadelphia in 1790, Morris's home became Washington's presidential mansion.

Like other prominent Americans, Morris speculated by buying up lands on the American frontier.[710] His first two forays into land speculation brought him huge returns.[711] But then his financial world began to unravel. He invested in millions of acres in five states and in what would become Washington, D.C. The Napoleonic Wars slowed immigration to a trickle, leaving fewer people to buy land and driving the value of Morris's land investments down.[712] It seemed he owed everybody.

He wrote, "My money is gone, my furniture is to be sold, I am to go to prison and my family to starve."[713] On February 16, 1798, he was escorted from his country estate to Philadelphia, where he was officially arrested and sent to Prune Street debtors' prison in Philadelphia.[714] It was, ironically, only a block away from where he had signed the Declaration of Independence.[715]

* * *

Washington visited Morris in that first year of confinement and had dinner with him in prison.[716] They would never meet again—Washington died the next year while Morris was still jailed. After he became president, Jefferson lamented that Morris couldn't now serve in the cabinet.[717]

Morris tried to meet his lot with courage. He wrote his son Thomas, "A man that cannot hear and face misfortune should not run risks. . . . But I have been too adventurous and therefore it is my duty to meet my Fate with Fortitude and I do it."[718]

Morris's reprieve came in 1800 when Congress passed the nation's first bankruptcy law. He got out of jail on August 26, 1801. His debts were about $3 million, but by December, he was cleared of it all under the new law.[719]

For the rest of his life, Morris lived on an annuity from his friend, Gouverneur. He and Roger Sherman were the only people to sign the Declaration of Independence, the Articles of Confederation, and the Constitution.[720] The debt his country owed him was huge, but with his fall came discouragement and a loss of influence. He died on May 8, 1806, with little public acknowledgment or mourning. He was seventy-two years old.[721]

Chapter 44
JOHN MORTON
Pennsylvania

Pennsylvania delegate John Morton knew how many of his constituents wanted him to vote. They were Quakers who didn't want war. There were also Loyalists who wanted reconciliation with Britain. On the side of independence stood Franklin and Wilson. On the side against independence were Dickinson, Morris, Humphreys, and Willing. Earlier on July 1, 1776, Morton voted against independence—five against, two for. By nightfall, he had changed his mind.

* * *

John Morton was born near Chester, Pennsylvania, in 1724.[722] He was named after his father, who, at the age of forty-one, died before Morton was born. His mother remarried to a man named John Sketchley. Morton's new stepfather was well educated and was kind to his new stepson. He taught him mathematics and surveying, giving Morton a trade to add to farming.

Around 1748, Morton married Ann Justis and started a family. Like many other surveyors, Morton was often called in to settle disputes, and he was soon made justice of the peace. From there, it was a small step into broader politics. He was thirty-two when first elected to the colonial general assembly of Pennsylvania. With only a brief stint out of office, he served for close to two decades.

When the Stamp Act caused consternation, Morton was sent as a delegate to the 1765 Stamp Act Congress in New York. He served in local capacities, such as acting as high sheriff from 1766 to 1770, and in state offices, such as being a judge and even becoming the associate justice of the Supreme Court of Appeals of Pennsylvania in April 1774. The latter appointment was the reason he turned down being colonel of the militia in Chester County.

* * *

In 1774, he was sent as a delegate to the first Continental Congress. Rush said Morton was "a plain farmer" but that he "was well acquainted with the principles of government, and of public business."[723]

When the first vote for independence came up on July 1, 1776, Morton, a moderate, voted nay. With five against and only two for it, Pennsylvania looked to put a kibosh on the independence movement. If Pennsylvania hadn't backed it, the other states would have had to back down. Then delegates Morris and Dickinson decided to be absent for the next vote on July 2. This left two against and two for. Morton felt personally inclined toward independence, although many of his constituents were not.[724]

His vote would make or break independence—and make or break his reputation back home.

He voted for independence.

On August 2, Morton joined the other delegates in signing the Declaration of Independence.[725]

Later, Morton headed the Committee of the Whole that adopted the Articles of Confederation. He wouldn't live to see the document ratified.[726]

* * *

At home, Morton's vote turned long-time friends and supporters against him. Not too long after this, he contracted a fever—probably tuberculosis. On his deathbed, he addressed himself to his critics, speaking words that would be chiseled into an obelisk monument at his grave. He said, "Tell them that they will live to see the hour when they shall acknowledge it to have been the most glorious service I ever rendered to my country."[727]

John Morton died in April 1777 at the age of fifty-three. Shortly after his death, his family fled his home, fearing an attack from the British.[728]

Chapter 45
THOMAS NELSON JR.
Virginia

Thomas Nelson Jr., governor and commander-in-chief of Virginia's military, watched as the American artillery pounded Yorktown in 1781. The British were getting no rest, it seemed, except for in one untouched house. Nelson asked why that house was not being fired upon. The soldiers answer that it was his home and they wanted to show respect for their governor and commander.

Family tradition says Nelson then told them to fire on his home—and he would pay them for each cannonball that hit its mark. Then he watched as the projectiles rained down, driving the British officers off his property as it was being pummeled.[729]

* * *

Nelson was born in Yorktown, Virginia, on December 26, 1738. He was the oldest son of William Nelson, a successful merchant and landholder.[730] He was called "Jr." because his uncle Thomas also lived in Yorktown.[731] At fourteen, Nelson was sent for a proper English education in Britain. He studied for eight years and graduated from Cambridge University in 1761. He returned to Virginia and married Lucy Grymes on July 29, 1762. They would have eleven children together. Life looked like it would be comfortable. His father gave him a plantation and a townhome in Yorktown. He had money, land, slaves, and connections.

This sort of life meant, of course, that he became a member of the House of Burgesses of Virginia only a few years later. His father was even acting governor from 1770 to 1771.

But that didn't prevent Nelson and his fellow legislators from angering the royal governor, Lord Dunmore, in 1774. Dunmore didn't like the resolutions the legislators passed against the British Parliament for closing Boston Harbor, so he dissolved the legislature. The governor's actions didn't stop Nelson. He, with eighty-nine other legislators, went to the nearby Raleigh Tavern and passed more resolutions—including one that called on the other colonies to send delegates to a new Continental Congress.

On November 7, 1774, Nelson learned that a ship had come to Yorktown with two small chests of British tea onboard for delivery to a merchant in Williamsburg.

Nelson and other Patriots from Yorktown followed the Boston example by boarding the ship and dumping the two chests into the sea.[732]

Nelson was soon in the new Virginia Provincial Congress in Williamsburg in 1774 and 1775.

The Provincial Congress named Nelson colonel and put him in command of one of three new regiments being formed, but he resigned the next month when he was named a delegate to the 1775 Continental Congress.

* * *

Adams said Nelson was "a fat man, a speaker, and alert and lively for his weight."[733] He also had a reputation of being jovial.[734]

In the spring of 1776, Nelson introduced a resolution Edmund Pendleton drafted to Virginia's provincial congress. The resolution called for permission for Virginia's delegates to the Continental Congress to declare independence from Britain. They adopted his resolution, and he brought it to Philadelphia. Fellow delegate Richard Henry Lee abridged the resolution and introduced it to Congress on June 7.[735] The vote for the resolution was delayed until July.

Nelson voted for independence and later signed the Declaration of Independence with other delegates on August 2.

Later in 1776, as a member of Virginia's legislature, Nelson was angry with his fellow legislators for passing a law that confiscated British merchants' property. Nelson felt it was unfair to the merchants who had, in many instances, extended credit to Americans. "I hope the bill will be rejected, but whatever be its fate, by God, I will pay *my* debts like an honest man," Nelson said.[736]

In 1777, Nelson experienced a severe headache and a loss of memory. He took a leave of absence from Congress and returned home. He had long suffered from chronic asthma, and this new trouble may have been a mild stroke. He was home by August, when a British fleet was sighted on Virginia's coast.

* * *

Virginia Governor Henry made Nelson brigadier general and commander-in-chief of the state's militia, but the state of emergency dissipated before a proper militia force could be fully organized. The British sailed off to attack Philadelphia instead.

A similar situation happened again when the Continental Congress requested states to raise cavalry troops, which the states were supposed to form at their own expense. Nelson recruited and outfitted about seventy horsemen with his own money and led his troops to Philadelphia in August 1778. By the time he arrived, the British had gone north and the Congress had decided the cavalry units were no longer needed.

Nelson paid his soldiers and sent them home. The exercise and activity, however, had one good effect: it seemed to have restored his health—if only temporarily.[737]

In 1779, Nelson was sent back to the Continental Congress, but it didn't last. After three months, his health failed again, and he had to come home.

His service to his country was not over though.

* * *

Congress needed money to help pay a French fleet to enter the war. Nelson set out to raise $2 million for Virginia's share. Nobody wanted to loan the unproven government the money, but people did agree to loan the money to Nelson. Nelson turned over the money in return for securities that ended up being worthless.[738]

Lord Cornwallis and Arnold attacked Virginia in 1781. Jefferson resigned as the state's governor so a person with more military experience could lead the state during the emergency. Nelson was elected governor and made commander-in-chief of the state's military, giving him almost dictatorial powers.[739]

The British attacked in multiple places throughout Virginia, and relief came from the French. By September, Washington's forces—including 3,000 Virginians under Nelson and French forces—had trapped Lord Cornwallis in Nelson's hometown, Yorktown, Virginia. Cornwallis surrendered in October.

Nelson's health continued to decline. About a month after the victory at Yorktown, he resigned as governor. A fellow Signer of the Declaration of Independence, Benjamin Harrison, was made governor in his stead.

* * *

After Nelson resigned, some people accused him of illegally taking supplies to give to the troops. The legislature acted quickly and exonerated him, citing the necessities of war.

Asthma continued to plague Nelson for the remainder of his life. Creditors plagued him as well, since the war had ruined his fortune. Although he was elected a delegate to the Constitutional Convention in 1787, he declined serving.[740] He moved to a small estate called Offley Hoo in Hanover County, where he died on January 4, 1789, at the age of fifty.

His house in Yorktown was repaired and still stands today. The holes the cannonballs made in its walls in that last major battle of the Revolutionary War are still visible.[741]

Chapter 46
WILLIAM PACA
Maryland

William Paca knew how to play to the crowds.

In 1771, Paca was a new member of Maryland's provincial assembly. He opposed the governor's proclaiming laws on his own without the legislature's approval, and when the governor proclaimed public officials were to collect certain fees, Paca and Chase led a crowd to the public gallows, where they hanged the governor's proclamation in a mock execution. After the proclamation breathed its last, as it were, it was buried in a coffin under the gallows. All during the execution, Paca fired guns from a model sailing schooner.[742]

* * *

Paca was born to a wealthy family near Abingdon, Maryland, on October 31, 1740. He studied law in Annapolis, Maryland, and then at Middle Temple in London. By 1764, he had his own law practice started. His career flourished quickly, he won friends easily, and even his opponents liked him.[743] He was elected to the Provincial Assembly in 1771 and to the Continental Congress in 1774.

In the spring of 1776, Paca was frustrated because he was unable to vote for independence. The Maryland legislature forbade it.

Paca and his friend Chase again plied their political expertise to convince the people of the need for independence. The people then applied pressure on their legislature. On June 28, 1776, the Maryland delegation was free to vote for independence.

* * *

In 1778, Paca's judicial career began when he was appointed chief judge of the Superior Court of Maryland. He was then chief justice of the Court of Appeals in prize and admiralty cases. Paca continued his climb up the state political ladder and became governor just in time to see the Revolutionary War end. He was, by this time, twice a widower. His first wife, Mary Chew, died in 1774 after about a decade of marriage. He married his second wife, Anne Harrison, in 1777. She died in 1780.[744] As governor, he was known for grand social events, such as balls and receptions.[745]

The year after he left the governor's office in 1785, he helped establish Washington College in Chestertown,

Maryland. He also opposed the ratification of the new Constitution, but once it had been ratified, he supported it enough that President Washington felt confident in appointing him judge of the United States Court for Maryland in 1789. Or perhaps it is more accurate to say Washington felt confident enough in Paca after he asked James McHenry's opinion of the man. McHenry replied that Paca would "carry much respectability and legal dignity into the office."[746]

Paca continued in that office for ten years until he died on October 23, 1799, in the same house in which he was born. He was only eight days shy of his fifty-ninth birthday.

Chapter 47
ROBERT TREAT PAINE
Massachusetts

Five people were dead, shot by British soldiers. Now, in 1770, two attorneys squared off in court over the Boston Massacre: Adams on the defense team and Robert Treat Paine on the prosecution team. Local public sentiment was with Paine but may have died down somewhat due to a seven-month delay before the trial began. The captain of the soldiers who fired on the crowd, Thomas Preston, was tried separately from his men. Paine tried in vain to prove Preston ordered his men to fire, and Preston was acquitted. Then it was time for the trial of the eight soldiers. Paine tried to show the soldiers were itching for a fight and looking for opportunity, but Adams countered that they had acted in self-defense against a rowdy mob. Six of the soldiers were acquitted. Paine was slightly more successful with two of the soldiers, who were convicted of manslaughter and treated leniently.

Paine and his friend Adams had squared off over an event that helped spark a revolution—a revolution on which they both ended up on the wrong side of British law.

* * *

Paine was born on March 11, 1731, in Boston, Massachusetts, and entered Harvard at age fourteen. After graduating from Harvard in 1749 at age eighteen, he tried teaching but soon left the country for health and adventure. He traveled to the Carolinas, England, Spain, the Azores, and even worked as a whaler in Greenland. In 1755, during the French and Indian War, he acted as chaplain for troops on an expedition to Crown Point, New York, on the northern frontier.[747] But after that, he turned to the study and practice of law.

As events led up to the break from Britain, Paine was close to the center of the Massachusetts rebels and was a friend of Adams, notwithstanding their being on opposing sides of the Boston Massacre case.

During the Continental Congress in 1776, Rush said Paine "rarely proposed anything and opposed nearly everything anybody else proposed."[748] Paine argued against so many proposals he was nicknamed the "Objection Maker."[749]

Paine was one of the signers of the Olive Branch Petition, an attempt to avoid the impending conflict. King George III burned the petition.[750]

That petition failing, Paine supported the Revolution and signed the Declaration of Independence.

He was the attorney general of Massachusetts from 1777 to 1790, when Governor Hancock appointed him to the Massachusetts Supreme Court. John Quincy Adams wrote his father, John Adams, that Paine's appointment "was rather popular."[751] Paine served in that position until he resigned at seventy-three because of the onset of deafness.[752]

Paine was often seen as stern, but he could change. He began as a Congregationalist clergyman but later embraced Unitarianism.[753] He became estranged from his son, Robert Treat Paine Jr., who was a poet and committed the crime of marrying a stage actress. But before Paine's son died in 1811, they reconciled their differences.

Before Paine died on May 11, 1814, Adams wrote to Rush and told him of a visit with Paine. Adams had been losing the ability to speak. "It would divert you to witness a conversation between my ancient friend and colleague, Robert T. Paine, and me. He is above eighty. I cannot speak, and he cannot hear. Yet we converse."[754]

Chapter 48

JOHN PENN
North Carolina

What caused the duel challenge in 1778 wasn't clear What was clear, however, was John Penn, a delegate from North Carolina to the Continental Congress, was at odds with the president of the Congress at the time, Laurens of South Carolina.

There were plenty of controversies that could have caused the duel. Maybe it was about Silas Deane, who had been one of the commissioners to France and was accused of misusing funds. Or maybe it had to do with several delegates trying to replace Washington as the leader of the army.

Penn and Laurens lived at the same boardinghouse in Philadelphia. They ate breakfast together and then walked to the field designated for the duel. Penn was in his mid-thirties. Laurens was in his mid-fifties and was an old hat at duels. In his previous three duels, his opponents had shot at him, but he'd refused to return fire.

Now, as they were crossing Fifth Street, Penn reached out to help the older Laurens over a large puddle in the road. Penn's act of kindness made him realize the ridiculous thing they were about to do, and he spoke with Laurens and made amends. The duel was averted.

* * *

John Penn was born on his father's small plantation outside Fredericksburg in Caroline County, Virginia, in May 1741.[755] He was an only child. His father died when Penn was eighteen and left him an inheritance, yet his education was lacking. When he decided to become a lawyer, his uncle Edmund Pendleton was luckily a justice of the peace and had what Jefferson and Adams called one of the best private libraries in the colonies.[756] Penn applied himself rigorously to his conservative uncle's law books, and by the time he was twenty-one, he was admitted to the bar. Penn began his law practice in Bowling Green, Virginia, and married Susannah Lyme in 1763.

Things went well until early in 1774 when he was charged with disrespecting King George. He was found guilty but refused to pay the token one-cent fine.[757] Penn was excited about independence, so perhaps to save embarrassment to his uncle and perhaps to avoid further ire from Loyalist law, he moved to new opportunities in North Carolina.

* * *

Penn settled northeast of Durham near Stoval, North Carolina. About a year later, he had so impressed his new neighbors that they sent him to the provincial convention for North Carolina.[758] In another year, he was on his way to Philadelphia as a delegate for the 1775 Continental Congress.[759]

In Congress, Penn worked on finances and on a number of committees. Although he had a reputation back home for speaking, he did not participate much in these debates.

By 1776, events were hastening toward independence. On February 12, Penn expressed his feelings about the importance of the struggle to a general in the North Carolina militia. "My Good Sir, encourage our People, animate them to dare even to die for their country. Our struggle I hope will not continue long—may unanimity and success crown your endeavors."[760]

Two months later, North Carolina passed the Halifax Resolves, instructing Penn and his fellow delegates, William Hooper and Joseph Hewes, to vote for independence. Penn and Hewes did (Hooper was out of town).

Penn signed the Declaration of Independence on August 2 and, a few years later, was still a delegate and signed the Articles of Confederation as well.

* * *

By 1780, the British were taking the war to the South. Penn returned to North Carolina in 1780 to join the defense. In August, he was made one of a three-member board of war, which had great powers to recruit troops and raise money. The other two board heads left most of the job to Penn, who used his almost-dictatorial powers with effectiveness and restraint. This, of course, made him enemies among the civilian and military leaders.

In January 1781, the North Carolina legislature dissolved the war board. Penn was asked to serve on the Council of State, but his health had declined, and he refused.

After Lord Cornwallis's forces withdrew to Virginia and eventually surrendered, Penn spent the remainder of his life with his family and practicing law. Penn died at his home near Stovall, North Carolina, on September 14, 1788, at the age of forty-seven.[761]

Chapter 49
GEORGE READ
Delaware

The British warship spotted George Read as he and his family tried to cross the Delaware River on October 13, 1777. The Signer of the Declaration of Independence hired a boat at Salem, New Jersey, to take them five miles across the river. It was low tide, and the boat became stuck in shallow water. The warship had sent a smaller boat in pursuit, and it was getting closer. Read barely had enough time to scratch his name off the luggage. As the vice president of Delaware, Read was well known—and in danger. The British had already captured the state's president (equivalent to governor) and would delight in having the next person in line captured as well.

The sailors hailed the boat and asked who they were and where they were going. Read represented himself as a mere country gentleman on his way home. The presence of Read's mother, wife, and small children must have convinced the British. The sailors didn't ask another question. Instead of capturing a high-profile leader in the American Revolution, they helped his family get to shore, along with all their unsearched baggage.[762]

* * *

George Read was born near North East, Cecil County, Maryland, on September 18, 1733, and was the eldest of six boys.[763] While he was still an infant, his family moved to New Castle, Delaware.[764] When he was older, he was sent to Reverend Francis Allison's academy in New London, Pennsylvania, where he met another future Signer of the Declaration of Independence, McKean.[765] Just after his sixteenth birthday, Read went to study law in Philadelphia with John Morland.[766] Dickinson was a fellow student.

Read passed the bar and began his law practice in New Castle. In his thirtieth year, he married a young widow, Gertrude Ross Till, the sister of George Ross, another future Signer of the Declaration of Independence.[767] Read's marriage also gave him a connection to Gertrude's brother, John Ross, who was the royal attorney general of Pennsylvania and Delaware. Ross helped Read replace him as attorney general of Delaware about three months after the marriage, a job Read kept until the war.

With all of his political connections, it wasn't a surprise that Read became a member of the General Assembly of Delaware a few years later.[768]

Read was a cautious man but firm in principle. He opposed Britain's Stamp Act and supported nonimportation.[769] He wrote in July 1765 about the Stamp Act, "If this law should stand unrepealed . . . the colonists will entertain an opinion that they are to become the slaves of Great Britain by the Parliament's making laws to deprive them of their property without their assent, by any kind of representation. This will naturally lead them into measures to live as independent of Great Britain as possible."[770] To Read, this independence didn't mean a different government; it meant Americans making their own products like cloth and iron. He didn't want things to get out of hand and disliked extremism.

Read was also a religious man. In one surviving letter, he chided a kinsman for breaking the Sabbath day, telling him, "Believe me, it is dangerous to indulge ourselves in *small* breaches of that duty we owe to the Divinity."[771] He also warned that chewing tobacco "is very hurtful."[772]

* * *

Read was a natural choice for the Continental Congress. He served well beginning in 1774 and was the chairman of the Naval Committee. True to form and temperament, he gladly signed the Olive Branch Petition a year before independence, seeking reconciliation with Great Britain.[773]

The instructions from the colonial legislatures often restricted the delegates for the Congress. Some gave latitude for their representatives to vote for independence; others did not. On June 14, 1776, the Delaware delegates received permission to vote for independence—if they deemed it necessary.[774]

Read didn't deem it so. He sided with his old school friend Dickinson of Pennsylvania against what they thought was premature independence. This stance caused a split in the Delaware vote between him and his other old schoolmate, McKean. If Read and McKean were deadlocked, it would mean Congress would not get the symbolic unanimous vote for independence.[775]

Then Rodney arrived, after an exhausting horse ride, in time to cast his vote with McKean for independence.[776]

After the vote, Read threw his support to independence and became the only delegate who voted against independence to sign the Declaration of Independence. On August 2, when he signed, Read knew the consequences. His argument had been one of timing. Now, when the time was at hand, he assented to the principle and signed. Pennsylvania delegate Joseph Galloway tauntingly said Read "had done so with a rope about his neck." Read replied, "I know the risk, and am prepared for all consequences."[777]

* * *

With independence came new state governments. Although Read was offered the position of the president of Delaware, he declined so he could still serve in Congress. Instead, he accepted the position of vice president of Delaware.[778] He was also elected speaker of the upper house of the Delaware legislature.

In September 1777, the British, on their way to Philadelphia, captured John McKinley, the president of Delaware. McKean, the chief justice of Pennsylvania, took charge of Delaware temporarily. Read was in Philadelphia when this happened and hurried home to Delaware with his family.

After his near capture on the Delaware River, Read served as Delaware's chief executive for about a year. McKean was glad to have Read take over and wrote to tell him he was "wishing you all manner of success in saving our country in general, and the Delaware State in particular."[779]

Success was not easy. Read complained to Washington about his yearlong job. "My situation is rather an unlucky one, in a government very deficient in its laws, and those greatly relaxed in their execution, and a Legislature as yet incomplete, and not disposed to unite and give aid to the executive authority."[780]

Read was happy to see Rodney elected to the post in 1778.

* * *

By 1779, Read was ill. He resigned from the legislative council and refused reelection to the Congress.[781] He became a judge in the United States Court of Appeals in admiralty cases in 1782.

He never liked the Articles of Confederation because he thought they would have to be changed to give more power to the federal government.[782] He jumped to be a delegate for the Constitutional Convention in 1787. He thought the best government would be one that eliminated all state governments and only had one strong, national government. Madison reported that Read thought, "If the States remain, the representatives of the large ones will stick together and carry everything before them. . . . These jealousies are inseparable from the scheme of leaving the States in existence. They must be done away."[783]

Read didn't get what he wanted, but the new federal government had more essential powers.

His friend Dickinson asked him to sign for him because he had to return home.[784] This made Read the only person to have signed the Constitution twice—once for himself and the second time for Dickinson.

Back home, it was Read's urgent advocacy that helped Delaware become the first state to ratify the Constitution.

Read became a senator at the beginning and served until he resigned on his sixtieth birthday on September 18, 1793, in order to take over as chief justice of Delaware.

He lived five more years.

Read had never been a wealthy man. He said, "I am a poor man, but, poor as I am, The King of England is not rich enough to purchase me."[785]

Read died suddenly on September 21, 1798, three days after his sixty-fifth birthday.

Chapter 50
CAESAR RODNEY
Delaware

Caesar Rodney was away from the Continental Congress the day before the July 2, 1776, vote on independence. He was busy leading Delaware militia as they chased down trouble-making Tories who were trying to spread insurrection in the colony. But he was also one of three delegates from Delaware. The other two, McKean and Read, were deadlocked. McKean was for immediate independence, and Read wanted to delay it.

But Rodney was seventy to eighty miles away—a trip that would normally take two days. A strong express rider could have reached him by night, but the prospects of Rodney making it back in time for the vote must have seemed unlikely at best. If the tie could not be broken, the colonies would not have a unanimous vote for breaking away from Great Britain, and the Revolution's cause would be weakened.

* * *

Rodney's father wrote in his journal about October 7, 1728, the night Rodney was born: "Hung some tobacco. Came in, got dinner and killed some squirrels.... About eleven o'clock at night, my wife awakened me for she was very bad. I got up and sent for ye midwife and women. But before any came, ye child was born and it was a SON. There was no soul with her but myself, being I believe just about midnight."[786]

Rodney was born into wealth on an 800-acre plantation; however, his father died in 1745 before Rodney was twenty. This meant he, as the eldest, inherited everything and eventually owned about 200 slaves. With wealth came influence and public duty—and Rodney's public service is still legendary. He was high sheriff of Kent County, registrar of wills, recorder of deeds, clerk of Orphans' Court, justice of the peace, and captain in the Kent County militia. And with each year, he seemed to take on new roles.[787]

Luckily, his younger brother, Thomas Rodney, was able to manage the family properties.

Rodney became a member of the colonial legislature as early as 1758. Like his friend McKean, he found himself on the Patriot side of issues like Britain's Stamp Act taxes and called for reforms from Great Britain.

In late 1766, a bill taxing the importation and exportation of slaves was proposed in the Delaware legislature. Rodney supported an amendment to the bill that would end all importation of slaves, but he couldn't get more legislators to sign on to the idea.[788]

He never married and spent his health on his work. He had asthma, and cancer began on his nose and spread to the left side of his face. After doctors cut away much of the tumor, Rodney hung a green silk scarf across the gaping wound.

In 1774, Parliament closed Boston Harbor, and Rodney went around the proprietary governor's authority and called a special session of the legislature himself to set up a provisional government. The group then voted Rodney, McKean, and the more cautious Read as delegates for the just-forming Continental Congress in Philadelphia.[789]

* * *

Adams, another strong independence advocate, was impressed with Rodney and wrote in his diary on September 3, 1774: "Caesar Rodney is the oddest-looking man in the world; he is tall, thin and slender as a reed, pale; his face is not bigger than a large apple, yet there is sense and fire, spirit, wit, and humor in his countenance."[790]

Rodney was a fiery revolutionary, but he was also busy in the Delaware militia. In May 1775, he was elected a colonel in the militia. By September, he was a brigadier general.[791] His duties kept him absent from Congress during much of 1775 and 1776—it seemed he was always busy trying to block Loyalists at home in Delaware.[792] On June 22, 1776, Rodney again left Congress to quell the beginnings of a Loyalist uprising in Sussex County, Delaware.[793]

The weather had been hot for weeks when, on the night of July 1, Rodney received an urgent message from McKean at the family plantation. McKean said Rodney had to come to Philadelphia at once to vote for independence and break the tie between Read and him. The vote was set for the next day. Tradition says Rodney started at once and rode by horseback, although some historians believe he probably took a carriage for at least part of the way.

In any case, it was a mad dash through the middle of the night. The roads turned to mud as thunderstorms drenched the midnight rider—alone, wet, asthmatic, galloping headlong into the darkness.

McKean remembered years later how he met Rodney at the state-house door, Rodney still wearing his riding boots and spurs. The members of Congress were assembling for the vote. The friends greeted each other and were the last to enter the hall. One can only imagine the look on Read's face when a muddy Rodney took his place next to McKean and him.

The proceedings immediately began, and before long, the vote was called. Rodney rose to give his vote and said, as best as McKean could remember, "As I believe the voice of my constituents and of all sensible and honest men is in favor of Independence and my own judgment concurs with them, I vote for Independence."[794]

It was a vote heard around the world.

On July 4, Rodney voted to adopt the Declaration of Independence.[795] He wrote to his brother Thomas, "I arrived in Congress (tho detained by thunder and Rain) time Enough to give my Voice in the matter of Independence. It is determined by the Thirteen United Colonies with out even one disenting Colony. We have now Got through with the Whole of the declaration and Ordered it to be printed, so that You will soon have the pleasure of seeing it. Hand bills of it will be printed and Sent to the Armies, Cities, Countys, Towns &c-to be published or rather proclaimed in form."[796]

After signing the engrossed copy of the Declaration of Independence on August 2, Rodney went back to his military duties in Delaware—but not with fanfare. The conservatives weren't happy about his vote and used their votes to get him out of Congress and the legislature and to keep him out of the state Constitutional Convention.[797]

* * *

Rodney served in the field throughout the winter of 1776, recruiting troops to support Washington and other actions. In September 1777, acting state president McKean made Rodney a major general.[798]

Rodney's political value rose once again when he was elected to replace McKean as president of Delaware and served through the rest of the Revolutionary War. This was not an easy task. Delaware was repeatedly under attack along its coast. It also didn't help that there were so many Loyalists in the state.

Meanwhile, Rodney's cancer grew worse, and he declined reelection in 1782. He wrote, "The doctor must conquer the cancer, or the cancer will conquer me."[799] Treatment in Philadelphia was not successful, and he continued his decline. The Delaware assembly further honored him, making him its leader and even meeting at his house when he was too ill to attend sessions.

Rodney finally died from cancer around June 26, 1784, on his plantation. He was fifty-five years old. He left most of his property to his brother Thomas's son, Caesar Augustus Rodney. His will also provided freedom for other people—the gradual emancipation of his 200 slaves.

RODNEY'S RIDE
By Elbridge S. Brooks[800]

In that soft midland where the breezes bear
The north and the south on the genial air,
Through the county of Kent, on affairs of State,
Rode Caesar Rodney, the delegate.

Burley and big, and bold and bluff,
His three-cornered hat and his coat of snuff,
A foe to King George and the English State
Was Caesar Rodney, the delegate.

Into Dover village he rode apace,
And his kinsfolk knew, from his anxious face,
It was matter grave that brought him there
To the counties three upon Delaware.

"Money and men we must have," he said,
"Or the Congress fails and our cause is dead.
Give us both and the King shall not work his will
We are men since the blood of Bunker Hill."

Comes a rider swift on a panting bay:
"Hollo, Rodney, ho! you must save the day,
For the Congress halts at a deed so great,
And your vote alone may decide its fate!"

Answered Rodney then: "I will ride with speed;
It is Liberty's stress; it is Freedom's need.
When stands it?" "To-night. Not a moment spare,
But ride like the wind on the Delaware."

"Ho, saddle the black! I've but half a day,
And the Congress sits eighty miles away—
But I'll be in time, if God grants me grace,
To shake my fist in King George's face."

He is up; he is off! and the black horse flies
On the northward road ere the "God-speed!" dies.
It is gallop and spur as the leagues they clear,
And the clustering mile-stones move a-rear.

It is two of the clock, and the fleet hoofs fling
The Fieldsboro' dust with a clang and cling,
It is three, and he gallops with slack rein where
The road winds down to the Delaware.

Four, and he spurs into Newcastle town.
From his panting steed he gets him down:
"A fresh one, quick; and not a moment's wait!"
And off speeds Rodney, the delegate.

It is five, and the beams of the western sun
Tinge the spires of Wilmington gold and dun;
Six, and the dust of the Chester street
Flies back in a cloud from his horse's feet.

It is seven, the horse-boat, broad of beam,
At the Schuylkill ferry crawls over the stream,
And at seven-fifteen by the Rittenhouse clock
He flings his rein to the tavern jock.

The Congress is met; the debate's begun,
And Liberty lags for the vote of one—
When into the hall, not a moment late,
Walks Caesar Rodney, the delegate.

Not a moment late, and that half-day's ride
Forwards the world with a mighty stride;
For the act was passed ere the midnight stroke
O'er the Quaker City its echoes woke.

At Tyranny's feet was the gauntlet flung;
"We are free!" all the bells through the colonies rung,
And the sons of the free may recall with pride
The day of Delegate Rodney's ride.

Chapter 51

GEORGE ROSS
Pennsylvania

George Ross began his career in Pennsylvania as a prosecutor on behalf of the king. His job was to uphold the laws with a very British bias. But biases can change. When Ross became a member of Pennsylvania's legislature, he found that the interests of royal appointees were not always in line with what was best for the colony.

* * *

George Ross was born the son of an Episcopal clergyman in New Castle, Delaware, in 1730. He studied law with his brother in Philadelphia and was admitted to the bar in 1750. He decided there were too many lawyers in Philadelphia, so he set up his new practice on the edge of the western frontier in Lancaster, Pennsylvania.[801]

One of his first clients was Anne Lawler, whom he married in 1751.

Ross worked for the British government as a prosecutor and served from 1768 to 1776 in the Pennsylvania Assembly. He was reluctant to join the Patriots at first because he believed the king and Parliament could be persuaded to give up its attacks on American freedom.[802]

Ross was a member of the Continental Congress in 1774 and wasn't a delegate in 1776, but when only three of Pennsylvania's delegates voted for independence, the Pennsylvania legislature decided to replace the other five delegates with supporters. Ross was sent to the Continental Congress in mid-1776—too late for the vote on independence but in time to sign the document in early August.[803] His niece, Betsy Ross, did her own part for independence by sewing flags for the new nation.

After this, Ross was vice president (Franklin was president) of the Pennsylvania constitutional convention to draft the state's new constitution.

* * *

By 1777, gout made Ross too ill for public service. After he recovered somewhat, Ross was appointed judge of the Court of Admiralty for Pennsylvania, where he faced complicated cases, including one about a mutiny aboard a British ship that, after the mutineers decided to surrender the ship to the Americans, was then captured by an American ship. The question was who deserved the award money for taking the ship from the British. That case dragged on for thirty years.[804]

But Ross did not.

A sudden and severe attack of the gout killed him on July 14, 1779. He was forty-nine years old. Although he had been reluctant to break with England, his legacy was one of independence.

Chapter 52
BENJAMIN RUSH
Pennsylvania

*I*n September 1775, Adams's impression of Benjamin Rush was, "He is an elegant, ingenious body. Sprightly, pretty fellow. . . . But Rush I think, is too much of a Talker to be a deep Thinker. Elegant not great."[805]

* * *

Not great? That certainly could have been the prediction when Rush was born on Christmas Eve near Philadelphia in 1745. He was the fourth of seven children born to the Rush family. His father was a farmer and a blacksmith who died before Rush was ten years old.

Rush was soon sent off to a private school at West Nottingham, Maryland. His uncle, Samuel Finley, a Presbyterian minister, ran the school. Finley later became the president of the College of New Jersey (now called Princeton University).[806] Rush went to the college and graduated at age fourteen in 1760. Everyone wanted him to be a lawyer, but his uncle Finley recommended medicine. So Rush spent six years with Dr. John Redman in Philadelphia, where he saw his first yellow fever (malaria) epidemic in 1762.

In 1766, he traveled to Scotland to study medicine at the University of Edinburgh. While he was there, his uncle Finley died. The trustees of the College of New Jersey needed a replacement and asked Rush if he could persuade John Witherspoon to come to America to take his late uncle's position as president. A trustee named Richard Stockton came from America to seal the deal. All three—Rush, Stockton, and Witherspoon—were destined to sign the Declaration of Independence.[807]

In the meantime, Rush graduated with a Doctor of Medicine degree in 1768. Then it was off to London, where he continued to study, training at St. Thomas Hospital and sitting in on medical lectures.

Rush began cultivating relationships with politicians. He approached Franklin, who was in London at the time, and convinced the famous statesman to give him letters of introduction, opening English life to the young doctor.[808]

But as English life was opening to Rush, relations between the colonies and Great Britain were deteriorating.

162

In one lecture Rush attended in London, so the story goes, a lecturer mocked that even if the Americans had cannons, they didn't have any cannonballs to fire. Rush retorted that if they did not have cannonballs, they could dig up and use the skulls of their ancestors who had left the old world for a new world of freedom.[809]

After his stint in London, Rush went to Paris and then finally home during the summer of 1768. Rush was now twenty-three years old, and he set up his medical practice in Philadelphia. People liked his personality, and as one of the best-educated physicians in the country, he was immediately successful.[810] He was also given the professorship of chemistry at the College of Pennsylvania, and he published the first American textbook on chemistry.

* * *

Rush began to assert himself politically, and although not a member of Congress, he became close friends with Adams, notwithstanding Adams's initial impressions that Rush spoke too much.

Rush agitated the patriotic movement, encouraging Paine to write an essay and suggesting the title be "Common Sense." And when most of the Pennsylvania delegation to the Continental Congress opposed independence, Rush supported it and urged the delegates to back it.[811]

On January 11, 1776, he married Julia Stockton, the daughter of Stockton, whom he had met in Europe. They eventually had thirteen children, four of whom died young.[812]

Rush was no doubt thrilled when the Continental Congress voted for independence in July that year. Pennsylvania cleaned out delegates who were opposed to splitting from Great Britain and replaced them. Rush was elected a new delegate for Pennsylvania and was able to sign the Declaration on August 2, even though he had never officially voted on it. He later recalled that day to his friend Adams. "Do you recollect," he wrote, "the pensive and awful silence which pervaded the house when we were called up one after another, to the table of the President of Congress to subscribe what was believed by many at that time to be our own death warrants?"[813]

* * *

Less than a year later, the new country put Rush to work in the Revolutionary Army as surgeon general of the middle department—one of the seven regional divisions of the army that included New Jersey, Pennsylvania, Delaware, Maryland, and parts of New York.[814] But Rush did not like the way things were run in the army's medical department.[815] He capitalized on dissatisfaction within the ranks of military doctors and accused Dr. William Shippen, who was chief physician of the army, of mishandling the department. Washington referred the matter to Congress, which dismissed the charges. Rush resigned in unhappy protest on January 3, 1778.[816] But he didn't stop there.

His mind was always bent on reform and change. He didn't like how things were being run in the army, so he began behind-the-scenes criticisms of Washington. Those criticisms aligned with the soon-to-be-discredited Conway Cabal. The *cabal* was more a term for people critical of Washington than it was for any organized group. It took its name from a particularly troublesome critic, a brigadier general named Thomas Conway.

Rush sent an anonymous letter to Henry, heavily criticizing Washington. Henry showed the letter to Washington, who recognized the handwriting as Rush's. This basically meant the end of Rush's stint in the army, and it wasn't a surprise that Washington never approved any federal post for Rush when he was president.[817]

* * *

Rush returned to his private practice as a doctor. Notwithstanding the falling out with Washington, Rush's reputation grew as he continued to work on education and medicine, helping establish the Pennsylvania Hospital and setting up the first free medical clinic for the poor.[818] He also helped Presbyterians found Dickinson College, named after Rush's friend Dickinson.[819]

Rush supported the new Constitution in 1787 and was a member of the state convention to ratify it. After it was ratified, he helped Wilson write Pennsylvania's new constitution.

Rush was central in treating the 1793 yellow fever epidemic in Philadelphia. He advised fleeing the city, and his treatment involved bleeding and strong laxatives called "Rush's thunderbolts."[820] While other doctors fled the city, he was one of only two or three who stayed. He also fell ill but recovered.

Rush had a scientific and perhaps spiritual interest in dreams. While he was convalescing, he had a dream in which a poor woman told him, "Oh, Doctor! Don't turn away from the poor! You were doomed to die of the yellow fever; but the prayers of the poor were heard by heaven, and have saved your life!"[821]

Five years later, in 1798, the yellow fever was back.

Rush later blamed the 1798 yellow fever epidemic on what he thought was the public's too-high regard for Washington. "We ascribe all the attributes of the Deity to the name of General Washington," he complained. "[He] is considered by our citizens as the bulwark of our nation. God would cease to be what He is, if he did not visit us for these things."[822]

But regardless of what he thought the cause was, he again stayed among the ill when other doctors fled. And though he had the best of intentions, contemporary critics calculate that many died under Rush's treatments because he followed the medical wisdom of his day, including using bleeding.

* * *

When Adams became president, he made Rush treasurer of the United States Mint in Philadelphia, a post Rush also held under President Jefferson and President Madison. William Stephens wrote, when he heard Rush had been appointed, "I hope he won't bleed that to death also."[823]

One of Rush's greatest accomplishments was bringing Adams and Jefferson back into a friendship that had been lost over political wrangling during their presidencies. He repeatedly encouraged the two to bury the hatchet. They finally did so and struck up a correspondence that enriched their lives and illuminated their history.

It seemed there wasn't any social improvement that didn't have Rush at the forefront. In 1803, he founded one of the country's first antislavery societies, the Pennsylvania Society for the Abolition of Slavery. He campaigned against alcohol and tobacco use. He advocated better education for girls, saying they should study science in addition to their other subjects.[824] And he pushed for prison reform and condemned public and capital punishment.[825]

On top of this were the more than 3,000 students he taught.[826]

In the end, however, he fell suddenly to an epidemic himself. Rush died of typhus in Philadelphia on April 19, 1813. He was sixty-seven years old. Adams, learning of the death of his friend, wrote to Elbridge Gerry about Rush: "As a man of Science, Letters, Taste, Sense, Philosophy, Patriotism, Religion, Morality, Merit, Usefulness, taken all-together Rush has not left his equal in America, nor that I know in the World. In him is taken away, and in a manner most sudden and totally unexpected a main prop of my life."[827] To Rush's son Richard, Adams added, "He has done more good in this World than Franklin or Washington."[828]

Chapter 53
EDWARD RUTLEDGE
South Carolina

The Continental Congress of the United States of America chose three upstarts to meet with British Admiral Lord Richard Howe and his brother General William Howe in September 1776. Adams, Franklin, and Edward Rutledge went to Staten Island in New York to listen to the Howes' proposals. The British commanders wanted peace. The only necessary precondition to the negotiations was for the United States to renounce its independence.

Rutledge convinced his fellow South Carolina delegates only a few months earlier to change their vote against independence to a vote *for* independence. There was now no way he, Franklin, and Adams would turn back those days in July. The peace negotiations broke down before they began. The war would continue.

* * *

Edward Rutledge was born in Christ Church Parish in South Carolina in or near Charles Town (later called Charleston) on November 23, 1749, the youngest of seven children. His father died on Christmas Day the next year. When Rutledge came of age, his brother John, who was a decade older, put him to work as a clerk in his law office in Charleston.[829] Rutledge followed in his brother's footsteps, studying law at Middle Temple in London when he was nineteen. He passed the English bar in 1772.

When he came back to South Carolina, he rose quickly in prominence as he defended Thomas Powell, publisher of the *South Carolina Gazette*. Powell ran into trouble with the upper house of the colony's legislature because he published some of their debates. Rutledge successfully helped Powell go free, making both friends and enemies.

In March 1774, Rutledge's star continued to rise as he married Henrietta Middleton, daughter of the richest man in South Carolina, Henry Middleton. Her dowry of 70,000 pounds suddenly made him the wealthiest person in his family and tied him to a powerful dynasty.

It wasn't a surprise when he was elected to the colonial legislature and sent off with his brother John and his father-in-law, Middleton, as a delegate to the Continental Congress in 1774.[830]

* * *

Adams was not impressed with the group of moderate delegates from South Carolina, although he had a tendency to not be impressed with anyone who had different views about independence. He described the twenty-four-year-old Rutledge: "Young Ned Rutledge is a perfect Bob-o-Lincoln—a swallow, a sparrow, a peacock; excessively vain, excessively weak, and excessively variable and unsteady; jejeune, inane, and puerile."[831]

Rush, however, called him a "sensible young lawyer."[832]

Rutledge and company represented the ideals of the Southern aristocracy and often butted heads with Adams and the New England delegates.[833] Rutledge, for his part, disapproved of the "violent" and "wrong-headed" delegates who wanted independence and added, "But you may thank your stars you sent prudent men; and I trust that the youngest is not the least so."[834]

Rutledge and his brother were elected again for the 1775 Congress. John Rutledge, however, left his little brother behind and returned to South Carolina to attend to other business. With other delegates replaced for other reasons, Rutledge became the senior member of the delegation and led the fight against what he thought was premature independence.[835]

In March 1776, South Carolina drafted its own constitution, with John Rutledge's help, and also authorized its delegates to vote for independence if they deemed it necessary. Rutledge believed independence would come but wanted a confederation formed first and wanted allies.[836]

Then came Lee's thunderbolt of a resolution for independence on June 7, 1776. Rutledge wasn't ready for this and wasn't sure which way he should vote, so he moved to postpone the resolution until July 1.[837]

But when July came along, Rutledge was still hesitant, voting with the other delegates from South Carolina against independence in the July 1 vote as a Committee of the Whole. The next day, however, was the official vote, not as a committee but as Congress. It seemed clear the measure would pass, and understanding the importance of a unanimous vote, Rutledge convinced his fellow delegates to change their minds for the July 2 vote. Two days later, on July 4, he voted approval of the Declaration of Independence. Not long after, he wrote his brother John, "Enclosed also is a very important Declaration which the King of Great Britain has at last reduced us to the necessity of making."[838]

On August 2, when the official written copy was presented, Rutledge was possibly the youngest Signer of the Declaration of Independence, at the age of twenty-six (George Walton may have been younger, though his exact birthdate is unknown).

* * *

After the signing, Rutledge turned his attention to his home state. He became a captain in the Charleston Battalion of Artillery in South Carolina's militia that had been formed to repel Sir Henry Clinton's invasion. In 1779, Rutledge helped

General William Moutrie successfully fight against the British at Port Royal Island, South Carolina. But he was taken prisoner by the British on May 12, 1780, when Charleston fell. Fellow Signers of the Declaration of Independence Heyward and Rutledge's brother-in-law Arthur Middleton were also captured. Even his mother was kept under house arrest with the hopes that she might have useful information.[839]

John Rutledge, however, escaped.

Rutledge, Heyward, and Middleton were sent to prison in St. Augustine, Florida, until they were freed in a prisoner exchange in July 1781.

* * *

After the war, Rutledge practiced law and served in the state house of representatives, where, among other measures, he opposed reopening Africa to slave trade.

In April 1792, his wife, Henrietta, died. Six months later, he married a widow named Mary Shubrick Eveleigh.

His brother, John Rutledge, was made an associate justice of the U.S. Supreme Court in 1789 but resigned in 1791 to become chief justice of the South Carolina Court of Common Pleas and Sessions. President Washington asked Rutledge to become an associate justice of the Supreme Court in 1794, but he did not accept. The next year, his brother was named chief justice of the Supreme Court and presided at the August term, but his unstable public statements, provoking concerns of mental illness, caused the Senate to reject his confirmation.

Rutledge, however, didn't suffer politically under his older brother's advancing mental illness. In 1798, he retired from his law practice and was elected governor.

He didn't finish his term, however. He died January 23, 1800, at fifty years old.[840]

Chapter 54
ROGER SHERMAN
Connecticut

Roger Sherman believed in the importance of the Continental Congress, but something else was more important to him. Rush remembered once when Sherman objected to Congress considering a nonurgent matter on a Sunday. "He gave as a reason for his objection," Rush wrote, "a regard of the commands of his Maker."[841]

* * *

Roger Sherman was a shoemaker and the son of a shoemaker.[842] He was born on April 19, 1721, in Newton, Massachusetts, and moved with his family two years later to Stoughton (now Canton), Massachusetts. Sherman didn't have much of a formal education until a schoolhouse opened nearby when he was thirteen,[843] but he loved to read books. A local cleric, Reverend Samuel Danbar, helped him study as well.

When Sherman's father died in 1741, Sherman, only nineteen years old, became responsible for his younger siblings. He continued his father's shoemaking business for a few years and then moved the family closer to an older brother in New Milford, Connecticut. The story goes that he walked the whole way—about 150 miles—with his cobbler tools in a bag on his back.

Sherman loved math and became the surveyor of New Haven County. He even made astronomical calculations and had them printed in an almanac.[844]

He was married on November 17, 1749, to Elizabeth Hartwell, who lived 150 miles away back in Stoughton, Massachusetts. They had seven children.

Sherman's survey work was often used when landowners disagreed. One lawyer was impressed with Sherman's notes on a dispute and encouraged him to go into the law. He did and was admitted to the bar in 1754 at the age of thirty-three. The next year, his rise in public service began in earnest. He took office after office—often concurrently. Always competently.

He was a member of the Connecticut Assembly for decades and was justice of the peace for Litchfield County.

Then his wife died in 1760.

He abandoned his law practice and his old home and moved to the larger town of New Haven, Connecticut. There, he managed a store aimed at students of Yale College.[845]

In 1763, he married Rebecca Prescott, and they had eight children.

He continued his political rise in the state senate or governor's council while serving as judge of the Superior Court and as treasurer of Yale College.

*　*　*

Sherman was a practical man, and this added weight to his support of the Revolution. In 1774, he attended the first session of the Continental Congress as a delegate from Connecticut. Adams's impression in 1774 was that "he is between fifty and sixty, a solid, sensible man."[846]

Sherman signed the Continental Congress's Articles of Association—a call for the boycott of trade with Great Britain.

Four days after Lee's famous June 7, 1776, resolution for independence, a committee was appointed to draft a declaration in case the resolution passed when it came up for a vote in July. Sherman was on the committee, along with Livingston, Franklin, Adams, and Jefferson.[847] That same day, June 11, another committee was formed to draft a plan of confederation. Sherman was on that committee as well.

If there was an important committee, Sherman was on it—Indian affairs, national finance, military, and so forth. Jefferson said, "He was a very able and logical debater in that body, steady in the principles of the revolution, always at the post of duty, much employed in the business of committees, and, particularly, was of the committee of Dr. Franklin, Mr. J. Adams, Mr. Livingston, and myself, for preparing the Declaration of Independence."[848]

Adams said, "The honourable Roger Sherman was one of the most cordial friends which I ever had in my life. Destitute of all literary and scientific education but such as he acquired by his own exertions, he was one of the most sensible men in the world. The clearest head and the steadiest heart. . . . One of the soundest and strongest pillars of the revolution."[849]

Jefferson said Sherman was "a man who never said a foolish thing in his life."[850]

Naturally, Sherman voted for independence and for the declaration his committee had prepared.

He signed the Declaration of Independence on August 2, 1776, with the majority of Congress. He also signed the Articles of Confederation in 1778, although it was not finally ratified until 1781.

*　*　*

In 1784, Sherman became mayor of New Haven, Connecticut, a post he held, with all his other ensuing positions, until his death.

In 1787, at age sixty-six, he became a delegate to the Federal Constitutional Convention in Philadelphia and was a voice of compromise there. And compromise was needed when the larger and smaller states reached an impasse over how they should be represented in the federal legislature. The larger states wanted to have the number of representatives tied to the population of the states. This would give them a larger voice and equally represent the people. The smaller states wanted representatives to be by the states, with each state having an equal vote.

Sherman took several of the proposals, mixed and matched them together, and proposed to have the lower house—the House of Representatives—be based on population, giving the larger states the advantage, and the upper house—the Senate—be more equal, with two representatives per state whether large or small. The idea was called the Connecticut Compromise, the Great Compromise, or even the Sherman Compromise. It eventually won the day and made the Constitution's passing possible.

Sherman signed the Constitution on September 17, 1787, and after the Constitution was adopted, Sherman served in the first Congress. At sixty-eight, he was the oldest man in that body.

But that didn't slow him down.

He worked for the Bill of Rights and published an essay supporting it under the name "A Citizen of New Haven." He wrote, "Every thing that tends to disunion, ought to be carefully avoided. Instability in government and laws, tends to weaken a state, and render the rights of the people precarious. The Constitution which is the foundation of law and government ought not to be changed without the most pressing necessity."[851]

Naturally, Sherman was on the committee to finalize the Bill of Rights amendments. He also helped draft the Judiciary Act of 1789. This law established the federal courts system.[852]

* * *

Sherman's interests were not limited to government. He published "A Short Sermon on the Duty of Self-Examination, Preparatory to Receiving the Lord's Supper" that year as well.[853]

He then replaced Senator William S. Johnson, who had resigned, and served until his death two years later.

Sherman died in his sleep in New Haven, Connecticut, on July 23, 1793, at the age of seventy-two. He is the only person to have signed the four major documents of freedom: the 1774 Articles of Association, the 1776 Declaration of Independence, the 1778 Articles of Confederation, and the 1787 Federal Constitution. It is no wonder that Adams described Sherman as "an old Puritan, as honest as an Angel and as staunch as a blood Hound firm as a Rock in the Cause of American Independence, as Mount Atlas."[854]

Chapter 55
JAMES SMITH
Pennsylvania

On July 5, 1776, James Smith took one of the newly printed copies of the Declaration of Independence and rode the two-days' journey back to his hometown of York, Pennsylvania. On the evening of July 6, a crowd of about 300 to 400 older men, boys, and women gathered in the town square to hear the news fresh from Philadelphia. After a few speeches and a reading of the Declaration, Smith addressed his fellow citizens and explained the advantages of independence. Then, in jubilation, he threw his hat high into the night air.[855]

* * *

James Smith was born in Ireland on September 17 sometime between 1713 and 1719. He was the second son in a large family and came to America with his father when he was about ten or twelve. The family settled on the wilder west side of the Susquehanna River in York County, Pennsylvania.[856]

Smith was educated at Reverend Francis Alison's Academy[857] in New London, Pennsylvania and at the Philadelphia Academy (now the University of Pennsylvania).[858] After that, he became a surveyor and studied law with his older brother, George, in Lancaster, Pennsylvania. He was admitted to the bar in 1745 and probably thought he had a great plan to make his fortune. He moved to the frontier: Shippensburg, Pennsylvania. He tried practicing law and surveying, but he wasn't successful. Or so he thought. His stint on the frontier didn't make him much money at the time, but it later gave him the political loyalty of the backcountry folk.[859] Five years later, he moved to York, Pennsylvania, and became the only lawyer in town. When he didn't find a lot of success as a lawyer, he tried his hand at iron manufacturing. That didn't work out either.

In the meantime, around 1760, he married Eleanor Armor from New Castle, Delaware. They had three sons and two daughters.

Slowly his fortunes and reputation grew. In 1774, he was sent to Philadelphia to see how to help Boston, which was under the so-called Coercive Acts that were devastating the city's economy. Smith supported a boycott of British goods in response.[860] Smith was so wound up about the

172

British that he came back home and raised one of the first groups of Revolutionary troops in Pennsylvania. In return, his troops made him captain and later, as they swelled in ranks, colonel.

Smith attended and participated in various state conventions, conferences, and meetings, helping draft resolutions that called for independence, but he was not yet a delegate to the Continental Congress. That would soon change.

* * *

After Congress voted for independence on July 2 and for the Declaration of Independence on July 4, the Pennsylvania delegates who didn't vote for independence were out of favor with the populace. Smith took a copy of the Declaration of Independence to York, Pennsylvania, on July 6 and enthusiastically read it and defended it to any hearers. On July 20, he was elected as a replacement delegate to Congress. He arrived in Philadelphia in time to sign the Declaration of Independence on August 2.

Smith was known in Congress for his excellent memory and his good sense of humor. In fact, he would often make his points by relating humorous anecdotes.

Smith was reelected in 1777. That year the Continental Congress fled Philadelphia for fear of the British. They went first to Lancaster and then to Smith's town, York. In York, the board of war held its meetings in Smith's law office.

But Smith's political career was winding down. He spent one year, 1780, in the State House of Representatives and then was briefly a judge in the Pennsylvania High Court of Errors and Appeals.

* * *

Smith went back to his law practice in York—only taking local political office. When he was elected to be a delegate again in the Continental Congress in 1785, he declined because of age. He continued practicing law until he retired in 1801, when he was probably the oldest practicing lawyer in the state.

In 1805, a fire started in a barn near his law practice. It spread to his office and destroyed all his papers, including letters and papers from Franklin, Samuel Adams, and, no doubt, his friends Washington and Wilson.

Smith died the next year on July 11, 1806. He was between eighty-seven and ninety-two years old. Even if he had never signed the Declaration of Independence, he would stand as one of the many patriots who supported freedom by word and deed. His signing only solidifies it more completely in the annals of history.

Chapter 56

RICHARD STOCKTON
New Jersey

*I*n the dead of winter, four months after he signed the Declaration of Independence, Richard Stockton was a prisoner of the British. Inside the squalid and cold stone walls of the infamous Provost Prison in New York City, he was deprived of food and was failing in health.[861] He was a New Jersey delegate to the Continental Congress, but he was being treated as a common criminal.

His son-in-law, fellow Signer Rush, was incensed and wrote to Lee in Congress. Rush said he didn't want the news to rouse his own resentment against the British. "But it has encreased it," he wrote. "Every particle of my blood is electrified with revenge—and if justice cannot be done to him in any other way, I declare I will in defiance of the Authority of the congress, & the power of the army drive the first rascally tory I meet with a hundred miles bare footed thro the first deep Snow that falls in our country."[862]

Stockton was the first and the only person who was specifically targeted, captured, and basically tortured because he was part of the group of men who signed the Declaration of Independence. Others were imprisoned for fighting in the war. Others suffered losses of property, health, and family as a result of the Revolution. But only Stockton lost his personal liberty directly because of his role in the Continental Congress and its declaring independence.

* * *

Stockton was born at Morven Estate near Princeton, New Jersey, in October 1730. He was the eldest son of John Stockton.[863] He was well educated and graduated from the College of New Jersey (later Princeton University) in Newark, New Jersey, in 1748. From there, he studied law under David Ogden in Newark and was admitted to the bar in 1754 at the age of twenty-three.

Later that year, he married Annis Boudinot.[864] They had six children.

In 1764, Stockton thought the best solution to rising tensions between America and Great Britain was to have American representation in Parliament. Parliament's Stamp Act changed his mind about that.[865]

Stockton became a trustee of the College of New Jersey and went to the

British Isles in 1766 to search for a new president for the college. While there, he met Rush, who was studying medicine in Scotland. With Rush's help, the two eventually persuaded a well-known Presbyterian minister, Witherspoon, to accept the position.[866]

On the trip, Stockton also met King George III.[867]

Back in Princeton, New Jersey, Stockton avoided public life. It just didn't interest him. "The publick is generally unthankful," he said, "and I will never become a servant of it, till I am convinced that by neglecting my own affairs I am doing more acceptable service to God and man."[868]

* * *

As the problems between the colonies and England grew, so did Stockton's involvement in politics. He served for eight years in the executive council of New Jersey under Franklin's son, William, the royal governor of New Jersey. He was among staunch Loyalists on the council, but he left it when it became clear there would be no reconciliation. He also became associate justice of New Jersey's Supreme Court in 1774.

The year of 1776 was an eventful year for the new nation and for Stockton. In January, Rush married Stockton's oldest daughter, Julia. In June, New Jersey's royal governor, William Franklin, was imprisoned under the direction of the provincial congress of New Jersey. The congress also appointed two new delegates to the Continental Congress—Stockton and the man he brought from Scotland a decade earlier, Witherspoon.

When Stockton and Witherspoon arrived in Philadelphia on July 1, the debate was in full force between pro-independence Adams and the more cautious Dickinson. Stockton called Adams "the Atlas of American Independence."[869]

His son-in-law, Rush, described Stockton as someone who loved law and order, but "he was timid where bold measures were required."[870] Yet there were few bolder measures that anyone could take than when Stockton voted for independence on July 2 and for the Declaration of Independence on July 4. He signed it on August 2. Like many, he knew it could mean imprisonment and perhaps death.[871]

* * *

In August, the new state of New Jersey held an election for a new governor in its legislature. Rush wrote to his wife that he thought it was inevitable Stockton would win.[872] The first meeting of the New Jersey state legislature pitted Stockton against Livingston for the state's first governor. The first ballot was tied. His supporters struck a deal that if Livingston won the vote, Stockton would be named chief justice of the state's Supreme Court. Stockton was unanimously made chief justice, but when he learned of his election, he declined. He wanted to stay in Congress.[873]

Congress sent Stockton on a fact-finding mission in September and October to inspect the state of the troops in upper New York. Clymer went with Stockton to meet with General Schuyler's army in the north. When Stockton saw the poor conditions of the New Jersey contingent of troops, he wrote, "There is not a single shoe or stocking to be had in this part of the world or I would ride a hundred miles through the woods to purchase them with my own money."[874]

At the same time, British military commander General Howe had his army on the move and invaded New Jersey.

When Stockton came back to New Jersey, he first helped get supplies for the American troops in the area.[875] He evacuated his family from the Princeton area to the home of his friend John Covenhoven in Monmouth County. The British overran Princeton, and Stockton's estate, Morven, became their headquarters. They looted it and burned his library, one of the finest collections of books in the new country.

Unfortunately Stockton was still in danger. Some Loyalists learned that the rebel delegate in the Continental Congress was staying with Covenhoven. Stockton and Covenhoven were captured and led away in the winter night some time near the beginning of December 1776.[876] Stockton was taken to Brunswick and thrown in jail.[877] He was later transferred to Provost Prison in New York City.

Provost Prison became infamous for the terrible treatment of its prisoners. There was no heat. The food was foul—what little they were given. The commander was sadistic, and sudden beatings were common. The guards even beat people who attempted to visit their jailed family members.

* * *

When word of his new father-in-law's treatment came to Rush, he informed Congress in hopes that it would take some action. "I have heard from good Authority that my much [honored] father in law who is now a prisoner with Gen Howe suffers many indignities & hardships from the enemy from which not only his rank, but his being a man ought to exempt him," he wrote.[878] Rush asked for a resolution in Stockton's favor and received one. Congress ordered General Washington to investigate and to threaten Howe with similar treatment to British prisoners if something wasn't done.[879]

Meanwhile, Stockton's health was failing. Hancock blamed General Howe. "He now openly assumes the Character, & copies the Manners of a Military Tyrant," he wrote. "His Treatment of Mr. Stockton is, to the last Degree shocking and inhuman, if Report is to be depended upon."[880]

In some ways, Stockton was the victim of the nature of the war. Normally, when two nations fought each other, they agreed upon rules for how to treat prisoners. But such agreements were between nations, and Britain wouldn't make such an agreement with the Continental Congress because then it would have to admit the United States were independent. Instead, prisoner exchanges and other wartime happenings were handled ad hoc—with agreements between generals or on a case-by-case basis.

At the time, a captured prisoner could be freed on parole—meaning he wasn't kept in a jail under guard, but on his word of honor, the prisoner promised to not take up arms. In some cases, the prisoners were lodged in homes and not allowed, again by their word of honor, to leave certain areas. During part of the war, for example, the United States had 4,000 British and Hessian prisoners in private homes instead of prisons—all kept there because they were on parole.[881] Nothing more than their word kept them there. They could do nothing. So strong, in fact, was the concept of parole that Washington ordered his own soldiers who broke parole to return to the British.[882]

Prisoner exchanges also followed this idea of parole. After the British were defeated at Yorktown, they were allowed to sail back to England under parole. They were still considered prisoners and stayed prisoners until they were exchanged for American prisoners.[883]

Stockton was in this dual murky world of real prisons and honor-bound parole prisons. One thing was clear: he was not being treated the way a high-ranking official should be treated—but by the middle of January 1777, he was released and made his way back to his wife and family at Morven.

* * *

Why Stockton was suddenly let go is a bit of a mystery. Some historians casually call him a traitor and a betrayer of the American cause, saying he repudiated his signature on the Declaration of Independence and swore allegiance to King George III of England.

On November 30, 1776, just a few days before Stockton was captured, General Howe and his brother Admiral Richard Howe issued a joint proclamation that for sixty days people could be pardoned of treason and/or not in danger of having their property or liberty taken by British troops if they swore this oath: "I (_____) do promise and Declare that I will remain in peaceable Obedience to his Majesty and will not take up arms, nor encourage Others to take up Arms in Opposition to this Authority."[884] Part of the mystery of Stockton's release is whether or not he took this oath and, if he did, what it says about his integrity and loyalty to the American cause. If he did take the oath, he was not alone. About 4,800 Americans signed the oath or, as it was sometimes described, "took Howe's protection."[885]

It isn't clear if Washington's inquiry (and the threat to treat British prisoners similarly) influenced Stockton's release. It is very likely that it had some effect. Whatever instruments were used to formalize Stockton's release, the basic nature of it clearly falls under the category of parole.

One account of his leaving prison came from his son-in-law, Rush: "At Princeton I met my wife's father who had been plundered of all his household furniture and stock by the British Army, and carried a prisoner to New York, from whence he was permitted to return to his family upon parole."[886] So the only definitive description from someone who said they spoke with Stockton and knew of the situation firsthand plainly identified it as "parole."

On February 8, Abraham Clark mentioned Stockton in a letter to John Hart. Clark said New Jersey would have to send two new delegates and explained, "Mr. Stockton by his late procedure cannot Act."[887] Saying "late procedure" fit the concept of parole perfectly; if Stockton took parole, he was still technically a prisoner and could not act in any capacity. He was released but not really free.

Others, however, identified Stockton's acts as signing Howe's declaration or taking Howe's protection. Hancock, for example, the very next day wrote, "Stockton it is said, & truly, has Rec'd General How's protection."[888]

The most enlightening information on the question comes from Witherspoon. He stopped by Princeton to take care of business and, while there, heard rumors about Stockton. It isn't clear if he had time to speak with Stockton at Morven outside of town. "Judge Stockton is not very well in health & much spoken against for his Conduct," Witherspoon wrote to his teenage son David. "He Signed Howes declaration & also gave his Word of honour that he would not meddle in the least in American affairs during the War."[889]

What was odd about Witherspoon's statement was that Stockton was accused of both signing the oath and giving his word of honor. If he signed the oath, there was no need for a parole's word of honor. If he gave his word of honor, there was no need to sign the oath. It was a possibility, with the lack of formal parole rules, that the British had him do both as part of the parole procedure. It could be that in order to travel safely through British-controlled territory, he needed to carry a certificate of Howe's protection order.

It was also possible that Witherspoon was just reporting a rumor. With thousands of people in New Jersey taking Howe's oath, it is not surprising that people would assume this was how Stockton got away from the British as well.

In any case, whether he took Howe's oath or gave his word of honor as part of a standard parole procedure, or both, Stockton was being spoken against. Those who knew him, though, did not seem to make much of it beyond it being one of the reasons he had to resign from Congress. The British never made anything of it. The Loyalist newspapers never mentioned anything about it. And Washington never mentioned it. He had made his own declaration that anyone who signed Howe's oath had thirty days to either repudiate it or go to areas controlled by the British.[890] He made no such demand of Stockton.

But Stockton *had* been held prisoner behind enemy lines, so as a matter of formality, he was required to reaffirm his loyalty before the New Jersey Committee of Safety. More than a year after his capture, on December 22, 1777, his health still not quite recovered, Stockton stood before a committee and declared publicly and on record his allegiance to the United States of America.[891] If he had faltered, if imprisonment, deprivation, near starvation, and sickness led him to sign Howe's oath of "peaceful obedience," then this new declaration reaffirmed his signature on the Declaration of Independence.

* * *

It wasn't until two years after his imprisonment that Stockton's health returned. But as he attempted to rebuild his legal practice, another trial came. In 1778, a small cancer appeared on his lip. A surgeon removed it, but it came back later in his throat. There was nothing he could do but suffer.[892] He died in Morven, the home in which he had been born, on February 28, 1781.

Stockton suffered for two years before his death. In his will, he purposely gave his "last words" to his children. He told them of his faith in God and the "redemption purchased by the Blessed Saviour."

"In the bowels of a father's affection," he charged and encouraged them to remember, "The fear of God is the beginning of wisdom."[893]

Chapter 57
THOMAS STONE
Maryland

Thomas Stone was looking forward to having his wife, Margaret, visit him in Philadelphia in April 1776. He was thirty-three years old and a delegate to the Continental Congress from Maryland, and he set out to meet her on April 27 or 28. But she became very ill.

While in Philadelphia, there was a smallpox scare. Margaret, the daughter of a doctor, decided to get vaccinated. The procedure was dangerous, to say the least. A doctor took the pus from a smallpox victim and shoved it into cuts made on the arm of the healthy person. If everything worked right, the person would develop a mild case of smallpox but recover quickly.

Margaret didn't.

The issues facing Stone, one of the most conservative members of Congress, were daunting. To him, it seemed everything was going too fast toward separation from Britain. He thought having his wife in town would be the only comfort in his political service. He wrote on May 20, 1776, how distressed he was about what he speculated was going to happen in America. "And this mortifying Speculation is not the greatest uneasiness I suffer at present," he wrote. "The Illness of a wife I esteem most dearly preys most severely on my Spirits, she is I thank God something better this afternoon, and this Intermission of her Disorder affords me Time to write to you. The Doctr. thinks she is in a fair way of being well in a few days. I wish I thought so."[894]

* * *

Thomas Stone was born at Poynton Manor, Charles County, Maryland, in 1743. As a boy, he rode twenty miles on horseback from his family's plantation to school. When his father died, the law of primogeniture gave the bulk of the estate to his older brother, and Stone had to make his own way in the world.

Which he did.

He studied law in Annapolis, Maryland, under Thomas Johnson and was admitted to the bar in 1764 at the age of twenty-one. He practiced in Frederick, Maryland, for a few years, and then in 1768, he married eighteen-year-old Margaret Brown. With her 1,000-pound dowry, the young couple established a farm near his family's old plantation in Port

Tobacco, Maryland. It featured a beautiful home he called *Habre-de-Venture*, "dwelling place in the winds."[895]

As the events of the Revolution rolled forward, counties and colonies across America created committees of correspondence to help the various colonies work in concert on similar goals. Stone served on Charles County's committee of correspondence in 1773.

In the next year, however, he irked some Patriots when he acted on behalf of the royal governor of Maryland and prosecuted Joseph H. Harrison, a Maryland legislator. Harrison refused to pay a poll tax to support clergy in the Anglican Church. Stone sided with Britain. Three other future Continental Congress delegates—Paca, Chase, and Stone's old mentor, Johnson, defended Harrison.

Stone lost the case but must have maintained some level of esteem among the people and legislature of Maryland because he was chosen as a delegate to the second Continental Congress in 1775.

* * *

In 1775, Stone signed the failed Olive Branch Petition to Britain. By 1776, events had placed the colonies on a run toward independence, and Stone thought things were going too fast, which weakened the possibility of either reconciliation or a successful independence the general population would support.

He thought, however, that war was preferable to surrendering rights.

"The Dye is cast. The fatal Stab is given to any future Connection between this Country & Britain: except in the relation of Conqueror & vanquished, which I can't think of without Horror & Indignation," he wrote in May 1776. "[But] when the Minds of Men are not prepared for such an Event, to cut the only Bond which held the discordant Members of the Empire together, appears to me the most weak and ill judged Measure I ever met with in a State which had the least Pretention to wisdom or Knowledge in the Affairs of Men."[896]

The tall, thin, and pale man still gave his vote for independence on July 2 and signed the Declaration of Independence on August 2.

But his heart was still distressed over his wife, who did not recover from the mercury poisoning she received during the smallpox inoculation process.

Stone served on the committee that drafted the Articles of Confederation, but he didn't end up signing them.

* * *

After Stone's turn in Congress, he served for several years in the Maryland state senate. In 1784, he went briefly back to Congress, even taking part as acting president for a short time. The next year, he was a representative from Maryland at the Mount Vernon Conference, a meeting Washington called to discuss water transportation issues between Virginia and Maryland.

When the Constitutional Convention was set, Stone refused to go. His sickly wife was getting worse. Margaret died at age thirty-four on June 1, 1787. Stone was devastated and withdrew from life, abandoning his legal practice and retreating to his home, *Habre-de-Venture*.

His doctors encouraged him to take a trip abroad to break out of his depression and halt his own decline in health. On October 5, 1787, he went to the port of Alexandria, Virginia, to begin his journey to England, but it was there, while waiting for the ship to sail, that Stone died suddenly—four months after his wife died. He was forty-four years old.

Chapter 58
GEORGE TAYLOR
Pennsylvania

When George Taylor came to America in 1736, he couldn't afford the passage from Ireland. He was about twenty years old and started his new life in Pennsylvania as an indentured servant. Sometimes such servants were treated like slaves. Taylor had a better go at it.

Samuel Savage Jr. purchased Taylor's contract and put him to work shoveling coal at the Warwick furnace—an ironworks in Chester County, Pennsylvania. Taylor had some education; he was the son of a clergyman and may have begun studying medicine back in Europe. Savage soon had him acting as a clerk. Within three years, Taylor was the manager and bookkeeper at Savage's Coventry Forge.

Then Savage died. About a year later, in 1742, Taylor married Savage's widow, Ann, and took over the ironworks. It had taken him six years to get from the bottom of the coal heap to the top of the company.

Ann and Taylor had two children, a daughter who died young and a son who later became a lawyer. After ten years, Savage's son, Samuel Savage III, took over his rights in the two ironworks. Taylor became partners with Samuel Flower and took out a ten-year lease on the Durham furnace near Easton, Pennsylvania, in 1754 or 1755.

* * *

As usually happened to somewhat prosperous business people, Taylor began dabbling in political affairs. In 1761, he became justice of the peace. He became better known while he was in charge of the construction of the Northampton Courthouse.[897] In 1764, he became more active in the revolutionary-minded local activities, such as a committee of correspondence and the Pennsylvania Colonial Legislature, which started the next year.

Then, in 1768, his wife, Ann, died. In his loneliness, he began an openly acknowledged relationship with his housekeeper, Naomi Smith, who became his common-law wife. They had five children together.

In 1774, the fighting in Massachusetts caused Taylor to jump to the defense of the colony—and he was elected a colonel in the county militia, although it was in name only. Taylor was itching for independence by

October 1775 when he became a member of the Provincial Congress. He must have been irritated when, in July 1776, only three of the eight Pennsylvania delegates voted for independence.[898]

He was elected on July 20 as one of five delegates to replace the hesitant delegates. His instructions from the provincial legislature were clear: he was to go to the Continental Congress in Philadelphia and sign the Declaration of Independence. He did this gladly, along with most of the delegates, on August 2.

He went from indentured servant to Signer of one of the most important documents of freedom in history. But Taylor didn't distinguish himself much among his colleagues. Rush described him as "a respectable country gentleman. Not active in Congress."[899]

* * *

In January 1777, Congress received word that chiefs from the "Minisink, Chockonit, Shinango, Mohawk and Quykunk" Native American tribes were on their way to Easton, Pennsylvania, to solidify friendly relations with the colony and Congress.[900] Taylor was chosen to meet with the tribes, probably in part because they were coming to his hometown. He and delegate George Walton were to offer a large number of presents to show Congress's friendship and confidence. On January 30, Walton and Taylor not only met with the tribes and offered the gifts, but they also struck a treaty with them.

This did not please their fellow members of Congress, who had not authorized any such treaty negotiations. The Committee on Indian Affairs was afraid the unauthorized treaty could upset the neutral stance and diplomatic balance it wanted the various American Indian tribes to maintain. Congress refused to ratify the treaty and instructed representatives to try to repair any possible political damage with the tribes.

Taylor resigned in March 1777.[901]

* * *

He wasn't long without a political job. The Pennsylvania legislature made Taylor a member of Pennsylvania's first Supreme Executive Council—its chief executive body under the new state's constitution.

His stint there didn't even last a year because he resigned due to illness.

Aside from signing the Declaration of Independence, Taylor's greatest help in the cause of the Revolution was his ironworks. Taylor's Durham Furnace turned out cannonballs, grapeshot (smaller iron balls in a canvas bag that shot out of a cannon like a shotgun discharge), and bar shot (two balls linked by a bar so it looked like a small dumbbell—used in naval warfare to cut down the masts of enemy ships as the projectile spun through the air).

However, the struggling government never paid him sufficiently for the ammunition. To add insult to his financial injury, Pennsylvania also confiscated the ironworks because the owner, John Galloway, was a Loyalist. The state didn't honor Taylor's lease, leading him to lease another ironworks, which he did in New Jersey.

Taylor's health began to fade. In 1780, he came back to Easton and leased a home, where he died on February 23, 1781, at the age of sixty-five. Although his will provided for his five grandchildren and his common-law wife, Naomi, and their five children, he had no assets to provide for their futures. His property, including two slaves named Tom and Sam, was sold to pay for the estate's debts.

In the end, he went from penniless to penniless, but the in between . . . .

Chapter 59
MATTHEW THORNTON
New Hampshire

Matthew Thornton spent his first winter in the Maine region of Massachusetts living on a ship in the harbor. He was born four years earlier, in 1714, to a Scottish Presbyterian family in Ireland; religious intolerance had driven the family across the Atlantic.

But coming to America did not solve their religious persecution. The family settled in Worcester, Massachusetts, where they were part of a Presbyterian minority in a Puritan community. His religious roots shaped his view of the significance of what the colonies would attempt when he was in his sixties. To him, the call of independence was the voice of God.

* * *

Thornton grew up and studied medicine in Leicester, Massachusetts, under a doctor named Thomas Green. In 1740, his family and many other Scottish Presbyterians left Worcester. They decided to start their own village away from the persecution and disputes of their Congregationalist neighbors. Thornton, however, began practicing medicine that year in Londonderry, New Hampshire (now Derry Village), at about the age of twenty-six.[902]

His skills as a surgeon came in handy when disputes in Europe soon spilled over into America. In King George's war with the French, Thornton traveled with New Hampshire troops in an expedition against the French in Nova Scotia, and he was there when the French surrendered their massive fort at Louisbourg in June 1745. Thornton stayed in the militia and rose to the rank of colonel by the time the Revolution started.

He returned to Londonderry and his medical practice, but his true interest seemed to be real estate, as he bought up land throughout New Hampshire.[903] Thornton finally found love with an eighteen-year-old woman named Hannah Jack and married her in 1760, when he was about forty-six years old. They had five children.

Meanwhile, as Thornton's economic cache rose, so did his political influence; he became one of New Hampshire's major leaders of the Revolution.

* * *

In 1775, Thornton was sent as a delegate to the New Hampshire Provincial Congress the same month as the battles of Lexington and Concord occurred. Within months, he was elected president of the provincial congress—head of one of the most pro-independence colonies in America. On May 23, 1775, Thornton sent a letter to the Continental Congress expressing "the voice of God and Nature to us, since the late hostile design and conduct of Great Britain, is, *that we are bound to look to our whole political affairs*."[904] Or, in other words, they were bound to take charge of all aspects of running the colonies (i.e. independence).

It was no wonder the royal governor fled New Hampshire.

On June 2, 1775, Thornton wrote a proclamation to the people of New Hampshire expressing resolve and reliance upon God. "You must all be sensible that the affairs of *America* have at length come to a very affecting and alarming crisis.—The *horrors* and *Distresses* of a *Civil War*, which, till of late, we only had in contemplation, we now find ourselves obliged to realize. Painful, beyond expression, have been those *Scenes of blood and devastation*, which the barbarous cruelty of British troops have placed before our eyes. Duty to GOD—to ourselves—to Posterity—enforced by the *cries of slaughtered Innocents*, have urged us to take up arms in our own defence," he wrote. "In a word—We seriously and earnestly recommend the practice of that pure and undefiled *religion*, which embalmed the memory of our pious ancestors, as that alone, upon which we can build a solid hope and confidence in the *Divine protection* and *favour*, without whose *blessing*, all the measures of safety we have, or can propose, will end in our shame and disappointment."[905]

When the Provincial Congress wasn't in session, Thornton served as chairman of New Hampshire's Committee of Safety. He was so busy he wrote once that he went ten days without having time to change his clothes.[906] As 1776 began, Thornton helped put together a new constitution to run New Hampshire on its own. The new government and written constitution were announced on January 5, 1776. It was the first written constitution adopted by any of the colonies.

New Hampshire's delegates to the Continental Congress had instructions to vote for independence. But Thornton wasn't one of them. Yet.

Thornton was an associate justice of the New Hampshire Superior Court, but after one delegate, who hadn't been in Congress to vote or sign the Declaration, resigned, Thornton was elected as his replacement. He arrived in Congress in November 1776.

Adams was impressed with Thornton, who was famous for his wit. "We have from New Hampshire a Colonel Thornton, a physician by profession, a man of humor. He has a large budget of droll stories with which he entertains company perpetually," Adams wrote.[907]

Although the vote for independence and the bulk of the signing were long since past, the sixty-two-year-old received permission to add his name to the Declaration of Independence, which he did on November 4, 1776.

It may look to some like Thornton was the last person to sign the Declaration of Independence, but he was not. Signers signed in groups according to their state, but Samuel Adams signed too closely under New Hampshire delegate William Whipple's name, leaving no room for Thornton. So Thornton signed at the bottom right of the document.

McKean, from Delaware, was the last to sign, probably in 1781.

Four days after he had signed the document, Thornton was inoculated for smallpox. The result of the illness was a "weakness of his eyes," which made it difficult for him to do his duties.[908]

* * *

Thornton left Congress in the spring of 1777, but it wasn't until fall that he was able to resume his judicial duties.

His appearance on the national stage had been brief.

In 1779, he moved to Exeter, New Hampshire, and in 1780, he bought the confiscated estate of Loyalist Edward Lutwych. He continued acting as a judge until 1782 and served in a few more state positions, including serving in the New Hampshire state senate or president's council at age seventy-one.

Then, in December 1786, his wife, Hannah, died at the age of forty-four. Thornton was seventy-two. The next year, his twenty-two-year-old son, Andrew, died.

* * *

A few years later, Thornton retired and began to pursue writing, such as political essays for newspapers. He also wrote an unpublished manuscript on sin and free agency, which was most noteworthy for its very long title: *Paradise Lost; or the Origin of the Evil called Sin examined; or how it ever did or ever can come to pass, that a creature should or could do anything unfit or improper for that creature to do; or how it ever did, or ever can come to pass, that a creature should or could omit, or leave undone what that creature ought to have done, or was fit and proper for that creature to do; or how it ever was, or can be possible for a creature to displease the Creator in Thought, Word or Action.*[909]

On June 24, 1803, while visiting his daughter Hannah in Newburyport, Massachusetts, Thornton died. He was eighty-nine years old.

At his funeral sermon, the reverend praised him for, among other things, "his constancy in attending the public worship, where he trod the courts of the house of God with steps tottering with age and infirmity."[910]

On his original gravestone was engraved "An Honest Man."

Chapter 60
GEORGE WALTON
Georgia

In 1783, the newly elected chief justice of Georgia, George Walton, was attacked on the streets of Savannah by William McIntosh, the son of Lachlan McIntosh, a former friend. William McIntosh beat Walton with a horsewhip because he thought he was "a Coward and a Villian" and that only someone "filled with an Unblemished Character" should sit on the bench of Georgia's highest court.[911]

Fortunately, not everyone in Georgia felt this way about Walton, a Signer of the Declaration of Independence.

* * *

Walton was born in late 1749 or perhaps early 1750 in Cumberland County, Virginia.[912] Within a few months of Walton's birth, his father died. Before he was seven, his mother had died as well.[913] Walton's uncle, also George Walton, raised him. When he was fifteen, Walton apprenticed himself to Christopher Ford, a carpenter,[914] and legend says he worked from sunup to sundown, and his master wouldn't allow him any candles so he could read at night. So Walton resorted to collecting scraps of wood from carpentry work and burning them so he could read borrowed books by night.[915] Other stories say his master recognized his abilities and gave him money to attend a local school.[916]

In any case, Walton ended his apprenticeship at age nineteen and moved to Savannah, Georgia, where his brother John lived. He studied law with Henry Yonge Jr., and in 1773, he was admitted to the bar.[917]

In July 1774, Walton and a few other patriots put a notice in the newspaper, calling people to meet at the Liberty Pole at Tondee's tavern. The object of the meeting was to support the people in Boston who were resisting British rule.[918] He organized another meeting in August, but general support was tepid, and no official delegates were sent to the first Continental Congress.

* * *

After the battles of Lexington and Concord, enthusiasm for the revolutionary cause increased. Walton became secretary in Georgia's Provincial Congress but was not one of its five delegates to Congress in July 1775; however, one man turned out to be a Loyalist, so Walton replaced him in Congress in February 1776.

Walton's position in the militia delayed him until June, but on the way to Congress, Walton took the time to write to his friend Colonel Lachlan McIntosh. "I am not too late for the great American question—If a question now it may be called!" He told McIntosh how he had recruited more Virginia soldiers for McIntosh's battalion in Georgia.[919] Walton arrived in time for the vote on independence and, at twenty-six years old, was possibly the youngest person to sign the Declaration on August 2, 1776.[920]

In the spring of 1777, another Georgia Signer, Button Gwinnet, was killed in a duel with McIntosh. McIntosh, then over Georgia's forces, was replaced. Walton stepped in on McIntosh's behalf, which helped him secure a place in Washington's army. "He [McIntosh] is a man of sense and judgment," Walton wrote General Washington, "with a great experience of the world; and, in point of bravery, he is fit to fight under the banners of General Washington."[921]

Walton returned to Georgia in 1778 to help defend it against the British. His brother John served in Congress that year and signed the Articles of Confederation.

In September, Walton married a teenage girl named Dorothy Camber, but the honeymoon didn't last long.[922] Walton was the senior colonel in Georgia's militia. This made him the acting commander during the Siege of Savannah from November to December 1778.

When the British attacked, they hit the state's militia hard. The Georgians were no match for the British troops. Walton received a bad wound in his thigh and was captured. The British surgeons worked on him, and he had soon recovered enough to be transferred to Sunbury with the rest of the captured prisoners. He was held for nine months before being exchanged for a British navy captain in September or October 1779.

* * *

When Walton was released, the British were still holding Savannah, but a group of Georgia conservatives formed a government of sorts in Augusta. Walton and other radicals thought the resulting executive council was not organized legally under the state's constitution. He gathered a group of the Georgia legislature, and they voted for Walton to be governor. This enabled Walton's government to receive funds from Congress and infuriated the other government, including one of its supporters, McIntosh.[923]

Walton determined to reduce McIntosh's influence, who became his most vocal critic in Georgia. In a November 30, 1779, letter from Georgia's legislature that requested funds from Congress, someone tacked on a paragraph requesting General McIntosh be sent away from Georgia. "The common dissatisfaction is such, and that founded on weighty reasons, it is highly necessary that Congress would . . . direct some distant field for the exercise of his abilities."[924] The letter was sent with the speaker of the assembly's signature—even though the speaker had just left town. It didn't matter that the letter accurately contained the sentiments of the assembly; the speaker's signature was forged, and this breach of legislative etiquette would come back to haunt Walton.[925]

Congress complied with the letter and ordered McIntosh away from Georgia. McIntosh struggled to clear his name—and sully Walton's—for years afterward.

In January 1780, the Georgia legislature chose from Walton's faction a new and legally legitimate governor.

By May 1780, Walton was back in Congress.[926]

In 1782, the British abandoned their plans in Georgia, and Savannah was once again under U.S. control.

* * *

On February 1, 1783, the House of Assembly agreed with McIntosh and his supporters that evidence indicated that the signature on the infamous 1779 dispatch to Congress was a forgery. It ordered Georgia's attorney general to take legal action against those responsible—meaning, of course, Walton. But the attorney general didn't take action. This would not have been a surprise to the assembly because just the day before, it had elected Walton to be chief justice of Georgia. This meant Walton presided over any legal action taking place on this issue.[927] The Georgia legislators' act was similar to a judge finding someone liable and then fining him only one dollar.

This infuriated McIntosh's supporters, including his son, who promised that if Walton tried to act as chief justice, he would "assist in pulling him of[f] of a Bench which ought to be filled with an Unblemished Character."[928] Instead, young William defended his father's honor by horsewhipping Walton on the streets of Savannah.

Thus, the father killed one Signer of the Declaration of Independence,[929] and the son whipped another.

McIntosh eventually felt he had cleared his name. Walton, it seemed, had been publically humiliated. Yet Walton continued to be elected from 1783 to 1789 by the legislature to be Georgia's chief justice—none the worse for wear.[930]

* * *

Walton's political career continued.

He became governor of Georgia again in 1789 and served until 1790. He served as a justice in the state Superior Court from 1790 to 1795 and then from 1799 to 1804. He was elected as delegate to the Constitutional Convention in 1787 but declined, although he was a delegate to Georgia's State Constitutional Convention the next year. Walton was even briefly a senator, from November 1795 to February 1796, temporarily filling in for a senator who resigned.[931]

Walton's son Thomas suddenly died in December 1803, right after he had become a lawyer. This greatly affected Walton, and he died in Augusta, Georgia, two months after his son on February 2, 1804.[932]

Walton once wrote to his then-friend General McIntosh: "The demon, discord, yet presides in this country, and God only knows when his reign will be at an end. I have strove so hard to do good with so poor a return, that, were the liberties of America secure, I would bid adieu to all public employment, to politics, and to strife; for even virtue itself will meet with enemies."[933]

Chapter 61

WILLIAM WHIPPLE
New Hampshire

In the summer of 1778, William Whipple was sitting at a table with other officers in the Continental Army and was about to get another lesson in how declaring independence had its risks. Whipple was involved in General John Sullivan's campaign to try to free Rhode Island from the British. Even with French allies along for the ride, the expedition failed but not before a cannonball smashed through Whipple's headquarters and landed right under the table where he sat—missing him, but taking the leg of another staff member.

* * *

William Whipple was born on January 14, 1730, in Kittery, York County, Maine (then in Massachusetts), not too far from Portsmouth, New Hampshire. Kittery was a harbor town with plenty of sailing ships to watch coming in and going out. The oldest of five children, Whipple went to sea and rose to become a captain by his twenties. He made his fortune fast; his voyages included Africa, the West Indies, and England. The destinations have led some to speculate he was engaged in the slave trade—ships to Africa would take on slaves and then sell them in the West Indies, where molasses was purchased and brought back to England or New England to be made into rum.

In any case, he left the sea in 1760 at age thirty and joined his brothers in the mercantile business in Portsmouth, New Hampshire. Business boomed.

But his love life did not. Whipple was left at the altar once, and he was thirty-seven before he married his thirty-five-year-old cousin, Catherine Mofatt, and had a child who died in infancy. They lived in Catherine's aging parents' large home overlooking the harbor.

* * *

As events in the colonies sped toward independence, Whipple was a strong and locally prominent revolutionary. In 1764, he helped prevent British tea from entering the port. In 1775, he put his merchant days behind him to become a revolutionary leader.[934] He had made his wealth; now he was going to make a country.

He represented his town at the Provincial Congress at Exeter in 1775, where he was placed on the Committee

193

of Safety. From his position in that revolutionary group, it was a short jump in January 1776 for the New Hampshire legislature to send him to Philadelphia as a delegate to the Continental Congress.[935] In Congress, Whipple was an active delegate and was busy with the marine, commerce, secret correspondence, military affairs, and finance committees.[936]

It didn't take a lot of soul searching for Whipple to vote for independence on July 2 and to sign the Declaration of Independence on August 2. He believed in a strong war effort and did his part. "This year, my Friend, is big with mighty events," Whipple wrote from Baltimore in January 1777 to his fellow New Hampshire delegate, Josiah Bartlett. "Nothing less than the fate of America depends on the virtue of her sons, and if they have not virtue enough to support the most Glorious Cause ever human beings were engaged in, they don't deserve the blessings of Freedom."[937]

At times, as brigadier general in 1777, Whipple left Congress to fulfill military responsibilities over one of New Hampshire's two militia brigades.[938] He marched in August 1777 and was with his troops in the battle of Saratoga in New York. The siege General Horatio Gates put up against British General Burgoyne was effective. Gates appointed Whipple to help arrange the surrender and escort the thousands of British prisoners to Boston, where they would be sent back, under parole, to Britain.

It was a major turning point in the war, and it convinced the French to align with the fledgling United States.

* * *

By his side through the fighting was one of Whipple's slaves, Prince Whipple (slaves often took their master's surname), who had been with him since he was a boy.

The story goes that Whipple told Prince he expected him to fight for his country. Prince replied, "Sir, I have no inducement to fight; but if I had my liberty, I would endeavor to defend it to the last drop of my blood."

Whipple gave him his freedom immediately.[939]

Except he didn't.

Whipple, like many of his day, had conflicting ideas and ideals about slavery. For example, Whipple approved of the Congressional plan to recruit slaves to fight in the war, with the promise that they would be emancipated. He wrote that such a plan "will I suppose lay a foundation for the emancipation of those poor wreches in that Country, & I hope be the means of dispensing the Blessings of freedom to all the Human Race in America."[940]

For whatever reason, Whipple didn't truly free Prince until 1784, and that was about five years after Prince had petitioned in vain for the New Hampshire legislature to free him and other slaves.

* * *

After dodging a cannonball that ripped through his headquarters in Rhode Island in 1778, Whipple left Congress the next year. He was no fan of Loyalists and favored the military solution. He wrote Josiah Bartlett, "I think it high time they were all hung or banished."[941]

Congress tried to appoint Whipple as commissioner of the board of admiralty in 1780. He declined the position. But he wasn't averse to taking a spot in New Hampshire's state legislature.

Congress wouldn't leave him alone, though. Morris made him New Hampshire's receiver of finances in 1782, the thankless job of collecting money from the state to send to Congress to pay war expenses. Naturally, it was difficult to get money out of the legislature, but eventually, in 1784, Whipple was able to gather $3,000 to send. He then quit the post. After that, he took on judicial work as an associate justice of the New Hampshire Superior Court.

In July of 1782, he was appointed president of a court of commissioners trying to find a solution to a border dispute between Connecticut and Pennsylvania. During the last few years of his life, Whipple suffered from a heart ailment and couldn't do his rounds as a circuit judge. By 1785, he no longer left his home in Portsmouth, New Hampshire, where he died on November 28, 1785. He was fifty-five years old.[942]

Whipple's instructions to his wife were to always provide a place for the now emancipated Prince and his family at their home overlooking the ships in the harbor.

Chapter 62
WILLIAM WILLIAMS
Connecticut

William Williams and his two guests discussed the chances of defeating the British. In late 1776, the prospects didn't look very good. "Well," Williams said calmly, "if they succeed, it is pretty evident what will be my fate. I have done much to prosecute the contest, and one thing I have done, which the British will never pardon—I have signed the Declaration of Independence. *I shall be hung.*"

One guest expressed the hope that the colonies would be successful. The other boasted he would escape the gallows because he didn't sign the Declaration of Independence or anything else against the British.

Williams shot back, "Then, sir, you deserve to be hanged, for not having done your duty."[943]

* * *

Williams was born on April 8, 1731, in Lebanon, Connecticut.

Originally, Williams wanted to be a minister like his grandfather and father, and like many other Signers of the Declaration of Independence, he went to Harvard, where he graduated in 1751.[944] A stint in the military during the French and Indian War in 1755 put him on a different career path. He served on the staff of his uncle Colonel Ephraim Williams, whose estate founded Williams College. His uncle was killed in an ambush at the battle of Lake George.

Williams developed a distaste for his British commanders and came back home to become a merchant. He also married a daughter of Connecticut Governor John Trumbull, the only British-appointed governor to support the Revolution.

In 1776, Williams replaced the ailing Oliver Wolcott at the Continental Congress in time to sign the Declaration of Independence on August 2.

He was free with his fortune in supporting the troops in the war. He also worked hard locally and visited the homes of all 4,000 residents of Lebanon to solicit donations of blankets for the troops and clock weights to melt into bullets.[945]

Williams did his public duty, serving about fifty years in public offices—usually three at a time—including functioning as town clerk of his hometown Lebanon, Connecticut; serving in various judgeships; participating as a deacon in the Congregationalist church; and serving as a member of the Connecticut Assembly.

His last years were devoted to reading, meditation, and prayer.[946]

When his son, Solomon, died in 1810, Williams took it hard and declined in health. Days before his death, he lost the ability to speak. Right before he died, however, he called out for his deceased son to come to him.[947] Williams died on August 2, 1811, exactly thirty-five years after he signed the Declaration of Independence. Ultimately, he cheated the British gallows.

Chapter 63
JAMES WILSON
Pennsylvania

The force of about 200 American militiamen surrounded the three-story brick home of James Wilson, a Signer of the Declaration of Independence. Inside the besieged home, standing by Wilson's side, were two other Signers, Morris and Clymer, as well as about twenty-eight other prominent and heavily armed Philadelphians. Although the British had at one time occupied Philadelphia and the Revolutionary War was not yet concluded, the first pitched battle in the "City of Brotherly Love" took place in 1779 between its own citizens.

* * *

James Wilson was born at Carskerdo, near St. Andrews, Scotland, in September 1742. His father was a prosperous farmer, and Wilson became a scholar. Starting in 1757, he attended the University of St. Andrews, then the University of Glasgow, and finally the University of Edinburgh, finishing his studies there in 1765. That year, at the age of twenty-three, Wilson came to New York around the time the Stamp Act taxation had everybody agitated.

Capitalizing on his scholarly credentials, Wilson moved the next year to Philadelphia and became a Latin tutor in the College of Philadelphia (now the University of Pennsylvania). He also began studying law with Dickinson, a political moderate, and was admitted to the bar at the end of 1767. Wilson specialized in real estate law and began to speculate in land—something that would later prove to be his downfall.[948]

He prosperity, sadly, included owning a slave. Later, in 1771, he married Rachel Bird. They had six children.

* * *

With the onset of the troubles between Great Britain and the colonies in 1774, Wilson became a chairman of his local committee of correspondence and then attended the Provincial Convention of Pennsylvania. He wrote a pamphlet titled "Considerations on the Nature and Extent of the Legislative Authority of the British Parliament."[949] The pamphlet argued against Parliament having authority over the colonies, yet, at the same time, asserted allegiance to the king.[950]

The next year, Wilson became a colonel in the Cumberland County militia, although he never saw any action in that group. After the April 1775 battles of Lexington and Concord, he was elected to the second Continental Congress. Adams said he was someone whose "Fortitude, Rectitude, and Abilities too, greatly outshine his Masters."[951] Rush said of Wilson, "His mind, while he spoke, was one blaze of light. Not a word ever fell from his lips out of time, or out of place, nor could a word be taken from or added to his speeches without injuring them."[952]

Wilson's position was complicated. He was well known as a champion of independence, yet he felt it was too soon to take the step.[953] On June 7, 1776, he voted for a delay in considering Lee's resolution on independence. In July, however, Wilson voted for the Declaration of Independence even though his old friend and law teacher, Dickinson, voted against it. Wilson signed the official handwritten copy of the Declaration on August 2, 1776.

Wilson opposed the new constitution for his state of Pennsylvania because he thought it was too democratic. This made him unpopular in Philadelphia, and he was removed from Congress in February but reinstated when it couldn't come up with a replacement. On September 14, 1777, he was removed again.

Around that time, British General Howe invaded Philadelphia, causing the Continental Congress to flee. Wilson left the city, the British, and his unpopularity to practice law in Annapolis, Maryland, for a year until the British strategically withdrew.

* * *

When he returned to Philadelphia, Wilson didn't find his popularity gaining.

The continental currency was suffering from inflation, and committees were set up by popular demand to set fixed prices. Wilson, Morris, and others argued that price fixing worked against liberty and free markets. They said price fixing only made things worse—as was evident in the food shortages in the city. On top of this less-than-popular position, the fact that Wilson had recently legally defended some wealthy Loyalists made him a symbol of the wealthy financiers and merchants.

On Monday morning, October 3, 1779, handbills were distributed throughout Philadelphia calling for the militia to gather and "drive from the city, all disaffected persons [Loyalists], and all who supported them."[954] Hungry, frustrated, and liquored up, the 200 militiamen set out looking for their enemies. Meanwhile, Wilson, Morris, Clymer, and other targets of the militia's wrath gathered their own forces.

When the parade of inebriated militia turned a corner and saw Wilson's group of thirty armed men opposing them—sober, smartly dressed, and ready to fight back—they were surprised. But when Wilson and the others took one look at the advancing mob, they retreated a block east to Wilson's home. The mob shouted "Huzzah! Huzzah! Huzzah!" and made their way after them, surrounding Wilson's house.

Lieutenant Robert Campbell, a veteran of the Continental Army who had lost an arm in battle, opened a third-story window and shouted down at the mob. Then someone shot his gun—possibly Campbell, though it could have been someone in the mob. Either way, the Patriot was shot dead, and both sides opened full fire.

Just then, the high-crust First City Troop arrived on horseback and crashed through the lower-crust mob, cutting and slashing. Twenty-seven militia were captured, and the rest fled. There were severe injuries on both sides. One was dead in Wilson's home; at least four militia mobbers were killed; and one bystander, "a black boy," died from crossfire.[955]

The attack had a sobering effect on the city.

Wilson fled, but by spring, the legislature had pardoned everybody.

* * *

Political opinions shifted in time, and a few years later, Wilson helped establish the Bank of North America and was elected once again to the Continental Congress.

In 1786, his wife, Rachel, died. The next year Wilson achieved the height of his career when he became a delegate for the Constitutional Convention. He was a leader in the debates on the floor and in the final drafting committee. He even acted as Franklin's voice, reading speeches on behalf of the aging statesman.

As a delegate, Wilson argued for a popular election of the Congress and president so people would have more confidence in their officials. He argued for checks and balances and the idea that power resided in the people. He also wrote a draft of the Constitution, which drafting committee chairman John Rutledge edited heavily. Wilson polished it and presented it to the delegates on August 6, 1787. The Constitution of the United States of America was approved and signed on September 17, 1787.

Wilson was also a leading voice in the Pennsylvania State Convention that considered the new Constitution. He told delegates, "Regarding it, then in every point of view, with a candid and disinterested mind, I am bold to assert, that it is the *best form of government which has ever been offered to the world.*"[956]

Many thought that when the new government under the Constitution was formed, Washington would honor Wilson with the chief judgeship of the U.S. Supreme Court. The Philadelphia *Federal Gazette* thought his appointment was inevitable and praised him. "To his laborious investigations into the principles and forms of every species of government that has ever existed in the world—and to his powerful reasonings in the late federal convention, the United States are indebted for many of the perfections of the new constitution."[957]

Rush noted that the anticipation of his appointment as chief justice was the reason Wilson was left out of the Senate and House.[958]

But Washington appointed John Jay chief justice instead and made Wilson an associate justice of the Supreme Court.

* * *

Wilson never again rose to the heights he had achieved while working on the Constitution. His speculations in land continued to increase, and some who wanted him impeached even accused him of trying to influence laws to favor land speculators.

Then Adams wrote to a friend on June 23, 1793, that Wilson, fifty years old, had "fallen most lamentably in love with a young Lady in this town, under twenty, by the name of Gray. He came, he saw, and was overcome." Adams concluded, "Cupid himself must laugh at his own absurdity, in producing such an Union."[959]

Wilson married nineteen-year-old Hannah Gray that year.

He bought large amounts of land in western New York, as well as in Pennsylvania and Georgia. His idea was to recruit European colonists and have them settle on his western lands. The plan involved huge amounts of capital from European investors. But the land speculation market collapsed, and like his friend Morris, Wilson saw his wealth disappear overnight. Creditors chased after him. He told a friend he was "hunted like a wild beast."[960]

At the time, justices on the Supreme Court also went out on circuit, traveling to various states to hear cases. Wilson left Pennsylvania and went to Burlington, New Jersey, to get away from creditors, probably in hopes that he could somehow get his financial life back on track. But, unfortunately, in the summer of 1797, he was arrested for alleged drunkenness and debt and spent time in debtors' prison until December of that year.

Wilson visited fellow Supreme Court justice James Iredell's home in Edenton, North Carolina, but the stress was too much for him, and he broke down and died of a "violent nervous fever" a month before his fifty-sixth birthday.

Wilson's young wife, Hannah, was left with nothing. His estate had the staggering amount of debt totaling $70,000.

Wilson survived many political attacks and even mob violence in his life, but his legacy remained intact—a new nation and a strong Constitution. "Fiery energy went into his declamations," Rush wrote in 1776. "Though his voice was not melodious, it was powerful, and his blue eyes gleamed through heavy spectacles rimmed in metal."[961]

Chapter 64

JOHN WITHERSPOON
New Jersey

John Witherspoon's first taste of a revolution against England took place not in America but in Scotland, where he was captured and locked in a prison tower. But that was mostly because of bad luck, not because Witherspoon had committed any crimes. It was 1746 and the twenty-three-year-old reverend just wanted to watch a battle.

Charles Edward Stuart, also known as "Bonnie Prince Charlie" or the "Pretender," invaded Scotland as part of his plan to regain the British throne for the Stuart family line and become known as "Bonnie *King* Charlie." He recruited some Highlanders of Scotland to fight the battle of Falkirk on January 17, 1746.

Witherspoon went out, as did others, to watch the battle and was captured by Stuart's forces and put into Doune Castle. He helped some of his fellow prisoners escape from the tower by tying their bed sheets together to make a rope, but he decided to wait rather than risk his extensive weight on the rope.

He was soon released. The fact that Stuart is still called the "Pretender" shows how the invasion went. Years later and an ocean away, Witherspoon would help mount a more successful attempt against the English.

* * *

John Witherspoon was born near Edinburgh, Scotland, on February 5, 1723. His father was a Presbyterian clergyman, and Witherspoon followed in his footsteps. He started at the University of Edinburgh in his midteens and graduated with a master of arts in 1739 and a divinity degree in 1743. Two years later, at twenty-one, he was ordained the minister of Beith Parish.

Five years later, and after his short stint in the prison tower, Witherspoon married Elizabeth Montgomery. They had ten children, five of whom lived to adulthood.

* * *

Witherspoon's fame rose as word of his sermons and writings spread as far as America. He stood against moderates he thought were trying to change doctrine and practices in the Presbyterian Church in Scotland, and, it turns out, there was a Presbyterian college in New Jersey

202

looking for just such a prominent person to be its new president. The College of New Jersey (later Princeton University) sent Stockton, a future Signer of the Declaration of Independence, to visit Witherspoon and urge him to accept the college presidency.

Witherspoon's wife, Elizabeth, however, did not want her husband to accept. She didn't want to risk her life crossing the ocean to live in a wild place. She overreacted but later relented, in part due to the influence of Rush, another future Signer, who happened to be in Scotland studying medicine.

Two years after the first invitation to come to New Jersey, the Witherspoon family set sail for America, arriving in Philadelphia on August 6, 1768. Eleven days later, Witherspoon was in Princeton, New Jersey, and became the sixth president of the College of New Jersey.

The move was good for the college. Witherspoon put it on sound financial and academic ground.

The move was also good for the country—the college became a hotbed of patriotic fervor.

* * *

"The great object of the approaching Congress should be to unite the colonies," Witherspoon wrote in 1774, "and make them as one body, in any measure of self-defence, to assure the people of Great Britain that we will not submit voluntarily, and convince them that it would be either impossible or unprofitable for them to compel us by open violence."[962]

Witherspoon worked on the Somerset County committee of correspondence and then in the Provincial Congress of New Jersey, where he helped orchestrate the arrest of New Jersey's royal governor (and son of Franklin), William. He was then made a delegate to the Continental Congress and arrived just in time in June 1776 to hear the debates between Adams and Dickinson.

Tradition holds that Witherspoon heard a delegate, possibly Dickinson, say the colonies were not yet ripe for independence. Witherspoon then broke into the speech and exclaimed, "Not ripe, sir! In my judgment we are not only ripe but rotting. Almost every colony has dropped from its parent stem and your own province needs no more sunshine to mature it."[963]

Naturally, he voted for and signed the Declaration of Independence. He was the only active clergyman to sign it.

In his years in the Continental Congress, Witherspoon sat on more than 100 different committees, including secret committees on foreign relations and the board of war.

The fight wasn't just academic for the scholar. He knew intimately what was at stake when his twenty-six-year-old son, James, died at the battle of Germantown, Pennsylvania, on October 4, 1777.

Witherspoon worked on a new constitution for New Jersey. He also signed the Articles of Confederation in 1778. He left Congress in 1782.

* * *

As the war concluded, Witherspoon worked to rebuild the college in Princeton. The war had devastated it. The British had occupied the campus, and the library—including many books Witherspoon had donated—had been burned. On a nine-month journey to England in 1783 to raise funds for the college, Witherspoon ran into a storm. He was thrown against the side of the ship and hurt his eye.[964] The insult to this injury was that the British were still not in a generous mood toward American institutions, and he barely raised enough money to pay only for the trip.[965]

Back in America, he served in the New Jersey State Assembly and in the 1787 State Convention to ratify the Constitution.

He also continued his religious leadership, uniting the Presbyterians in America and presiding over its first general assembly in 1789. That year, his wife, Elizabeth, died. Two years later, the sixty-eight-year-old married again—to a twenty-three-year-old widow named Ann Dill. They had two girls together, one of whom died in infancy.

Not long after his daughter died, Witherspoon fell from a horse and injured his other eye, leading to blindness. He continued to preach, though he had to be led by hand to the pulpit.

Witherspoon died on his farm, Tusculum, outside Princeton, New Jersey, on November 15, 1794. He was seventy-one.

His voice during the Revolution was essential, combining scholarship, religion, and passion for freedom.

Chapter 65
OLIVER WOLCOTT
Connecticut

Oliver Wolcott fell ill in June 1776 and had to leave the Continental Congress just when things were getting interesting.[966] On the way back to Connecticut, he passed through New York City, where a crowd tore down the statue of King George III. The head was sent off to Britain as a show of rebellion. The body went with Wolcott back to Litchfield, Connecticut, where he had it melted down and made into 42,022 bullets.

* * *

Wolcott was born in Windsor, Connecticut, in November 1726. He graduated from Yale College at the head of his class in 1747. That same year, the governor of New York commissioned him to be a captain during "King George's War," a precursor to the French and Indian War. Wolcott's company of volunteers served on the Northwestern frontier for about a year.[967] Around that same time, his father served as royal governor of Connecticut from 1751 to 1754.

Wolcott studied medicine with his brother R. Alexander but did not actually commence a practice. Instead, he became the Litchfield county sheriff in 1751 and continued in various positions in state offices.

On the cusp of the Revolution, Wolcott said all members of Congress should protect their colony's constitutions. "Experience, Nature's sure hand maid, will guide us right," he said. "We shall do our Duty."[968]

As war encroached on the colonies, Wolcott divided his time between the Continental Congress, illness, and military affairs. He wasn't present for the vote on independence, although he was in favor of it. Later, in the fall of 1776, after his illness, he returned to Congress and signed the Declaration of Independence.[969]

A year later, in fall 1777, Wolcott commanded a brigade of militia that helped defeat General Burgoyne at Saratoga, New York.[970]

One task Congress gave Wolcott was to be one of the commissioners of Indian affairs, with the assignment to convince the Iroquois to be neutral. After the war, he again worked with the Iroquois, drawing up peace terms with those who had sided with the British in the war.

Wolcott served Connecticut for a decade as its lieutenant governor and supported the new Constitution. His son, Oliver Wolcott Jr., served as secretary of the Treasury with President Washington and then President Adams.[971]

In 1796, Wolcott was elected governor but died in office on December 1, 1797, at the age of seventy-one.

Chapter 66
GEORGE WYTHE
Virginia

On Sunday morning, May 25, 1806, George Wythe, a Signer of the Declaration of Independence, was poisoned by arsenic. By the time his friend and former student President Jefferson heard the sad news, Wythe was already dead and buried.

* * *

George Wythe was born near Black River, Elizabeth City County, Virginia, in 1726. He had an older brother and a younger sister. His father, a wealthy plantation owner, died when Wythe was three. His mother was a well-educated Quaker and gave him an excellent education—but she also died when he was young.

Wythe grew up under his brother, Thomas's, guardianship, and Thomas sent Wythe to study law with a relative. In 1746, at the age of twenty, Wythe passed the bar. He soon married his law partner's sister, Ann Lewis. She died eight months later. When Thomas died less than ten years later, Wythe became a wealthy man with the inheritance of his father's estate. But instead of moving to the plantation, he moved to Williamsburg, Virginia, to practice law and politics. He also found a new wife to share life with, Elizabeth Taliaferro. They had a son, but he died as an infant.

Wythe became a member of the Virginia House of Burgesses and was soon taken up by revolutionary ideals.

* * *

In the midst of this, a young redheaded youth named Thomas Jefferson applied to Wythe to take him on as a law student. Jefferson and Wythe became fast friends. Jefferson, whose father had also died when he was young, considered Wythe a second father. Over his lifetime, Wythe was also the teacher of others who changed the face of the country, such as Marshall, Monroe, and Clay. His students shaped the country's freedom and government.

As Wythe grew in political influence and became the clerk of the House of Burgesses, he was chosen as a delegate for the Continental Congress in 1775. Rush said, "He [Wythe] seldom spoke in Congress, but when he did, his speeches were sensible, correct and pertinent.

I have seldom known a man [to] possess more modesty or a more dovelike simplicity and gentleness of manner."[972]

Wythe assisted Adams and Lee in arguing for the resolution for independence on June 7, 1776. The vote on the resolution was postponed until July.

Jefferson was tapped to write a declaration of independence in case the vote was in the affirmative, but he was also concerned about Virginia's creation of a new written constitution. He gave a draft of his proposed version of Virginia's constitution to Wythe, who took it back to the colony in late June.

Wythe participated in writing the constitution for Virginia and designing a seal for the soon-to-be-state. He missed the July vote but returned to Congress by August, in time to sign the Declaration of Independence.[973] He may have signed it with the others on August 2 or later in the month.

* * *

In November 1776, along with Jefferson and other lawyers, Wythe began a three-year project to help revise Virginia's laws to coincide with its new constitution. They considered abolition of slavery but knew it wouldn't be approved. They also failed to change some of Virginia's laws about witnesses—laws that prohibited blacks from testifying in court against whites.

In 1777, Wythe began a twenty-eight-year stint in the Virginia Chancery Court. A few years later, he became a law professor at the College of William and Mary, making him the first professor of law in American history.

A decade later, he was a delegate for the Federal Convention in Philadelphia, along with Washington and others. Wythe helped set the rules for the convention, then left and went back to Virginia, never to sign the Constitution. His second wife, Elizabeth, died that year.[974] Wythe worked to get the Constitution ratified and continued as chancellor. In 1789, Washington asked him to be a federal district judge, but Wythe declined the appointment.[975]

In 1791, Wythe resigned his professorship and moved to Richmond, Virginia, because of his judicial duties. But he opened a private law school so he could keep teaching.

Ten years later, he left the judgeship.

* * *

In 1806, Wythe was eighty years old, yet he was still a generous teacher at heart. His last pupil was a sixteen-year-old boy named Michael Brown. Brown was part white and part black and faced prejudice as a "mulatto," but Wythe took him under his wing as eagerly as he had students like then President Jefferson.

Wythe also tried to help his eighteen-year-old grandnephew, the grandson of his sister. The grandnephew had been given Wythe's name, George Wythe Sweeney, but not his character. Sweeney stole from his uncle and lived life on the edge. Still, he was slated to inherit Wythe's estate, except for some portions Wythe was going to leave to Brown and his housekeeper, Lydia Broadnax.

One morning in May, Broadnax was in the kitchen making breakfast when she noticed Sweeney fiddle with the coffeepot and then throw a slip of paper into the stove's fire. She didn't think much of it at the time. She brought Wythe his breakfast and then ate with Brown in the kitchen.

All three were soon racked in agony. The doctors came and thought it was cholera, even though Wythe insisted it had to be poison and was certain it was his grandnephew.

"I am murdered," he said.[976]

He lived long enough to take Sweeney out of his will.

Brown died after a week on June 1. Wythe died a week later on June 8, 1806. He was eighty years old. Broadnax recovered, and Sweeney was arrested and tried for the double murder.

But the trial did not go well.

All of the evidence was circumstantial. Yes, Sweeney had stolen from his uncle. Yes, he had arsenic, even in his room, but ironically, Broadnax—an eyewitness to Sweeney's treachery—was not allowed to testify against him because she used to be a slave. Wythe had freed her twenty years earlier, but under Virginia's laws, blacks could not testify against whites. So the murderer went free.

After the huge funeral, Jefferson heard of the death of his "second father." In a biographical sketch, he wrote of Wythe: "No man ever left behind him a character more venerated than George Wythe. His virtue was of the purest kind; his integrity inflexible, and his justice exact; of warm patriotism, and, devoted as he was to liberty, and the natural and equal rights of man, he might truly be called the Cato of his country, without the avarice of the Roman; for a more disinterested person never lived. Temperance and regularity in all his habits, gave him general good health, and his unaffected modesty and suavity of manners, endeared him to every one."[977]

Epilogue

When the Signers of the Declaration of Independence appeared to Woodruff in recurring dreams in 1877, they appeared as individuals without, for the most part, any familial connection to any Mormons. What bound them to the members of The Church of Jesus Christ of Latter-day Saints was a love for liberty. From those visits, Woodruff learned two things: First, he learned the Signers were good men. Second, he learned the ordinances of salvation were meant for everybody.

As time went on, Woodruff returned to his memories of these visions and saw them as tokens of not only God's approval of the Latter-day Saints but of the fidelity of the Church to the principles of freedom and fraternity with the Founding Fathers. It was as if the Signers had come to plant a seed that would bear fruit when Woodruff later became President of the Church. They were there to emphasize that temple work was to bind families together, that very few would reject the gospel when it was preached to them after this life, and that the love of Christ knows no bounds.

That the Signers were good people should be an encouragement to us today. They were born into a very different world from the one we live in. They had different prejudices, many of which, like slavery and some attitudes toward women, are utterly repugnant to us. Yet, ultimately, they strove for goals bigger than their own interests. They risked everything for freedom, but they were still weak. They still needed a greater freedom.

Like them, we probably have repugnant prejudices and ideas we are not aware of. It is perfectly fine to condemn some of the Signers' actions while praising others. But we need to ask ourselves how we would have fared had we been born into their circumstances. We, like them, are weak and need that same freedom they sought among those red rocks in the gleaming white temple in St. George, Utah. If Christ makes us free, we are free indeed.

True "independence forever" is choosing to love and serve each other.

The End

APPENDIX 1

Extracts from Wilford Woodruff's Journal

The extracts in this and other appendixes attempt to maintain the original spelling, punctuation, and capitalization of the original sources.

August 19, 1877 to August 21, 1877

Sunday, August 19, 1877[978]

19 Sunday Met at the Tabernacle at 11 oclok. Prayer by Wm Smith. Augustus Hardy spoke 10 Minuts, Thomas Hall 10 M, B F Pendleton 14 Minuts. Afternoon. Prayer by James Nixon. Frank B. Woolly spoke 2 M, Moroni Snow 2 M, Seth Pimm 1. Erastus B. Snow spoke 6 M, W Woodruff 35 M D. H. Cannon 35. I wrote 2 Letters to Bulah & Emma.

I spent the Evening in preparing a list of the Noted Men of the 17 Centaury and 18th including the signers of the declaration of Independance and the Presidents of the United States for Baptism on Tuesday the 21 Aug 1877.

Monday, August 20, 1877[979]

20 I sent a letter to Presidet Young, L J Nuttall, Nellie Asahel Clarie and Owen. 6.

Tuesday, August 21, 1877[980]

Aug 21, 1877 I Wilford Woodruff went to the Temple of the Lord this morning and was Baptized for 100 persons who were dead including the signers of the Declaration of Independence all except John Hancock and _____ [The blank name was William Floyd. The temple work for both Hancock and Floyd had previously been completed in the St. George Temple.] I was Baptized for the following names

William Hooper
Joseph Hewes
John Penn
Button Gwinnett
Lyman Hall
Edward Rutledge
George Walton
Thomas Heywood Jr
Thomas Lynch Jr
Arthur Myddleton
Samuel Chase
William ~~Chase~~ Paca
Thomas Stone
Charles Carroll of Carrolton
George Wythe
Richard Henry Lee
Thomas Jefferson
Benjamin Harrison
Thomas Nelson Jr
Francis Lightfoot Lee
Carter Braxton
Robert Morris
Benjamin Rush

Benjamin Franklin
John Morton
George Clymer
James Smith
~~Francis Lightfoot Lee~~
George Taylor
James Wilsol
George Ross
Caezar Rodney

211

George Read
Thomas M Kean
Philip Livingston
Francis Lewis
Lewis Morris
Richard Stockton
John Witherspoon
Francis Hopkinson
John Hart
Abraham Clark
Josiah Bartlett
William Whipple
Samuel Adams
John Adams

Robert Treat Paine
Elbridge Gerry
Stephen Hopkins
William Ellery
Roger Sherman

Samuel Huntington
William Williams
Oliver Wolcott
Mathew Thornton

Baptized for the following Eminent Men

Daniel Webster
Washington Irving
Michael Faraday
William Makepeace Thackerey
John Calwall Calhoon
Baron Justus Von Liebig
Henry Clay
Edward George Earl Lytton Bulwer
George Peabody
Charles Louis Napoleon Bonapart
Thomas Chalmers
William Henry Seward
Thomas Johnathan Jackson

David Glascoe Farragut
Hiram Powers
Lewis John Rudolph Agassis
David Livingstone
Christopher Columbus
Americus Vespucius
John Wesley
Samuel Johnson
Oliver Goldsmith
Frederick 2d king of Prussia

Edward Gibbon
David Garrick
Sir Joshua Reynolds
Robert Burns
Johann Wolfgang Goethe
John Philip Kemble
Frederick Von Schiller
Henry Grattan
Robert Fulton
Lord Horatio Nelson
John Filpot Corran
George Stephenson
Frederic Henry Allexander Von Humboldt
Sir Walter Scott
Lord Henry Brougham
Lord George Gordon Byron
William Wordsworth
Daniel O Connell
Count Camillo Bonso di Cavour
Richard Cobden
Thomas Babington Macaulay
Benito Juarez
Count Demetrius Perepa

[369]
When Br McAllister had Baptized me for the 100 Names I Baptized him for 21, including Gen Washington & his forefathers and all the Presidets of the United States that were not in my

212

list Except Buchannan Van Buren & Grant.

It was a vary interesting day. I felt thankful that we had the privilege and the power to administer for the worthy dead esspecially for the signers of the declaration of Independance, that inasmuch as they had laid the foundation of our Government that we Could do as much for them as they had done for us.

Sister Lucy Bigelow Young went forth into the font and was Baptized for Martha Washington and her family and seventy (70) of the Eminent women of the world. I Called upon all the Brethren & Sisters who were present to assist in getting Endowments for those that we had been Baptized for to day.

I wrote Letters to D D MCArthur. I wrote to Susan Dunford. There were Baptized in all to day 682.

APPENDIX 2

Extract from John D. T. McAllister's Journal

August 21, 1877 to August 23, 1877

Tuesday, August 21, 1877:[981]

Tuesday 21 At the Temple as usual. 682 Baptisms for the dead my Self 170 Wilford Woodruff 21 Joseph Hammond 266 A P Winsor 225. Evening received a letter from my Brother in law James B Davis. Sent Circular of the 1st Presidency to the Bishops in St George Stake. this day I was Baptised for all the dead Presidents of the United States except Martin Van Buren & Jas Buchanan. this day Sister Lucy B Young was Baptised for Maria Fackrell.

Wednesday, August 22, 1877:[982]

Wednesday 22 At the Temple as usual, I recd Endowments for Genl George Washington and Sister Lucy B Young recd Endowments for Martha Washington and we acted for them in Sealing. My Wife Ann recd Endowments for Mary Ball Washingtons Mother. 6 living Endowments to day and 82 for the dead. total 88. I was ordained a High Priest for Washington 3 Living Elders ordained. 2 High Priests for the dead & 35 Elders for the dead. Sealings 2 Living 33 dead W Woodruff 9, D H Cannon 26 Sealing to Parents 6 Living 1 dead.

Thursday, August 23, 1877:[983]

Thursday 23 At the Temple as usual I received Endowments for Millard Fillmore. also acted for Augustine Washington & my Wife Ann for his 1st wife & 2nd Mary Ball in the Sealing. Ann also acted for Maria Fackrell who was sealed to me. Elder W Woodruff Officiating. 139 Endowments today 3 Living 136 dead. Bro Woodruff Sealed 3. D H Cannon 3 & My Self 18. total 24. Ordinations 60. B Franklin a High Priest.

APPENDIX 3

Extract from a discourse by Wilford Woodruff

In the Tabernacle in Salt Lake City
September 16, 1877
Journal of Discourses 19:228–229

Before I close, I want to say one thing to the Latter-day Saints, which is resting upon my mind. President Young having now passed away, his labors with us have ceased for the present. He, with his brethren, built and completed one Temple, also laid the foundation for one at Manti and one at Logan, and besides a great deal of work has been done on the one in this city. He left this unfinished work for us to carry on to completion; and it is our duty to rise up and build these Temples. I look upon this portion of our ministry as a mission of as much importance as preaching to the living; the dead will hear the voice of the servants of God in the spirit-world, and they cannot come forth in the morning of the resurrection, unless certain ordinances are performed, for and in their behalf, in Temples built to the name of God. It takes just as much to save a dead man as a living man. For the last eighteen hundred years, the people that have lived and passed away never heard the voice of an inspired man, never heard a Gospel sermon, until they entered the spirit-world. Somebody has got to redeem them, by performing such ordinances for them in the flesh as they cannot attend to themselves in the spirit, and in order that this work may be done, we must have Temples in which to do it; and what I wish to say to you, my brethren and sisters, is that the God of heaven requires us to rise up and build them, that the work of redemption may be hastened. Our reward will meet us when we go behind the vail.

"Blessed are the dead which die in the Lord from henceforth: Yea, saith the Spirit, that they may rest from their labors; and their works do follow them."

We have labored in the St. George Temple since January, and we have done all we could there; and the Lord has stirred up our minds, and many things have been revealed to us concerning the dead. President Young has said to us, and it is verily so, if the dead could they would speak in language loud as ten thousand thunders, calling upon the servants of God to rise up and build Temples, magnify their calling and redeem their dead. This doubtless sounds strange to those present who believe not the faith and doctrine of the Latter-day Saints; but when we get to the spirit-world we will find out that all that God has revealed is true. We will find, too, that everything there is reality, and that God has a body, parts and passions, and the erroneous ideas that exist now with regard to him will have passed away. I feel to say little else to the Latter-day Saints wherever and whenever I have the opportunity of speaking to them, than to call upon them to build these Temples now under way, to hurry them up to completion. The dead will be after you, they will seek after you as they have after us in St. George. They called upon us, knowing that we held the keys and power to redeem them. I will here say, before closing, that two weeks before I left St. George, the spirits of the dead gathered around me, wanting to know why we did not redeem them. Said they, "You have had the use of the Endowment House for a number of years, and yet nothing has ever been done for us. We laid the foundation of the government you now enjoy, and we never apostatized from it, but we remained true to it and were faithful to God." These were the signers of the Declaration of Independence, and they waited on me for two days and two nights. I thought it very singular, that notwithstanding so much work had been done, and yet nothing has been done for them. The thought never entered my heart, from the fact, I suppose, that heretofore our minds were reaching after our more immediate friends and relatives. I straightway went into the baptismal font and called upon brother McCallister to baptize me for the signers of the Declaration of Independence, and fifty other eminent men, making one hundred in all, including John Wesley, Columbus, and others; I then baptized him for every President of the United States, except three; and when their cause is just, somebody will do the work for them.

I have felt to rejoice exceedingly in this work of redeeming the dead.

APPENDIX 4

Extract from John D. T. McAllister's Journal

Dedicatory sessions of the Salt Lake Temple

April 7, 1893, and April 11, 1893, to August 23, 1877

Friday, April 7, 1893:[984]

<u>Evening session</u> Hymn page 143. Prest F.D. Richards dedicatory prayer. Prest Snow led the shout. Prest Woodruff related his manifestations in St George Temple. Referred to his and my baptisms for a number of Notable persons. Apostles B Young [Jr.], F.M. Lyman, & President Cannon, Apostle H.J. Grant dismissed.

Tuesday, April 11, 1893:[985]

<u>P.M.</u> Anthem "Joy to the World" Dedicatory prayer by Apostle A. H. Lund, Prest Snow led the shout. Bro. Easton and choir. "O My Father" Apostle N.W. Merrill spoke. President Woodruff a grand Sermon. Millenium. Work done in St George Temple. Prests Cannon and Smith spoke. the latter called a vote of the acceptance of the Temple by the Saints and the Lord <u>Unamious</u>. "Choir How Lovely is the Temple." Elder S. B Young dismissed.

APPENDIX 5

Extract from Joseph West Smith's Journal
April 11, 1893

Tuesday, April 11, 1893:[986]
Tues. 11. Afternoon I took Aunt Mary Jane and attended the Temple services. Not quite so crowded as on previous occasions. Anthon H. Lund offered the prayer.

Pres. Woodruff made a few remarks. Pres. Snow led the Hosanna Shout. "O My Father" was sung in a soul-inspiring manner by R. C. Easton.

Apostle Merrill: "I have felt like I wanted to go in a corner somewhere and weep for joy. We have built a few temples, but we are going to build other temples."

Pres. Woodruff: "Bro. Merrill talks of building other temples, yes that is the very work we are called to do. If we had put up a log cabin 200 x 100 ft. with a slab roof on it, and undertook to redeem our friends in it, we should not have been satisfied with it. The time is set when the Savior will come to earth, although it has not been revealed to us.

"While at St. George there was a class of men come to me in the night visions, and argued with me to have work done for them. They were the signers of the Declaration of Independence."

Pres. Cannon: "Each of us represents immense numbers when we count back a few generations.

Some of you may have come here with the expectation of seeing angels, or seeing the Elders transfigured before your eyes, or surrounded by a halo of light; but this is not equal to the testimony of the Spirit."

Pres. Joseph F. Smith asked all of the people who felt to accept this temple to say "yes," and if they felt to accept it if they felt that the Lord accepts it also. A hearty response, "Yes!" to both questions.

After meeting Ellen and I made a few purchases, $2.25. We took supper, and spent the evening at Cousin Clarissa's.

APPENDIX 6

Extract from President Wilford Woodruff's Remarks Made at the Salt Lake Stake Conference
Sunday, December 12, 1897[987]

I want to ask this congregation a question. Can you point me to any emperor, king, priest, denomination or power on the face of the whole earth, outside of the Church of Jesus Christ of Latter-day Saints, who has power to go forth and redeem one of their dead? There never was a soul anywhere that could do this until God organized His Church upon the earth. One of the leading principles with Joseph Smith, Brigham Young, John Taylor and Wilford Woodruff, and the Apostles and leading men of this Church, has been the redemption of their dead. The Lord said He would raise up saviors in the last days upon Mount Zion while the kingdom should be the Lord's. This is a duty resting upon all Israel, and one that we should comprehend. The signers of the Declaration of Independence and the men that laid the foundation of this great American government know full well that there has not been a power on earth where they could apply to have this principle carried out in their behalf, only the Apostles that held the keys of the kingdom of God in this generation. They have gone to them and plead with them to redeem them because there was no other power on earth could do it, and this has been accomplished. This principle is today with the Latter-day Saints. There is no more glorious principle given to man than the power which you have while holding the Priesthood, to go forth and redeem your fathers, your mothers, your progenitors. It will stand with you in the morning of the resurrection. Such principles are worthy of contemplation. There is no man living that can point to any church or people that have this power on the earth, but the Latter-day Saints. Whether the world believe it or not, it is true.

APPENDIX 7

Extract from President Wilford Woodruff's Discourse

In the Tabernacle in Salt Lake City April 10, 1898, 2:00 p.m. session
President Woodruff's last general conference address[988]

Brother Cannon has been laying before you something with regard to the nation in which we live and what has been said concerning it. I am going to bear my testimony to this assembly, if I never do it again in my life, that those men who laid the foundation of this American government and signed the Declaration of Independence were the best spirits the God of heaven could find on the face of the earth. They were choice spirits, not wicked men. General Washington and all the men that labored for the purpose were inspired of the Lord.

Another thing I am going to say here, because I have a right to say it. Every one of those men that signed the Declaration of Independence, with General Washington, called upon me, as an Apostle of the Lord Jesus Christ, in the Temple at St. George, two consecutive nights, and demanded at my hands that I should go forth and attend to the ordinances of the House of God for them. Men are here, I believe, that know of this, Brothers J. D. T. McAllister, David H. Cannon and James G. Bleak. Brother McAllister baptized me for all those men, and then I told those brethren that it was their duty to go into the Temple and labor until they had got endowments for all of them. They did it. Would those spirits have called upon me, as an Elder in Israel, to perform that work if they had not been noble spirits before God? They would not.

I bear this testimony, because it is true. The Spirit of God bore record to myself and the brethren while we were laboring in that way.

What has been said with regard to this nation and to our position is coming to pass. All the powers of earth and hell will not stay the hand of Almighty God in the fulfillment of those great prophecies that have to come to pass to prepare the way for the coming of the Son of Man....

I pray God my Heavenly Father that as Elders of Israel and as Latter-day Saints we may prize these principles, and that we may do our duty what time we spend here in the flesh. These Apostles and all the quorums of the Priesthood have a great work upon them. Every father and mother has a great responsibility resting upon them, to redeem their dead. Do not neglect it. You will have sorrow if you do. Any man will who neglects the redemption of his dead that he has power to officiate for here. When you get to the other side of the veil, if you have entered into these Temples and redeemed you progenitors by the ordinances of the House of God, you will hold the keys of their redemption from eternity to eternity. Do not neglect this! God bless you. Amen.

APPENDIX 8

James Godson Bleak Family History Account from Marvel Ruth Bleak Spiering

Purporting to be an account by James Godson Bleak taken from some of his own records. This account is uncertain, and the source has not yet been found. This James Godson Bleak account first appears as a handwritten document in the possession of his great-granddaughter Marvel Bleak Spiering.[989] Vera Taggart obtained a copy of the document and sent a photocopy to Vicki Jo Anderson, postmarked October 2, 1991. Anderson forwarded a copy to Ron Fox. It is not an original document Bleak created but purports to be a handwritten copy of Bleak's records and contains an account of the appearance of the Signers and others to Wilford Woodruff.

The account does not appear in any known and verified records Bleak created.

An examination of the account shows that it relies heavily upon President Woodruff's 1898 general conference address (see Appendix 7). It is, in many respects, more a pastiche than a first-person account. It grabs almost random phrases from Woodruff's 1898 address and even makes up a quote from Woodruff by sticking together bits and pieces from the address instead of just quoting what was there.

Although more research is required, it is our tentative opinion that this account appears to come from a forgery by someone outside the extended Bleak family—possibly by a third-party genealogist. There would be little reason for Bleak, a careful historian, to recreate his own memories of an event using someone else's words. It would also be surprising to find that Bleak had invented a jumbled and remixed quote from Woodruff in place of just simply quoting him.

In the event that an original of this document is found in Bleak's handwriting, the account may still have to be given little historical weight because the way it was constructed shows little original memory of the event. It also contradicts Woodruff's own accounts on multiple points. Historical safety remains in going with the earliest and most contemporary accounts that President Woodruff himself gave. We include the whole transcript here in hopes that others may be able to determine the sources used in this account. The available source was a photocopy that occasionally cut off the end of lines, so some word endings are in brackets. The source document also has missing parentheses, quote marks, and the like.

The account:

(James G. Bleak My g.grandfather)
Family History Offices, held by James Godson Bleak.

"This was copied from some of his own records."

James G. Bleak; born 15 nov. 1829 Southwark Surry co England. Bap. 8 Feb 1851 at London, Middlesex co. Eng. by Priest: Thomas Johnson, Confirmed: 11 Feb. 1851 by Elder: Richard Adams. Ordained Elder, 25 May 1851 by President Harry Savage.

Set apart as 2nd Counselor to President Thomas C. Armstrong of Whitechaple Branch London Eng. 1852 by Elder C. Armstrong—released—1854

Set apart as President of Whitechapel Branch, London Eng. 6 Feb 1854, by Pres. Robinson of London Conference. Released 9 Mar. 1856.

Clerk and Audior of Axies of Conference in London Eng. 7 aug 1854

Baptised into Law of Consecration in London Eng. 16 Mar. 1856.

Left London Eng. With my wife Elizabeth and our four children—on the Ship, "Horizon,["] for Boston Mass. en route to Utah 21 May 1856.

Ordained High Priest 30 apr. 1857 at North Ogden weber co. Utah—by Henry Mower.

Made—Sergeant in Nauvoo Legion—23 Apr. 1857—North Ogden. (see: Echo Canyon War. (Whitney's Popular History of Utah[.)]

Went out in Co. Chauncy West's Reg. in Oct 1857 to Ma[?] Valley, then in Ogden Territory to intercept U. S. Troops in Col. Alexander's Command, who were attempting to come into Utah against the Saints, by way of Mt. Horn route. Returned . . . went to Echo Canyon and—returned from there 4 Dec 1857—The Lord having placed a barrier of 16 ft of Snow between us and our enemies.

In the Spring 1858 we moved to Lehi, Utah and then that Summer returned to my home in North Ogden.

Made President of High Priests Quorum, North Ogden, Utah, 31 Dec. 1858. Set apart by John Young. Released 20 Feb. 1860

Endowed 3 Dec. 1859 at Salt Lake City Endowment House. Recieved Patriarchal Blessing 12 June 1859 North Ogden, by Patriarch Charles W. Hyde.

Called to Southern Utah to help settle that territory With my family I left for there, Oct 1861 after the Semi-Annual Conference, Salt Lake. Was set apart for said mission by Pres. George A. Smith: Left Nov. 18[?]

At Same Conference Oct 1861, I was set apart by Pres. George A. Smith as Clerk and Historian of Southern Utah Mission.

Received Second Anointing, 12 Oct 1868 by Erastus Snow in Historians Office Salt Lake City Utah.

Sent to Europe on a mission—also to be Assistant Editor of "Mellenial Star" and Journal of Discourses"—apr 1872. While I was there I gathered names of my people from that Country, to bring back to America and the Temple with me.

Returned home July 1873.

Was Secretary of United Order of St. Geo. Utah 1874. Commenced recording in St. Geo. Temple by appointment of Pres. Brigham Young—10 Mar. 1877. Held this position for many yrs.

Set apart by Pres. Wilford Woodruff to officiate in the sealings and other ordinances of the St. Geo. Temple 4 Mar. 1881—Witnesses—J. D. T. McAllister and David H. Cannon. Recorded by Mrs. Farnsworth.

Was Chief Recorder of St. George Temple by 1888.

While working there I spent all the time possible With my children, doing temple work on the names of our people, I brought from Europe while there on my Mission.

I was appointed by Pres. Edward Hunter, as St Geo. Stake agent, for Bishop—mon. 12 apr. 1880.

Ordained a Bishop of St. Geo. 12 June 1881—Salt Lake City Utah—by Pres. John Taylor—and apostle Francis M. Lyman. Also ordained in St George for said office—not knowing that Pres. Taylor had previously done this and not knowing what Apostle Lyman was about to do.

I was also present in the St. Geo. Temple and witne[ssed] the appearance of the Spirits of the Signers of the Declaration of Independence. And also the spirits of the Presidents of the U.S. up to that time. And also others, such as Martin Luther and John Wesley. (The man that started the Methodist Faith.) who came to Wilford Woodruff and demanded that their baptism and endowments be done. Wilford Woodruff was baptized for all of them—while I and Brothers' J. D. T. McAllister and David H. Cannon (who were witness[es] to the request.) were endowed for them. These men that we did work for, were Choice Spirits, not Wicked Men. They laid the foundation of this American Gov., and signed the Declaration of Independence And were the best spirits the God of Heaven could find on the face of the earth to perform this work. Martin Luther and John Wesley helped to release the people from religious bondage that held them during the dark ages. They also prepared the peoples hearts so they would be ready to receive the restored gospel when the Lord sent it again to men on the earth.

Wilford Woodruff, "Said, would those spirits have come to me and demanded at my hand as an Elder ordinances in the House of God, for them if they had not been noble spirits before God? They would not. I bear testimony, because its true. The Spirit of God bore record to myself and these brethren while we were laboring in their behalf.

by his gg.dag by Marvel Bleak Spiering

APPENDIX 9
The Temple Work

A listing of the individuals whose temple work was inaugurated by performing proxy baptisms for the dead on August 21, 1877, by Woodruff, McAllister, and Young follows. Although the dates are not listed here, the rest of the temple ordinances for most of these people were completed soon after in August and September. The last work appears to be completed in November.

The order below is as it appears in the temple records—and the most likely order in which they were performed.[990] *The order in Woodruff's journal is followed for those twenty-five eminent men that were accidently left off the temple baptism records. This list modernizes the spelling and identity of the names but retains the temple-record order.*

Wilford Woodruff baptized John D. T. McAllister on behalf of the following individuals:

George Washington (1732–1799) Commander in Chief of the Continental Army during the Revolutionary War. President of the Constitutional Convention. First president of the United States of America, 1789–1797. The essential figure of American history, Washington deserves his rightful title: Father of Our Country.

John Washington (cir. 1631–1677) The great-grandfather of George Washington. He emigrated from England to Virginia in 1656. He raised tobacco and was a member of the House of Burgesses.

Sir Henry Washington (cir. 1615–1664) Governor and colonel of the city of Worcester, England; Washington defended Worcester against Parliament's forces in 1646. Washington was first cousin to George Washington's great-grandfather, John Washington.

Rev. Lawrence Washington (1602–cir. 1653) The great-great-grandfather of George Washington. He was the rector in Purleigh, England, until Puritan Parliament's anti-Royalist policies removed him. He died in poverty. His wife was Amphyllis Twigden.

Augustine Washington (1694–1743) The father of George Washington. He was a tobacco planter, justice of the peace, and county sheriff in Virginia. His first wife was Jane Butler; his second was Mary Ball.

Lawrence Washington (1659–1697) The grandfather of George Washington. He was a tobacco planter, lawyer, and politician. He married Mildred Warner.[991]

Lawrence Washington (1718–1752) He was the older half-brother and mentor of George Washington. He named Mount Vernon after his commanding officer Edward Vernon. He married Anne Fairfax.

Daniel Parke Custis (1711–1757) The first husband of Martha

Washington. He was a wealthy Virginia planter. He died seven years into their marriage.

John "Jack" Parke Custis (1754–1781) Son of Martha Washington and her first husband, Daniel Parke Custis. Jack's father died when Jack was a toddler, and Jack's mother and stepfather, George Washington, raised him. Jack served as an aide to his stepfather at the siege of Yorktown and died from "camp fever" soon after the British surrendered.

James Madison (1751–1836) Father of the Constitution. Fourth president of the United States—1809–1817—and husband of Dolley Madison.

James Monroe (1758–1831) President of the United States—1817–1825.

John Quincy Adams (1767–1848) President of the United States—1825–1829.

Andrew Jackson (1767–1845) President of the United States—1829–1837.

William Henry Harrison (1773–1841) President of the United States—March 4, 1841–April 4, 1841.

John Tyler (1790–1862) President of the United States—1841–1845.

James Knox Polk (1795–1849) President of the United States—1845–1849.[992]

Zachary Taylor (1784–1850) President of the United States—1849–1850.

Millard Fillmore (1800–1874) President of the United States—1850–1853. He created Utah Territory and appointed Brigham Young as its first territorial governor.

Franklin Pierce (1804–1869) President of the United States—1853–1857.

Abraham Lincoln (1809–1865) President of the United States who wrote the Gettysburg Address, preserved the Union, and ended slavery in the United States. His term was 1861–1865.

Andrew Johnson (1808–1875) President of the United States—1865–1869.

John D. T. McAllister baptized Wilford Woodruff on behalf of the following individuals:

William Hooper (1742–1790) Signer from North Carolina.
Joseph Hewes (1730–1779) Signer from North Carolina.
John Penn (1741–1788) Signer from North Carolina.
Button Gwinnett (1735–1777) Signer from Georgia.
Lyman Hall (1724–1790) Signer from Georgia.
Edward Rutledge (1749–1800) Signer from South Carolina.
George Walton (cir. 1749–1804) Signer from Georgia.
Thomas Heyward Jr. (1746–1809) Signer from South Carolina.
Thomas Lynch (1749–1779) Signer from South Carolina.
Arthur Middleton (1742–1787) Signer from South Carolina.
Samuel Chase (1741–1811) Signer from Maryland.
William Paca (1740–1799) Signer from Maryland.
Thomas Stone (1743–1787) Signer from Maryland.

Charles Carroll of Carrolton (1737–1832) Signer from Maryland.
George Wythe (1726–1806) Signer from Virginia.
Richard Henry Lee (1732–1794) Signer from Virginia.
Thomas Jefferson (1743–1826) Signer from Virginia. President of the United States 1801–1809.
Benjamin Harrison (1726–1791) Signer from Virginia.
Thomas Nelson Jr. (1738–1789) Signer from Virginia.
Francis Lightfoot Lee (1734–1797) Signer from Virginia.
Carter Braxton (1736–1797) Signer from Virginia.
Robert Morris (1734–1806) Signer from Pennsylvania.
Benjamin Rush (1745–1813) Signer from Pennsylvania.
Benjamin Franklin (1706–1790) Signer from Pennsylvania.
John Morton (1724–1777) Signer from Pennsylvania.
George Clymer (1739–1813) Signer from Pennsylvania.
James Smith (cir. 1713/19–1806) Signer from Pennsylvania.
George Taylor (cir. 1716–1781) Signer from Pennsylvania.
James Wilson (1742–1798) Signer from Pennsylvania.
George Ross (1730–1779) Signer from Pennsylvania.
Caeser Rodney (1728–1784) Signer from Delaware.
George Read (1733–1798) Signer from Delaware.
Thomas McKean (1734–1817) Signer from Delaware.
Philip Livingston (1716–1778) Signer from New York.
Francis Lewis (1713–1803) Signer from New York.
Lewis Morris (1726–1798) Signer from New York.
Richard Stockton (1730–1781) Signer from New Jersey.
John Witherspoon (1723–1794) Signer from New Jersey.
Francis Hopkinson (1737–1791) Signer from New Jersey.
John Hart (1713–1779) Signer from New Jersey.
Abraham Clark (1726–1794) Signer from New Jersey.
Josiah Bartlett (1729–1795) Signer from New Hampshire.
William Whipple (1730–1785) Signer from New Hampshire.
Samuel Adams (1722–1803) Signer from Massachusetts.
John Adams (1735–1826) Signer from Massachusetts.
Robert Treat Paine (1731–1814) Signer from Massachusetts.
Elbridge Gerry (1744–1814) Signer from Massachusetts.
Stephen Hopkins (1707–1785) Signer from Rhode Island.
William Ellery (1727–1820) Signer from Rhode Island.
Roger Sherman (1721–1793) Signer from Connecticut.
Samuel Huntington (1731–1796) Signer from Connecticut.
William Williams (1731–1811) Signer from Connecticut.
Oliver Wolcott (1726–1797) Signer from Connecticut.
Matthew Thornton (1714–1803) Signer from New Hampshire.
Demetrius Parepa, Baron Georgiades de Boyescu (cir.1800–cir.1836) Father of opera singer Euphrosyne Parepa-Rosa.

Daniel Webster (1782–1852) American statesman, senator, secretary of state, and orator.

Washington Irving (1783–1859) American historian, essayist, and author of *The Legend of Sleepy Hollow* and *Rip Van Winkle*, among other works.

Michael Faraday (1791–1867) English scientist who worked with electricity and magnetism.

William Makepeace Thackeray (1811–1863) English novelist and satirist who wrote, among other things, *Vanity Fair*.

John Caldwell Calhoun (1782–1850) American senator and vice president and a proponent of states' rights and slavery.

Justus von Liebig (1803–1873) German chemist and teacher who worked on plant nutrition.

Henry Clay (1777–1852) American senator, statesman, and orator.

Edward George Earle Lytton Bulwer-Lytton (1803–1873) English novelist, poet, and politician who coined, "The pen is mightier than the sword."

George Peabody (1795–1869) American who became a British banker and philanthropist.

Charles Louis Napoleon Bonaparte, Napoleon III (1808–1873). France's first president and, after executing a coup d'état, its last monarch.

Thomas Chalmers (1780–1847) Scottish minister and theologian.

William Henry Seward (1801–1872) American secretary of state under Abraham Lincoln and Andrew Johnson, senator, and governor of New York. Helped the U.S. purchase Alaska from the Russians in 1867.

Thomas Jonathan "Stonewall" Jackson (1824–1863) American/Confederate general.

David Glasgow Farragut (1801–1870) American naval officer and admiral.

Hiram Powers (1805–1873) American sculptor who was famous for *The Greek Slave*.

Jean Louis Rodolphe Agassiz (1807–1873) Swiss-American naturalist.

David Livingstone (1813–1873) Scottish explorer and medical missionary in Africa.

Christopher Columbus (1451–1506) Italian explorer and colonizer.

Amerigo Vespucci (1454–1512) Italian explorer who showed that Columbus had discovered a new landmass later named America.

John Wesley (1703–1791) English theologian, reformer, abolitionist, and Anglican founder of the Methodist movement.

Samuel Johnson (1709–1784) English essayist, poet, and biographer who wrote an influential dictionary and who was the subject of James Boswell's classic *Life of Samuel Johnson*.

Oliver Goldsmith (1730–1774) English/Irish playwright, poet, and novelist.

Frederick II of Prussia, Frederick the Great (1712–1786) King of Prussia and military conqueror who improved bureaucracy at home and promoted religious tolerance.

Edward Gibbon (1737–1752) English historian and member of Parliament who wrote the six-volume

History of the Decline and Fall of the Roman Empire.

David Garrick (1717–1779) English actor and playwright who promoted more realistic acting. Husband of Eva Marie Veigel.

Sir Joshua Reynolds (1723–1792) English painter who was the first president of the Royal Academy.

Robert Burns (1759–1796) Scottish poet who wrote, among other things, "Auld Lang Syne."

Johann Wolfgang von Goethe (1749–1832) German writer, poet, philosopher, artist, and politician who was best known for his work *Faust*.

John Philip Kemble (1757–1823) English actor. Brother of actress Sarah Kemble Siddons.

Friedrich Schiller (1759–1805) German poet, dramatist, historian, and philosopher.

Henry Grattan (1746–1820) Irish politician.

Robert Fulton (1765–1815) American engineer and inventor who perfected the first commercially successful steamboat.

Horatio Nelson (1758–1805) English naval hero who died at the battle of Trafalgar.

John Philpot Curran (1750–1817) Irish politician, lawyer, and wit.

George Stephenson (1781–1848) English civil and mechanical engineer who developed railways.

Friedrich Wilhelm Heinrich Alexander von Humboldt (1769–1859) Prussian naturalist and geographer who explored Latin America.

Sir Walter Scott (1771–1832) Scottish novelist and poet who wrote *Ivanhoe*.

Lord Henry Peter Brougham (1778–1868) British statesman and Lord Chancellor.

Lord George Gordon Byron (1788–1824) English poet who wrote, among other things, the satirical poem *Don Juan*.

William Wordsworth (1770–1850) English poet who helped found the Romantic literary movement.

Daniel O'Connell (1775–1847) Irish politician who strove for Catholic rights in Great Britain.

Camillo Benso (1810–1861) Count of Cavour and Italian statesman who helped unite the country. He was the first Prime Minister of Italy.

Richard Cobden (1804–1865) British manufacturer and statesman who campaigned for peace.

Thomas Babington Macaulay (1800–1859) British historian, politician, and secretary at war.

Benito Juárez (1806–1872) Mexican lawyer, politician, and president of Mexico who resisted French colonialism.

John D. T. McAllister baptized Lucy Bigelow Young on behalf of the following seventy women:

Elisabeth Christine of Brunswick-Wolfenbüttel-Bevern (1715–1797) Queen of Prussia and Frederick the Great's neglected wife.

Eva Marie Veigel, stage name: Eva Maria Violette (1724–1822) Dancer and wife of David Garrick.

Jane Mary Nugent (1734–1812) Wife of Edmund Burke.

Jean Armour (1765–1834) Inspiration and wife of Robert Burns.

Christiane Vulpius (1806–1816) Wife of Johann Wolfgang von Goethe.

Priscilla Hopkins Brereton (1756–1845) Actress and wife of John Philip Kemble.

Martha Wayles (1748–1782) Wife of Thomas Jefferson.

Charlotte Von Lengefeld (1766–1826) Writer and wife of Friedrich Schiller.

Henrietta Fitzgerald (cir. 1758–1789) Wife of Henry Grattan.

Frances "Fanny" Wollward Nisbet (1761–1831) Wife of Horatio Nelson.

Sarah Creagh (1755–1844) Wife of Irish politician John Philpot Curran, who later left him.

Frances "Fanny" Henderson (1768–1806) First of George Stephenson's three wives. She died before he found fame and fortune in railroads.

Charlotte Genevieve Carpenter (born Charpentier) (1777–1826) Wife of Sir Walter Scott.

Mary Anne Eden Spalding (1785–1865) Wife of Lord Henry Peter Brougham.

Anne Isabella "Annabella" Milbanke (1792–1860) Wife of Lord Byron, but she separated from him after a tumultuous year of marriage.

Mary Hutchinson (1770–1859) Wife of William Wordsworth.

Catherine "Kitty" Pakenham Wellesley, Duchess of Wellington (1773–1831) Wife of Arthur Wellesley, First Duke of Wellington.

Elizabeth "Bessy" Dyke (1794–1865) Actress and wife of Thomas Moore and the inspiration for his poem "Believe Me, If All Those Endearing Young Charms."

Rachel Donelson (1767–1828) Wife of U.S. President Andrew Jackson. She died after his election but before he took office.

Mary O'Connell (1778–1836) Wife (and third cousin) of Irish politician Daniel O'Connell.

Emily Lamb Melbourne, Lady Cowper (1787–1869) Her father, Peniston Lamb, became Viscount Melbourne. Her first husband was Lord Cowper, but when he fell ill, she became the mistress of Lord Palmerston. After Lord Cowper died, she married Lord Palmerston, who later became British prime minister.

Margarita Maza Juárez (1826–1871) Wife of Benito Juárez and first lady of Mexico. (The St. George Temple records list "Princess Charlotte wife of Benito Juarez." This is the wrong name and is not Juárez's wife.)[993]

Abigail Eastman (1739–1816) Mother of senator and secretary of state Daniel Webster.

Grace Fletcher (1781–1828) First wife of senator and secretary of state Daniel Webster.

Matilda Hoffman (1791–1809) Fiancée of writer Washington Irving. She died at age seventeen before they married, and he remained single the rest of his life.

Sarah Barnard (1800–1879) Wife of scientist Michael Faraday.

Isabella Gethin Shawe (1816–1893) Wife of satirist William Makepeace Thackeray. She was institutionalized for mental illness after the birth of their third child.

Martha Caldwell (1730–1802) Mother of Vice President John C. Calhoun.

Elinor "Ellie" Junkin (1825–1854) First wife of "Stonewall" Jackson. She died after giving birth to a stillborn son.

Lydia Knapp Gibbs (1786–1846) Wife of Elijah Gibbs, who was the great uncle of Lucy Bigelow Young (who was baptized on Lydia Gibbs's behalf).[994] There are also connections to Woodruffs in the genealogy.[995]

Catharine Maria Sedgwick (1789–1867) American novelist.

Mary Russell Mitford (1787–1855) English author, poet, and dramatist.

Sydney Owenson, Lady Morgan (cir. 1781–1859) Irish novelist.

Mary Fairfax Somerville (1780–1872) Scottish scientist and mathematician who was known for her writings. Somerville College at Oxford, founded in 1879, was named after her.

Letitia Elizabeth Landon (1802–1838) English novelist and poet who signed her poems "L. E. L."

Sarah Margaret Fuller Ossoli (1810–1850) American journalist and supporter of women's rights.

Emily Chubbuck Judson (1817–1854) American poet and Baptist missionary to Burma who wrote under the pen name "Fanny Forrester."

Elizabeth Barrett Browning (1806–1861) English poet, wife of poet Robert Browning. She wrote "How Do I Love Thee?" and other works popular during her lifetime.

Frances Sargent Osgood (née Locke) (1811–1850) American poet.

Hannah More (1745–1833) English religious author and philanthropist who focused on helping children.

Marie Antoinette (1755–1793) Queen of France, wife of King Louis XVI, both of whom were beheaded during the French Revolution.

Maria Theresa (1717–1780) Mother of Marie Antoinette. Also empress consort of the Holy Roman Empire, Queen of Hungary and Bohemia, and ruler of the Habsburg Monarchy for four decades.

Frances "Fanny" Burney, Madame d'Arblay (1752–1840) English novelist and playwright.

Mary Ball Washington (1708–1789) Mother of George Washington and five other children. She lived to see Washington become the first president of the United States. She was the second wife of Augustine Washington.

Martha Dandridge Custis Washington (1731–1802) Wife of George Washington, her second husband. She was the first first lady of the United States.

Charlotte Corday (1768–1793) French assassin who stabbed a prominent French Revolution leader, Jean-Paul Marat, in his bathtub. At her trial, Corday stated, "I have killed one man to save a hundred thousand." Her act had the opposite effect. Marat, a driving force behind the appropriately named Reign of Terror, was hailed as a martyr by his supporters.

Anne Pope Washington (1635–1668) Great-grandmother of George Washington. (Identified as "Mrs. John Washington" in the St. George Temple records.)[996]

Elizabeth Pakington Washington (cir. 1630–n.d.) Wife of Sir Henry Washington, who was first cousin to George Washington's great-grandfather Colonel John Washington. After Sir

Henry died, Elizabeth married Samuel Sandys, Baron Sandys. (Identified as "Mrs. Henry Washington" in the St. George Temple records.)

Amphyllis Twigden Washington (cir. 1600–cir. 1655) The great-great-grandmother of George Washington. She was the wife of Rev. Lawrence Washington.

Jane Butler Washington (1699–cir. 1728) First wife of George Washington's father. She had four children, including George Washington's half-brother, Lawrence Washington. (She is identified as "Mrs. Washington" in the St. George Temple records.)[997]

Mildred Warner Washington (1671–1701) The grandmother of George Washington. She married Lawrence Washington and, after he died in 1698, remarried to George Gale and moved to England. After she died, her children, including George Washington's father, Augustine, returned to Virginia. (Identified as "Mrs. Mildred Warner Washington (Augustine's mother)" in the St. George Temple records.)

Anne Fairfax Washington (1728–1761) Wife of Lawrence Washington, George Washington's half-brother. She inherited Mount Vernon after her husband's death and remarried. George Washington, who had been leasing Mount Vernon from her, inherited it after her death.

Mary Philipse Morris (1730–1825) Early unrequited love of George Washington. She instead married British officer Roger Morris, who fled in 1775 to Britain in opposition to the Revolutionary War. She joined her husband in England in 1783. Their American home is the oldest surviving home in Manhattan, New York.

Martha "Patsy" Parke Custis (1756–1773) Daughter of Martha Washington and her first husband, Daniel Parke Custis. Patsy's father died when she was a baby, and her mother and George Washington, her stepfather, raised her. She died of what is believed to have been an epileptic seizure when she was seventeen years old.

Eleanor Calvert Custis Stuart (cir. 1758–1811) Wife of John Parke Custis and daughter-in-law of Martha Washington. After Eleanor became a widow, she married Dr. David Stuart. George and Martha Washington raised two of Eleanor and John Parke Custis's children, Eleanor "Nelly" Parke Custis and George Washington Parke Custis. (Identified as "Mrs. John Parke Custis" in the St. George Temple records.)

Maria Fackrell Possibly Ann Maria Fackrell (1833– n.d.). Ann Maria Fackrell was baptized a member of the Church on April 6, 1849, in Bristol, England, by George Halliday and may have died before coming to Utah. In any case, John D. T. McAllister probably knew Maria Fackrell because she was mentioned specifically in his journal, being singled out among all the other women whose work was done that day. (Identified as "Marie Fackrell" in the St. George Temple records.)[998]

Euphrosyne Parepa-Rosa (1836–1874) British opera singer who toured the United States, including Salt Lake City.

Elizabeth Sequinn, Countess Demetrius Parepa (cir.1815–1870) Mother of opera singer Euphrosyne Parepa-Rosa.

Sarah Ford Johnson (1669–1759) Mother of English essayist and poet Samuel Johnson.

Abigail Smith Adams (1744–1818) First lady and wife of John Adams, who was the first vice president and second president of the United States. Mother of John Quincy Adams, the sixth president. She is especially noted for her correspondence with her husband, documenting the times and people of the American Revolution and the new government.

Maria Edgeworth (1768–1849) Irish novelist who wrote for both adults and children.

Sarah Van Brugh Livingston Jay (1756–1802) Wife of the first chief justice of the United States, John Jay.

Jane Austen (1775–1817) English novelist who wrote *Sense and Sensibility* and *Pride and Prejudice*, among other works.

Sarah Kemble Siddons (1755–1831) Welsh actress famous for her portrayal of Lady Macbeth. Sister of actor John Philip Kemble.

Dolley Payne Todd Madison (1768–1849) Wife of U.S. President James Madison. She was a popular first lady.

Elizabeth "Betsy" Gurney Fry (1780–1845) English social activist and prison reformer.

Felicia Hemans, aka Felicia Dorothea Browne (1793–1835) English poet.

Lydia Huntley Sigourney (1791–1865) American poet.

Anna Brownell Murphy Jameson (1794–1860) Irish/British nonfiction writer.

Charlotte Brontë (1816–1855) English novelist and poet who wrote *Jane Eyre*, among other works.

APPENDIX 10
The Declaration of Independence

This text of the Declaration of Independence comes from the National Archives and retains original spellings

IN CONGRESS, July 4, 1776.

The unanimous Declaration of the thirteen united States of America,

When in the Course of human events, it becomes necessary for one people to dissolve the political bands which have connected them with another, and to assume among the powers of the earth, the separate and equal station to which the Laws of Nature and of Nature's God entitle them, a decent respect to the opinions of mankind requires that they should declare the causes which impel them to the separation.

We hold these truths to be self-evident, that all men are created equal, that they are endowed by their Creator with certain unalienable Rights, that among these are Life, Liberty and the pursuit of Happiness.—That to secure these rights, Governments are instituted among Men, deriving their just powers from the consent of the governed,—That whenever any Form of Government becomes destructive of these ends, it is the Right of the People to alter or to abolish it, and to institute new Government, laying its foundation on such principles and organizing its powers in such form, as to them shall seem most likely to effect their Safety and Happiness. Prudence, indeed, will dictate that Governments long established should not be changed for light and transient causes; and accordingly all experience hath shewn, that mankind are more disposed to suffer, while evils are sufferable, than to right themselves by abolishing the forms to which they are accustomed. But when a long train of abuses and usurpations, pursuing invariably the same Object evinces a design to reduce them under absolute Despotism, it is their right, it is their duty, to throw off such Government, and to provide new Guards for their future security.—Such has been the patient sufferance of these Colonies; and such is now the necessity which constrains them to alter their former Systems of Government. The history of the present King of Great Britain is a history of repeated injuries and usurpations, all having in direct object the establishment of an absolute Tyranny over these States. To prove this, let Facts be submitted to a candid world.

He has refused his Assent to Laws, the most wholesome and necessary for the public good.

He has forbidden his Governors to pass Laws of immediate and pressing importance, unless suspended in their operation till his Assent should be obtained; and when so suspended, he has utterly neglected to attend to them.

He has refused to pass other Laws for the accommodation of large districts of people, unless those people would relinquish the right of Representation in the Legislature, a right inestimable to them and formidable to tyrants only.

He has called together legislative bodies at places unusual, uncomfortable, and distant from the depository of their public Records, for the sole purpose of fatiguing them into compliance with his measures.

He has dissolved Representative Houses repeatedly, for opposing with manly firmness his invasions on the rights of the people.

He has refused for a long time, after such dissolutions, to cause others to be elected; whereby the Legislative powers, incapable of Annihilation, have returned to the People at large for their exercise; the State remaining in the mean time exposed to all the dangers of invasion from without, and convulsions within.

He has endeavoured to prevent the population of these States; for that purpose obstructing the Laws for Naturalization of Foreigners; refusing to pass others to encourage their migrations hither, and raising the conditions of new Appropriations of Lands.

He has obstructed the Administration of Justice, by refusing his Assent to Laws for establishing Judiciary powers.

He has made Judges dependent on his Will alone, for the tenure of their offices, and the amount and payment of their salaries.

He has erected a multitude of New Offices, and sent hither swarms of Officers to harrass our people, and eat out their substance.

He has kept among us, in times of peace, Standing Armies without the Consent of our legislatures.

He has affected to render the Military independent of and superior to the Civil power.

He has combined with others to subject us to a jurisdiction foreign to our constitution, and unacknowledged by our laws; giving his Assent to their Acts of pretended Legislation:

For Quartering large bodies of armed troops among us:

For protecting them, by a mock Trial, from punishment for any Murders which they should commit on the Inhabitants of these States:

For cutting off our Trade with all parts of the world:

For imposing Taxes on us without our Consent:

For depriving us in many cases, of the benefits of Trial by Jury:

For transporting us beyond Seas to be tried for pretended offences

For abolishing the free System of English Laws in a neighbouring Province, establishing therein an Arbitrary government, and enlarging its Boundaries so as to render it at once an example and fit instrument for introducing the same absolute rule into these Colonies:

For taking away our Charters, abolishing our most valuable Laws, and altering fundamentally the Forms of our Governments:

For suspending our own Legislatures, and declaring themselves invested with power to legislate for us in all cases whatsoever.

He has abdicated Government here, by declaring us out of his Protection and waging War against us.

He has plundered our seas, ravaged our Coasts, burnt our towns, and destroyed the lives of our people.

He is at this time transporting large Armies of foreign Mercenaries to compleat the works of death, desolation and tyranny, already begun with circumstances of Cruelty & perfidy scarcely paralleled in the most barbarous ages, and totally unworthy the Head of a civilized nation.

He has constrained our fellow Citizens taken Captive on the high Seas to bear Arms against their Country, to become the executioners of their friends and Brethren, or to fall themselves by their Hands.

He has excited domestic insurrections amongst us, and has endeavoured to bring on the inhabitants of our frontiers, the merciless Indian Savages, whose known rule of warfare, is an undistinguished destruction of all ages, sexes and conditions.

In every stage of these Oppressions We have Petitioned for Redress in the most humble terms: Our repeated Petitions have been answered only by repeated injury. A Prince whose character is thus marked by every act which may define a Tyrant, is unfit to be the ruler of a free people.

Nor have We been wanting in attentions to our Brittish brethren. We have warned them from time to time of attempts by their legislature to extend an unwarrantable jurisdiction over us. We have reminded them of the circumstances of our emigration and settlement here. We have appealed to their native justice and magnanimity, and we have conjured them by the ties of our common kindred to disavow these usurpations, which, would inevitably interrupt our connections and correspondence. They too have been deaf to the voice of justice and of consanguinity. We must, therefore, acquiesce in the necessity, which denounces our Separation, and hold them, as we hold the rest of mankind, Enemies in War, in Peace Friends.

We, therefore, the Representatives of the united States of America, in General Congress, Assembled, appealing to the Supreme Judge of the world for the rectitude of our intentions, do, in the Name, and by Authority of the good People of these Colonies, solemnly publish and declare, That these United Colonies are, and of Right ought to be Free and Independent States; that they are Absolved from all Allegiance to the British Crown, and that all political connection between them and the State of Great Britain, is and ought to be totally dissolved; and that as Free and Independent States, they have full Power to levy War, conclude Peace, contract Alliances, establish Commerce, and to do all other Acts and Things which Independent States may of right do. And for the support of this Declaration, with a firm reliance on the protection of divine Providence, we mutually pledge to each other our Lives, our Fortunes and our sacred Honor.

BIBLIOGRAPHY

Adams, Charles Thornton. *Matthew Thornton of New Hampshire: A Patriot of the American Revolution*. Philadelphia: Dando Printing and Publishing Co., 1903.

Adams, John and Charles Francis Adams, eds. *The Works of John Adams, Second President of the United States: with a Life of the Author, Notes and Illustrations, by his Grandson Charles Francis Adams*. 10 vols. Boston: Little, Brown and Co., 1856.

Addy, Caroline S. *James Godson Bleak: Pioneer Historian of Southern Utah*. MA thesis, Brigham Young University, 1953.

Adherents.com, various entries (accessed March 19, 2011).

Alexander, Thomas G. *Things in Heaven and Earth: The Life and Times of Wilford Woodruff, a Mormon Prophet*. Salt Lake City: Signature Books, 1991.

Allen, James B., Jessie L. Embry, and Kahllile B. Mehr. *Hearts Turned to the Fathers: A History of the Genealogical Society of Utah, 1894–1994*. Brigham Young University Studies: Provo, Utah 1995.

AmericanMusicPreservation.com http://www.americanmusicpreservation.com/FirstAmericansong.htm (accessed September 17, 2014).

"An American Time Capsule: Three Centuries of Broadsides and Other Printed Ephemera." Library of Congress website. http://memory.loc.gov/ammem/rbpehtml/ (accessed October 23, 2012).

Anderson, Devery S. *The Development of LDS Temple Worship 1846–2000: A Documentary History*. Salt Lake City: Signature Books, 2011.

Anderson, Devery S. and Gary James Bergera. *Joseph Smith's Quorum of the Anointed 1842–1845*. Salt Lake City: Signature Books, 2005.

Anderson, Vicki J., Karen Arnesen, and Valerie Holladay. *The Other Eminent Men of Wilford Woodruff*. Malta, ID: Nelson Books, 2000.

Axelrod, Alan. *The Real History of the American Revolution: A New Look at the Past*. New York: Sterling, 2007.

Barrett, Walter. *The Old Merchants of New York City*, vol. 4. New York: Thomas R. Knox & Co., 1885.

Barthelmas, Della Gray. *The Signers of the Declaration of Independence: A Biographical and Genealogical Reference*. Jefferson, North Carolina: McFarland and Company, Inc., Publishers, 1997.

Baugh, Alexander. "'Blessed Is the First Man Baptised in This Font': Reuben McBride, First Proxy to Be Baptized for the Dead in the Nauvoo Temple." *Mormon Historical Studies*, vol. 3, no. 2 (Fall 2002): 253–261.

Baugh, Alexander. "'For This Ordinance Belongeth to My House': The Practice of Baptism for the Dead Outside the Nauvoo Temple." *Mormon Historical Studies*, vol. 3, no. 1, (Spring 2002): 47–58.

Baugh, Alexander L. and Susan Easton Black, eds. *Banner of the Gospel: Wilford Woodruff*. Provo, Utah: Religious Studies Center, Brigham Young University, 2010.

Bennett, Richard E. "'Line upon Line, Precept upon Precept': Reflections on the 1877 Commencement of the

Performance of Endowments and Sealings for the Dead." *Brigham Young University Studies*, vol. 44, no. 3 (2005): 38–77.

Bennett, Richard E., "Wilford Woodruff and the Rise of Temple Consciousness among the Latter-day Saints, 1877–84." Chap. 7 in *Banner of the Gospel: Wilford Woodruff*. Edited by Alexander L. Baugh and Susan Easton Black. Provo, Utah: Religious Studies Center, Brigham Young University, 2010.

Bennett, William J., ed. *Our Sacred Honor: Words of Advice from the Founders in Stories, Letter, Poems, and Speeches*. New York: Simon & Schuster, 1997.

Biographical Directory of the United States Congress 1774–Present, online. http://bioguide.congress.gov (accessed March 19, 2011).

Bishop, M. Guy. "'What Has Become of Our Fathers?': Baptism for the Dead at Nauvoo." *Dialogue: A Journal of Mormon Thought*, vol. 23, no. 2 (1987): 85–97.

Black, Susan Easton and Harvey Bischoff Black. *Annotated Record of Baptisms for the Dead 1840–1845: Nauvoo, Hancock County, Illinois*. 7 vols. Provo, Utah: The Center for Family History and Genealogy, Brigham Young University, 2002.

Bleak, James Godson. *James Godson Bleak Journal*. L. Tom Perry Special Collections, 19th Century Western & Mormon Manuscripts. Harold B. Lee Library, Brigham Young University, Provo, Utah.

Bridges, Edwin C. "George Walton." Webpage about George Walton and his home, Meadow Garden. http://www.historicmeadowgarden.org/george_walton.php (accessed October 13, 2012).

Brown University Steering Committee on Slavery and Justice, Repository of Historical Documents. http://dl.lib.brown.edu/slaveryandjustice (accessed March 19, 2011).

Brown, Lisle G., "Chronology of the Construction, Destruction and Reconstruction of the Nauvoo Temple." Webpage (1999, 2000). http://users.marshall.edu/~brown/nauvoo/chrono.html (accessed September 8, 2014).

Brown, Samuel Morris. *In Heaven as it is On Earth: Joseph Smith and the Early Mormon Conquest of Death*. Oxford University Press: New York, 2012.

Burke, James. *American Connections: The Founding Fathers. Networked*. New York: Simon & Schuster, 2007.

Burnett, Edmund Cody. *Letters of Members of the Continental Congress*, vol. 1. Washington, D.C.: Carnegie Institution of Washington, 1921.

Burton, Richard F. *The City of the Saints and Across the Rocky Mountains to California*. New York: Harper & Brothers, 1862.

Cashin, Edward J. Jr. "George Walton and the Forged Letter." *The Georgia Historical Quarterly*, vol. 62, no. 2 (Summer 1978): 133–145.

Chadwick, Bruce. "The Mysterious Death of Judge George Wythe." *American History Magazine*. Weider History Group. Published online December 11, 2008. http://www.historynet.com/the-mysterious-death-of-judge-george-wythe.htm (accessed January 12, 2012).

Clemens, William Montgomery. *Button Gwinnett: Man of Mystery* Pompton Lakes, New Jersey: William M. Clemens Publisher, 1921.

ColonialHall.com (accessed March 19, 2011).

"Complete Sun and Moon Data for One Day," USNO Astronomical Applications Department. Online interactive database. http://aa.usno.navy.mil/data/docs/RS_OneDay.php (accessed December 10, 2011).

Conference Report of The Church of Jesus Christ of Latter-day Saints, Sixty-Eighth Annual Conference of The Church of Jesus Christ of Latter-day Saints, April 1898. Salt Lake City: Deseret News Publishing Company, 1898.

Cornelius, Elias. *Journal of Dr. Elias Cornelius, a Revolutionary Surgeon: Graphic Details of His Sufferings While a Prisoner in Provost Jail, New York, 1777 and 1778, with Biographical Sketch.* Washington, D.C.: Judge Charles M. Tompkins and Chester T. Sherman, 1903.

Curtis, Kirk M. *History of the St. George Temple.* MS thesis, Brigham Young University, 1964.

De Groote, Michael. "Patriotic Patriarch: Benjamin Franklin at the Constitutional Convention." Research Paper for Origins of the Constitution class at J. Reuben Clark Law School, Brigham Young University, 1992.

Descendants of the Signers of the Declaration of Independence website. www.dsdi1776.com/Signers (accessed March 19, 2011 and September 5, 2011).

Deseret Evening News. "President Woodruff is Dead." September 2, 1898, 1. udn.lib.utah.edu/cdm/compoundobject/collection/den1895/id/72072/rec/208 (accessed October 4, 2014).

Dictionary of Canadian Biography/Dictionnaire biographique du Canada. University of Toronto and the Université Laval, 1959. http://www.biographi.ca (accessed July 4, 2011).

Donovan, Frank. *The Thomas Jefferson Papers.* Cornwall, New York: The Cornwall Press, 1963.

Duyckinck, Evert A. *National Portrait Gallery of Eminent Americans.* 2 vols. New York: Johnson, Fry, & Company, 1862.

Duyckinck, Evert A. *Portrait Gallery of Eminent Men and Women of Europe and America.* 2 vols. New York: Johnson, Fry and Company, 1872.

Dwight, N. *The Lives of the Signers of the Declaration of Independence.* New York: Harper and Brothers, 1840.

Edwards, Virginia. "Stories of Old St. Augustine." St. Augustine, Florida: St. Augustine Historical Society/St. Augustine Record, circa 1971. http://augustine.com/history/old-st-augustine/minorcans-augustine.php (accessed April 25, 2011).

Ehat, Andrew F. and Lyndon W. Cook. *The Words of Joseph Smith: The Contemporary Accounts of the Nauvoo Discourses of the Prophet Joseph.* Orem, Utah: Grandin Book Company, 1991.

Endowment House Baptisms for the Dead, microfilm records at Family History Library, Salt Lake City, Utah.

Fackenthal, Benjamin Franklin. *The Homes of George Taylor, Signer of the Declaration of Independence.* Easton, Pennsylvania: Bucks County Historical Society Papers (Reprint), 1922.

Farmer, John, and Jacob Bailey Moore, eds. *Collections, Topographical, Historical and Biographical, Relating Principally to New-Hampshire*, vol. 1. Concord, New Hampshire: H. E. & J. W. Moore, 1831.

Ferguson, Elmer James. *The Papers of Robert Morris, 1781–1784: April 16–July 20, 1782.* Pittsburgh: University of Pittsburgh Press, 1980.

Ferris, Robert G. and Richard E. Morris. *The Signers of the Declaration of Independence.* Flagstaff, Arizona: Interpretive Publications, Inc., 1982.

Find a Grave website.. www.findagrave.com (accessed March 19, 2011).

Fire Island National Seashore—William Floyd (U.S. National Park Service) website. www.nps.gov/fiis/historyculture/williamfloyd.htm (accessed April 6, 2011).

Fleming, Thomas. *The Intimate Lives of the Founding Fathers.* New York: Smithsonian Books, 2009.

Ford, Worthington C., et al. *Journals of the Continental Congress, 1774–1789.* Washington, D.C., 1904–37. http://memory.loc.gov/ammem/amlaw/lwjc.html.

"Forges and Furnaces Collection, 1727–1921." Philadelphia: The Historical Society of Pennsylvania, 2005. http://www.hsp.org/sites/www.hsp.org/files/migrated/findingaid-212forgesandfurnaces.pdf (accessed December 28, 2011).

Franklin, Benjamin. *Benjamin Franklin: The Autobiography and Other Writings.* (Oxford New York: Oxford University Press, 1999.

Gaustad, Edwin. *Benjamin Franklin: Inventing America.* Oxford New York: Oxford University Press, 2004.

The General William Floyd House website. www.generalwilliamfloydhouse.org (accessed March 19, 2011).

Goodrich, Charles Augustus. *Lives of the Signers to the Declaration of Independence.* New York: William Reed and Company, 1829.

Grant, James. *John Adams: Party of One.* New York: Farrar, Straus and Giroux, 2005.

Green, Harry Clinton and Mary Wolcott Green. *The Pioneer Mothers of America: A Record of the More Notable Women of the Early Days of the Country, and Particularly of the Colonial and Revolutionary Periods.* New York: G. P. Putnam's Sons, 1912. Excerpts reprinted as *Wives of the Signers: The Women Behind the Declaration of Independence.* Aledo, Texas: WallBuilder Press, 1997.

Hagaman, Edward. *The Old Martyrs' Prison, New York; An Historical Sketch of the Oldest Municipal Building in New York City: Used As a British Prison During the War for American Independence: Built about 1756 and Known at Different Times As "the New Gaol," "the Debtors' Prison," "the Provost," "the Hall of Records" and "the Register's Office."* New York: American Scenic and Historic Preservation Society, 1902.

Hagerty, James. "Charles Carroll of Carrollton." *Catholic Encyclopedia*, vol. 3. New York: Robert Appleton Company, 1908.

Hartley, William G. *My Fellow Servants: Essays on the History of the Priesthood.* Brigham Young University Studies: Provo, Utah, 2010.

The Howes' Proclamation of November 30, 1776, at Todd Braisted's "The On-Line Institute for Advanced

Loyalist Studies." http://www.royalprovincial.com/military/facts/ofrproc2.htm (accessed November 4, 2012).

Huges, Samuel. "The Artful Rebel: Francis Hopkinson." *The Pennsylvania Gazette*, May/June 2012, 48–57.

Jesse, Dean C., ed. *The Papers of Joseph Smith: Volume 2, Journal, 1832–1842*. Salt Lake City: Deseret Book Company, 1992.

Journal History of The Church of Jesus Christ of Latter-day Saints. LDS Church Archives, Salt Lake City.

Journal of Discourses. 26 vols. London and Liverpool: Latter-day Saints' Book Depot, 1855–1886.

Judson, L. Carroll. *A Biography of the Signers of the Declaration of Independence and of Washington and Patrick Henry with an Appendix Containing the Constitution of the United States and Other Documents*. Philadelphia: J. Dobson, and Thomas, Cowperthwait and Company), 1839.

Kaminski, John P. *The Founders on the Founders: Word Portraits from the American Revolutionary Era*. Charlottesville, Va.: University of Virginia Press, 2008.

Kiernan, Denise and Joseph D'Agnese. *Signing Their Lives Away: The Fame and Misfortune of the Men Who Signed the Declaration of Independence*. Philadelphia: Quirk Books, 2009.

Knight, Betsy. "Prisoner Exchange and Parole in the American Revolution." *The William and Mary Quarterly*, Third Series, vol. 48, no. 2 (April, 1991): 201–22.

Koch, Adrienne and William Peden, eds. *The Life and Selected Writings of Thomas Jefferson*. New York: The Modern Library/Random House, 1944.

Lamplugh, George R. "George Walton, Chief Justice of Georgia, 1783–1785." *Georgia Historical Quarterly*, vol. 65 (Summer 1981): 82–91.

Laux, James B. "The Lost Will of George Taylor, the Signer." *The Pennsylvania Magazine of History and Biography*, January 1920, vol. 44, no. 173: 82–87. (Bound by Philadelphia: Publication Fund of the Historical Society of Pennsylvania, 1920.)

Ludlow, Daniel H. *Encyclopedia of Mormonism: The History, Scripture, Doctrine, and Procedure of the Church of Jesus Christ of Latter-day Saints*. 4 vols. New York: Macmillan, 1992.

Mackley, Jennifer Ann. *Wilford Woodruff's Witness: The Development of Temple Doctrine*. Seattle, Washington: High Desert Publishing, 2014.

Madison, James. *Notes of Debates in the Federal Convention of 1787 Reported by James Madison*. New York: W. W. Norton & Company, 1987.

Malone, Dumas. *Jefferson and His Time, Vol. 1: Jefferson the Virginian*. New York: Little, Brown and Company, 1948.

McAllister, John D. T. (John Daniel Thompson). *John D. T. McAllister Journal*. L. Tom Perry Special Collections, 19th Century Western & Mormon Manuscripts, 1851–1895. Harold B. Lee Library, Brigham Young University, Provo, Utah.

McClure, James. "1776 Declaration of Independence Reading in York Town Re-enacted in Annual Ceremony." YorkBlog.com, July 1,

2010. http://www.yorkblog.com/yorktownsquare/2010/07/01/james-smith/ (accessed December 20, 2011).

McClure, James. "Smith Brought Declaration to York." *York Daily Record/York Sunday News*, August 5, 2006. http://www.ydr.com/ci_4141726 (accessed December 20, 2011).

McCullough, David. *John Adams*. New York: Simon & Schuster, 2001.

Minutes of the Council of Safety of the State of New Jersey. Jersey City, New Jersey: J.H. Lyon, 1872.

Mulder, William and A. Russell Mortensen. *Among the Mormons: Historical Accounts by Contemporary Observers*. New York: Alfred A. Knopf, 1958. Reprinted Lincoln, Nebraska: University of Nebraska Press, 1973.

Olds, Fred A. "The Celebrated Edenton Tea Party." *Daughters of the American Revolution Magazine*, June 1922, vol. 56, no. 6. (Incorrectly identifies Isabella Johnston as the same Isabella Johnston [d. 1766] that was engaged to Signer Joseph Hewes.)

The Papers of Benjamin Franklin. Sponsored by The American Philosophical Society and Yale University. Digital Edition by The Packard Humanities Institute (online version). http://franklinpapers.org (accessed November 17, 2012).

Pickett, Russ. "Delaware's Hero for all Times: 'Soldier, Judge, Governor, Patriot' Caesar Rodney: 4th President of Delaware." 2007. www.russpickett.com/history/rodnbio.htm (accessed December 9, 2011).

Purcell, L. Edward. *Who Was Who in the American Revolution*. New York: Facts On File, 1993.

Rakove, Jack. *Revolutionaries: A New History of the Invention of America*. New York: Houghton Mifflin Harcourt, 2010.

Randall, Willard Sterne. *Thomas Jefferson: A Life*. New York: Henry Holt and Company, Inc., 1993.

Rappleye, Charles. *Robert Morris: Financier of the American Revolution*. New York: Simon & Schuster, 2010.

Ratzlaff, Robert K. *John Rutledge, Jr., South Carolina Federalist, 1766–1819*. Arno Press Inc., 1982.

Read, William Thompson. *Life and Correspondence of George Read: A Signer of the Declaration of Independence; With Notices of Some of His Contemporaries*. Philadelphia: J. B. Lippincott & Company, 1870.

Rush, Benjamin and George W. Corner, eds. *The Autobiography of Benjamin Rush*. Princeton, N.J.: The American Philosophical Society, Princeton University Press, 1948.

Sanderson, John and Robert Taylor Conrad. *Sanderson's Biography of the Signers to the Declaration of Independence*. Philadelphia: Thomas Couperthwaite Company, 1846.

Scheer, George F. and Hugh F. Rankin. *Rebels and Redcoats: The American Revolution Through the Eyes of Those Who Fought and Lived It*. Cleveland: The World Publishing Company, 1957. Reprint: Da Capo Press, Inc., 1987.

Smith, Joseph Smith Jr., *History of The Church of Jesus Christ of Latter-day Saints*. Edited by B. H. Roberts. 7 vols. Deseret Book: Salt Lake City, Utah 1971.

Smith, Joseph West. *Journal of Joseph West Smith*. 11 April 1893.

Special Collections and Manuscripts, Harold B. Lee Library, Brigham Young University, Provo, Utah.

Smith, Paul H., Gerard W. Gawalt, and Rosemary Fry Plakas. *Letters of Delegates to Congress, 1774–1789.* 26 vols. http://memory.loc.gov/ammem/amlaw/lwdg.html.

South Carolina Plantations, "Peachtree Plantation—McClellanville—Charleston County." http://south-carolina-plantations.com/charleston/peachtree.html (accessed on July 21, 2011).

Stapley, Jonathan A. "Adoptive Sealing Ritual in Mormonism." *Journal of Mormon History*, vol. 37, no. 3 (2011): 64.

St. George Temple Baptisms for the Dead, microfilm records at Family History Library, Salt Lake City, Utah.

Stoll, Ira. *Samuel Adams: A Life.* New York: Free Press, 2008.

Stuy, Brian H. "Wilford Woodruffs Vision of the Signers of the Declaration of Independence." *Journal of Mormon History*, vol. 26, no. 1 (2000): 64.

Talbott, Page, ed. *Benjamin Franklin: In Search of a Better World.* New Haven, Connecticut: Yale University Press, 2005.

Thomas, Isaiah and Benjamin Franklin Thomas. *The History of Printing in America.* Albany, New York: American Antiquarian Society, 1874.

Unger, Harlow Giles. *John Hancock: Merchant King and American Patriot.* Edison, N.J.: Castle Books, 2005.

Valis, Glenn. "New Jersey During the Revolution." Webpage about John Hart. http://www.doublegv.com/ggv/JHart.html (accessed March 19, 2011).

Vaughan, Dorothy Mansfield. "This Was a Man: A Biography of General William Whipple." Paper read at the National Society of the Colonial Dames in the State of New Hampshire on February 26, 1964. http://www.whipple.org/william/thiswasaman.html (accessed December 29, 2011).

The Voyage of the Slave Ship Sally website at Brown University. http://www.stg.brown.edu/projects/sally/ (accessed April 30, 2011).

Wallace, D. D. *Constitutional History of South Carolina from 1725 to 1775.* Abbevile, South Carolina: Hugh Wilson, Printer, 1899.

Whitney, David C. *Founders of Freedom in America: Lives of the Men Who Signed the Declaration of Independence and so Helped to Establish the United States of America.* Chicago: J. G. Ferguson Publishing Company, 1964.

Wilbor, Elsie M. *Werner's Readings and Recitations, No. 6.* New York: Edgar S. Werner, 1891.

Winder, Mike and Ronald L. Fox. *When the White House Comes to Zion.* American Fork, Utah: Covenant Communications, 2011.

Wood, Dale Glen, *Brigham Young's Activities in St. George During the Later Years of his Life.* MS thesis, Brigham Young University, 1963.

Woodruff, Wilford. "The Law of Adoption: Discourses Delivered at the General Conference of the Church, in the Tabernacle, Salt Lake City, Utah, Sunday Morning, April 8, 1894" *The Deseret Weekly*, vol. 48, no. 18 (April 21, 1894): 541–44. books.google.com/books?id=3WXUAAAAMAA-

J8pg=PA541#v=onepage&q&f=false (accessed October 4, 2014). Also see: *The Utah Genealogical and Historical Magazine*, vol. 13, no. 4 (October, 1922): 145–52.

Woodruff, Wilford. "Remarks Made at the Salt Lake Stake Conference Sunday, December 12, 1897." *Deseret Evening News*, December 18, 1897, 9. udn.lib.utah.edu/cdm/compoundobject/collection/den1895/id/138051/rec/296 (accessed October 4, 2014).

Woodruff, Wilford. *Wilford Woodruff's Journal, 1833–1898, Typescript*. Edited by Scott G. Kenney. 9 vols. Midvale, Utah: Signature Books, 1983–1985.

Woodruff, Wilford, and Brian H. Stuy, *Collected Discourses Delivered by Wilford Woodruff, His Two Counselors, The Twelve Apostles, and Others*. Burbank, Calif.: B.H.S. Pub, 1987.

Woods Jr., David Walker. *John Witherspoon*. New York: Fleming H. Revell Company, 1906.

Wright, Robert K., *The Continental Army*. Washington, D.C.: United States Army Center of Military History, 1983.

Wyllie, John Cook, ed. "New Documentary Light on Tarleton's Raid: Letters of Newman Brockenbrough and Peter Lyons." *The Virginia Magazine of History and Biography*, vol. 74, no. 4 (October 1966): 452–61.

Yorgason, Blaine M., Richard A. Schmutz, and Douglas D. Alder. *All That Was Promised: The St. George Temple and the Unfolding of the Restoration*. Salt Lake City: Deseret Book, 2013.

Source Notes
Abbreviations Used

FF Whitney, David C. *Founders of Freedom in America: Lives of the Men Who Signed the Declaration of Independence and so Helped to Establish the United States of America.* Chicago: J. G. Ferguson Publishing Company, 1964.

FOF Kaminski, John P. *The Founders on the Founders: Word Portraits from the American Revolutionary Era.* Charlottesville, Va.: University of Virginia Press, 2008.

IL Fleming, Thomas. *The Intimate Lives of the Founding Fathers.* New York: Smithsonian Books, 2009.

SD Ferris, Robert G. and Richard E. Morris. *The Signers of the Declaration of Independence.* Flagstaff, Arizona: Interpretive Publications, Inc., 1982.

SDB Barthelmas, Della Gray. *The Signers of the Declaration of Independence: A Biographical and Genealogical Reference.* Jefferson, North Carolina: McFarland and Company, Inc., Publishers, 1997.

STL Kiernan, Denise and Joseph D'Agnese. *Signing Their Lives Away: The Fame and Misfortune of the Men Who Signed the Declaration of Independence.* Philadelphia: Quirk Books, 2009.

WW Purcell, L. Edward. *Who Was Who in the American Revolution.* New York: Facts On File, 1993.

WWJ Woodruff, Wilford. *Wilford Woodruff's Journal, 1833–1898, Typescript.* Edited by Scott G. Kenney. 9 vols. Midvale, Utah: Signature Books, 1983–1985.

ENDNOTES

1. *Conference Report of The Church of Jesus Christ of Latter-day Saints*, Sixty-Eighth Annual Conference, 89 (April 10, 1898).

2. See, for example, Doctrine and Covenants 121:39, taken from an inspired letter of Joseph Smith: "We have learned by sad experience that it is the nature and disposition of almost all men, as soon as they get a little authority, as they suppose, they will immediately begin to exercise unrighteous dominion."

3. Woodruff, "The Law of Adoption," *The Deseret Weekly*, April 21, 1894, 544. Compare Woodruff, "Remarks Made at the Salt Lake Stake Conference," *Deseret Evening News*, December 18, 1897, 9.

4. Alexander, *Things in Heaven and Earth: The Life and Times of Wilford Woodruff, a Mormon Prophet*, 5–6.

5. *Journal of Discourses*, 22:332. This dream was recounted by Woodruff on October 8, 1881, in a discourse about dreams.

6. Alexander, *Things in Heaven and Earth*, 18–19.

7. Baugh, "Images of Wilford Woodruff's Life," in *Banner of the Gospel: Wilford Woodruff*, 7.

8. Alexander, *Things in Heaven and Earth*, 21.

9. Baugh, "Images of Wilford Woodruff's Life," in *Banner of the Gospel: Wilford Woodruff*, 7.

10. Bishop, "'What Has Become of Our Fathers?': Baptism for the Dead at Nauvoo," 86; Ehat, *The Words of Joseph Smith: The Contemporary Accounts of the Nauvoo Discourses of the Prophet Joseph*, 49.

11. Woodruff, "Remarks Made at the Salt Lake Stake Conference," *Deseret Evening News*, December 18, 1897, 9.

12. Modern practice and official LDS Church policies prohibit members of the Church from performing celebrity baptisms and ask Mormons to focus on their own family and ancestors.

13. Bishop, "'What Has Become of Our Fathers?': Baptism for the Dead at Nauvoo," 90. In an 1887 letter to James Henry Martineau, Woodruff discourages doing temple work for those "outside of his own kindred." He does, however, give "wise discretion" for allowing people to do work for friends "when they satisfy you that they have no representative in the Church." Anderson, *The Development of LDS Temple Worship 1846–2000: A Documentary History*, 67–68.

14. Black, *Annotated Record of Baptisms for the Dead 1840–1845: Nauvoo, Hancock County, Illinois*, 1:23 (1841 baptism).

15. Bishop, "'What Has Become of Our Fathers?': Baptism for the Dead at Nauvoo," 90.

16. George Washington was baptized by proxy in 1841 by Stephen Jones. Black, *Annotated Record of Baptisms for the Dead 1840–1845*, 3:2016. Washington was also baptized by John Harrington and by Don Carlos Smith that year. Black, *Annotated Record of Baptisms for the Dead 1840–1845*, 3:1573.

17. Black, *Annotated Record of Baptisms for the Dead 1840–1845*, 3:1565, 2015; Bishop, "'What Has Become of Our Fathers?': Baptism for the Dead at Nauvoo," 90.

18. Ehat, *The Words of Joseph Smith*, 79; Smith, *History of the Church*, 4:426. Emphasis in original.

19. Baugh, "'Blessed Is the First Man Baptised in This Font': Reuben McBride, First Proxy to Be Baptized for the Dead in the Nauvoo Temple," 253–259; Baugh, "'For This Ordinance Belongeth to My House': The Practice of Baptism for the Dead Outside the Nauvoo Temple," 53.

20. Baugh, "For This Ordinance Belongeth to My House," 54.

21. Black, *Annotated Record of Baptisms for the Dead 1840–1845*, 6:3915. Bulah Woodruff's work was done on April 21, 1842. See *WWJ*, 2:165, 177, where Woodruff was baptized, among others, for his mother and two brothers. He was baptized in the river for Robert Mason on August 26, 1842. His journal typescript says "1841," which would have been impossible since he was still returning from his mission to England. *WWJ*, 2:204–205.

22. Mulder, *Among the Mormons: Historical Accounts by Contemporary Observers*, 122–123.

23. Historian Richard E. Bennett described the endowment as "a ceremonial washing and anointing, a series of lectures and dramatizations on the purpose of earth life and the plan of salvation, the making of sacred covenants, and an enriching sense of the divine presence." Bennett, "'Line upon Line, Precept upon Precept': Reflections on the 1877 Commencement of the Performance of Endowments and Sealings for the Dead," 46; Alma P. Burton, "Endowment" in *Encyclopedia of Mormonism*, 2:455;

24. *Journal of Discourses*, 2:31 (April 6, 1853). Emphasis in original. Bennett, "Line upon Line, Precept upon Precept," 46.

25. *WWJ*, 2:326–327. Woodruff wrote about how Hyrum Smith performed their eternal marriage: "He sealed the marrige Covenant between me & my Wife Phebe W. Carter for time & eternity & gave us the principle of it which was interesting to us." Holzapfel, "Wilford Woodruff's 1897 Testimony," in *Banner of the Gospel: Wilford Woodruff*, 352–354.

26. Anderson, *Joseph Smith's Quorum of the Anointed 1842–1845*, 38–39, 44–45.

27. Alexander, *Things in Heaven and Earth*, 107.

28. Bennett, "Line upon Line, Precept upon Precept," 63.

29. Brown, *In Heaven as it is On Earth: Joseph Smith and the Early Mormon Conquest of Death*, 204.

30. See Stapley, "Adoptive Sealing Ritual in Mormonism," 58.

31. Alexander, *Things in Heaven and Earth*, 123–124.

32. Ibid., 124–125.

33. Alexander, *Things in Heaven and Earth*, 130–131; Brown, "Chronology of the Construction, Destruction and Reconstruction of the Nauvoo Temple."

34. Alexander, *Things in Heaven and Earth*, 178.

35. Bennett, "Line upon Line, Precept upon Precept," 49.

36. Bennett, "Line upon Line, Precept upon Precept," 50; Alexander, *Things in Heaven and Earth*, 177.

37. *Journal of Discourses*, 16:186.

38. Ibid., 16:186–187. Brigham Young said he and none of his siblings were sealed to their own father even though it could have been done in the Nauvoo Temple. The press of events in those days prevented their temple work from happening at that time—but Young trusted it would be done in the future.

39. *Journal of Discourses*, 16:187–188.

40. Hartley, *My Fellow Servants: Essays on the History of the Priesthood*, 438.

41. When the Endowment house was first built, it did not include a baptismal font. That font was added later and so some work for the dead was able to begin again—although the proxy work for the dead was still restricted to marriage sealings and baptism for the dead.

42. Alexander, *Things in Heaven and Earth*, 201. See *WWJ*, 6:477, 478, 485, for some of Woodruff's activity with temple ordinances in the Endowment House.

43. Stuy, "Wilford Woodruffs Vision of the Signers of the Declaration of Independence."

44. Ibid., 68.

45. "Endowment House Baptisms for the Dead," film number 183384; Stuy, "Wilford Woodruffs Vision of the Signers of the Declaration of Independence," 68.

46. Stuy, "Wilford Woodruffs Vision of the Signers of the Declaration of Independence," 68.

47. Jesse, *The Papers of Joseph Smith: Volume 2, Journal, 1832–1842*, 526.

48. Stuy, "Wilford Woodruffs Vision of the Signers of the Declaration of Independence," 68.

49. Ibid. Bernhisel was baptized for Benjamin Rush on July 8, 1874, right after Independence Day.

50. Stuy, "Wilford Woodruffs Vision of the Signers of the Declaration of Independence," 69. Stuy calls Bernhisel's work "a systematic program of proxy work for the Founding Fathers and other U.S. leaders."

51. *WWJ*, 7:282.

52. Stuy, "Wilford Woodruffs Vision of the Signers of the Declaration of Independence," 69. Woodruff was at a funeral. *WWJ*, 7:282.

53. Curtis, *History of the St. George Temple*, 106–107; Bennett, "Line upon Line, Precept upon Precept," 51; Hartley, *My Fellow Servants: Essays on the History of the Priesthood*, 438.

54. Bennett, "Line upon Line, Precept upon Precept," 51.

55. Wood, *Brigham Young's Activities in St. George During the Later Years of his Life*, 32.

56. Curtis, *History of the St. George Temple*, 20.

57. Ibid., 43, 74.

58. Ibid., 43.

59. *WWJ*, 7:289; Stuy, "Wilford Woodruffs Vision of the Signers of the Declaration of Independence," 75.

60. *WWJ*, 7:291 (November 9, 1876).

61. Ibid., 7:292.

62. Bennett, "Line upon Line, Precept upon Precept," 59.

63. *WWJ*, 7:303–320.

64. Ibid., 7:304.
65. Curtis, *History of the St. George Temple*, 86. Emphasis in original.
66. *WWJ*, 7:318.
67. Ibid., 7:318–320. Woodruff wrote in his journal that Young's feet "began to amend from the time he made his speech." The pulpit itself was removed from its place on the east of the St. George Temple second-floor assembly room in 1938 and put in storage.
68. *WWJ*, 7:303.
69. Bennett, "Line upon Line, Precept upon Precept," 61.
70. *WWJ*, 7:321.
71. Ibid., 6:390.
72. Ibid., 7:321.
73. Bennett, "Line upon Line, Precept upon Precept," 39–40.
74. Ibid., 62.
75. Ibid., 64.
76. *WWJ*, 7:322.
77. Bennett, "Line upon Line, Precept upon Precept," 64.
78. *WWJ*, 7:329; Bennett, "Line upon Line, Precept upon Precept," 64.
79. *WWJ*, 7:338. Eudora's first marriage ended in divorce. Her marriage to Woodruff did as well. Her third marriage was to a non-Mormon judge. Eudora's sister, Susa Young Gates, became well known for her work in the Church and nationally in striving for equal rights for women.
80. *WWJ*, 7:340–341.
81. Wood, *Brigham Young's Activities in St. George During the Later Years of his Life*, 58.
82. *WWJ*, 7:342.
83. Curtis, *History of the St. George Temple*, 92.
84. *WWJ*, 7:344.
85. Stapley, "Adoptive Sealing Ritual in Mormonism," 92; *WWJ*, 7:345. The sealing took place on April 13, 1877.
86. *WWJ*, 7:354–355.
87. *WWJ*, 7:358; McAllister, *John D. T. McAllister Journal*, 3:38–39.
88. All misspellings in this passage are part of the original source.
89. *WWJ*, 7:261.
90. Burton, *The City of the Saints and Across the Rocky Mountains to California*, 250.
91. *WWJ*, 7:358.
92. Hartley, *My Fellow Servants: Essays on the History of the Priesthood*, 237.
93. Ibid., 229–231.
94. Ibid., 231.
95. Hartley, *My Fellow Servants: Essays on the History of the Priesthood*, 229, 235; *WWJ*, 7:343.
96. Hartley, *My Fellow Servants: Essays on the History of the Priesthood*, 240.
97. Ibid.
98. McAllister, *John D. T. McAllister Journal*, 3:245
99. Hartley, *My Fellow Servants: Essays on the History of the Priesthood*, 236.
100. Ibid., 258.

101. See, for example, a talk Woodruff gave on October 6, 1896, in which he stated, "Joseph Smith visited me a great deal after his death, and taught me many important principles." In that talk, he mentioned that the last time he'd seen the Prophet was "in the night vision." Stuy, *Collected Discourses Delivered by Wilford Woodruff, His Two Counselors, The Twelve Apostles, and Others*, 5:237. Woodruff also wrote in his journal on March 19, 1894, about how he "met with Benjamin Franklin" and "spent several hours with him." However, in that same dream, Franklin appeared to die. "I thought then He died," Woodruff wrote, "and while waiting for burial I awoke." *WWJ*, 9:293.

102. *Journal of Discourses*, 22:331–332. Woodruff spoke for thirty-three minutes. *WWJ*, 8:59.

103. *Journal of Discourses*, 22:333.

104. Woodruff was obviously living somewhere outside the temple in May 1877. He had to take a carriage to it. *WWJ*, 7:350 (May 17, 1877). The descendants of the Thomas and Caroline Cottam family have a family tradition that Woodruff had his vision of the Signers while staying in the Cottams' upstairs room. Yorgason, *All That Was Promised: The St. George Temple and the Unfolding of the Restoration*, 304. See footnote 4. While this is possible, Woodruff said in 1898 that it took place in the temple. On the other hand, he could have had the dreams at a home and, in his dreams, been in the temple.

105. James G. Bleak, who kept many of the records for the St. George Temple, had a bed in his temple office. He went to the temple in the late afternoon and, as he described in his journal in the spring of 1888, "arrived there safely." He continued, "Found C. L. Walker asleep in my bed, which is a liberty he is not justified in taking. I have said nothing to him about it, but shall lock the door hereafter while he is about." Bleak, *James Godson Bleak Journal*, (Sunday, April 22, 1888). Bleak became temple recorder later that year. Addy, *James Godson Bleak: Pioneer Historian of Southern Utah*, 52.

106. *WWJ*, 7:366–367; *Conference Report of The Church of Jesus Christ of Latter-day Saints*, Sixty-Eighth Annual Conference, 89 (April 10, 1898).

107. *WWJ*, 7:373; *Journal of Discourses*, 19:223–230.

108. McAllister, *John D. T. McAllister Journal*, 6:153.

109. Smith, *Journal of Joseph West Smith*, 77. Compare to McAllister, *John D. T. McAllister Journal*, 6:154–155.

110. Woodruff, "Remarks Made at the Salt Lake Stake Conference," *Deseret Evening News*, December 18, 1897, 9.

111. *Conference Report of The Church of Jesus Christ of Latter-day Saints*, Sixty-Eighth Annual Conference, 89–90 (April 10, 1898); *WWJ*, 9:544.

112. *WWJ*, 7:367.

113. *WWJ*, 7:395 (January 14-15, 1878). "I spent the day mostly writing. I wrote up my Journal." *WWJ*, 7:353 (June 5, 1887).

114. *Journal of Discourses*, 19:228.

115. *Journal of Discourses*, 19:229.

116. *Journal of Discourses*, 19:229; Smith, *Journal of Joseph West Smith*, 77.

117. *Conference Report of The Church of Jesus Christ of Latter-day Saints*, Sixty-Eighth Annual Conference, 89 (April 10, 1898).

118. *Journal of Discourses*, 19:229.

119. Ibid.

120. *Conference Report of The Church of Jesus Christ of Latter-day Saints*, Sixty-Eighth Annual Conference, 89 (April 10, 1898).

121. *Journal of Discourses*, 19:229.

122. Smith, *Journal of Joseph West Smith*, 77.

123. See *Journal of Discourses*, 19:229.

124. "St. George Temple Baptisms for the Dead," film number 1262968 and film number 1262904.

125. Levi Ward Hancock, John Hancock's third cousin, performed John Hancock's baptism on May 29, 1877, and his endowment work on March 13, 1877. Addison Everret performed William Floyd's baptism on March 13, 1877. It also appears to have been done on February 14, 1877. Floyd's endowment was completed on June 14, 1877.

126. *Journal of Discourses*, 19:229. Woodruff used similar language in his journal—perhaps quoting the Signers when he wrote his August 21, 1877, entry: "I felt thankful that we had the privilege and the power to administer for the worthy dead esspecially for the signers of the declaration of Independance, that inasmuch as they had laid the foundation of our Government that we Could do as much for them as they had done for us." *WWJ*, 7:369.

127. *Journal of Discourses*, 19:229.

128. *Conference Report of The Church of Jesus Christ of Latter-day Saints*, Sixty-Eighth Annual Conference, 89–90 (April 10, 1898).

129. Historian Richard E. Bennett said, "Preliminary research into the diaries of the time indicate that most members were as unprepared for the doctrine as they were unschooled in the practice. When talk was made of redeeming the dead, most referred to it in terms of baptisms for the dead. Conspicuously absent in contemporary literature among the Latter-day Saints from 1850 to 1877 was any mention of endowments for the dead." (Bennett, "Line upon Line, Precept upon Precept," 57.)

130. *Journal of Discourses*, 19:228. Compare *WWJ*, 6:390.

131. Alexander, *Things in Heaven and Earth*, 215.

132. Bennett, "Line upon Line, Precept upon Precept," 66.

133. Woodruff, "Remarks Made at the Salt Lake Stake Conference," *Deseret Evening News*, December 18, 1897, 9.

134. *WWJ*, 7:367.

135. Ibid.

136. Winder and Fox, *When the White House Comes to Zion*, 11–13. On October 3, 1875, Ulysses S. Grant was the first president of the United States to visit Utah. Woodruff was impressed to see the two presidents, Brigham Young and Grant, meeting.

137. Van Buren was unpopular among Mormons for not helping the persecuted Saints who were driven from their homes in the late 1830s under Missouri's official sanction. Buchanan was unpopular for sending an army in 1857 to quell a nonexisting Mormon rebellion.

138. Stuy, "Wilford Woodruff's Vision of the Signers of the Declaration of Independence," 72–73, 75.

139. *WWJ*, 7:367–369.

140. Stuy, "Wilford Woodruff's Vision of the Signers of the Declaration of Independence," 73. Thirteen women were not mentioned in *Portrait Gallery*. Of those, Stuy said nine were related to George Washington.

141. See Appendix 8 for a discussion of an account that claims to be written by James Godson Bleak and that talks about others appearing to Woodruff, such as Martin Luther, who was not on any of Woodruff's lists. Compare to the analysis in Yorgason, *All That Was Promised*, 309–310.

142. *WWJ*, 7:367–369. The published transcript of Woodruff's journal scrambles the order of Signers and eminent men and omits Robert

143. McAllister, *John D. T. McAllister Journal*, 3:48. In his journal, McAllister said, "This day I was Baptised for all the dead Presidents of the United States except Martin Van Buren & Jas Buchanan. this day Sister Lucy B Young was Baptised for Maria Fackrell." McAllister did not mention he participated in 1871 in the baptisms of eleven of the Signers including Benjamin Franklin and two presidents Andrew Jackson and James K. Polk.

144. *WWJ*, 7:369; *Journal of Discourses*, 19:229.

145. Stuy, "Wilford Woodruff's Vision of the Signers of the Declaration of Independence," 80.

146. *WWJ*, 7:369.

147. Ibid.

148. Ibid.

149. McAllister, *John D. T. McAllister Journal*, 3:48; *WWJ*, 7:369.

150. *WWJ*, 7:369; McAllister, *John D. T. McAllister Journal*, 3:48.

151. *WWJ*, 7:367–369.

152. Bennett, "Line upon Line, Precept upon Precept," 67.

153. *WWJ*, 7:370–372.

154. Ibid., 7:373.

155. *Journal of Discourses*, 19:228.

156. *WWJ*, 7:373.

157. Bleak, *James Godson Bleak Journal*, (Friday, October 21, 1887).

158. Joseph West Smith recorded in his journal the words of Woodruff at a dedication session of the Salt Lake Temple: "The last ten days of my life have been the most interesting. I have learned why my life has been spared. The reason why a representative of the Woodruff family was called to preside is because the Lord could not find a weaker vessel. The devil is not always going to have power over us. The Presidency have never called themselves." (Smith, *Journal of Joseph West Smith*, 80 [Friday, April 14, 1893]). Compare President Woodruff's sentiments to 1 Corinthians 1:27: "But God hath chosen the foolish things of the world to confound the wise; and God hath chosen the weak things of the world to confound the things which are mighty."

159. McAllister, *John D. T. McAllister Journal*, 6:153 (Friday, April 7, 1893).

160. Ibid., 6:154–155 (Tuesday, April 11, 1893).

161. Smith, *Journal of Joseph West Smith*, 77–78 (Tuesday, April 11, 1893).

162. Woodruff wrote about Brigham Young's views on the law of adoption at a meeting on February 16, 1847: "The Lord introduced the law of adoption for the benefit of the children of men as a school master to bring them back into the covenant of the Priesthood," Brigham Young said. "This Principle I am aware is not clearly understood by many of the Elders in this Church at the present time as it will Hereafter be: And I confess that I have had ownly a smattering of those things but when it is necessary I will attain to more knowledge on the subject & consequently will be enabled to teach & practice more and will in the mean time glorify God the bountiful giver." *WWJ*, 3:134.

163. Stapley, "Adoptive Sealing Ritual in Mormonism," 100.

164. Ibid., 103.

165. Ibid., 104. See also footnote 141.

166. Woodruff, "The Law of Adoption," *The Deseret Weekly*, April 21, 1894, 542.

167. Allen, *Hearts Turned to the Fathers: A History of the Genealogical Society of Utah, 1894–1994*, 42.

168. Woodruff, "The Law of Adoption," *The Deseret Weekly*, April 21, 1894, 543. Woodruff added, "When you get to the end, let the last man be adopted to Joseph Smith, who stands at the head of the dispensation. This is the will of the Lord to this people." The idea of adopting

to Joseph Smith was later clarified, and this requirement was dropped for the moment—perhaps because it would be easy for people to give up on their family history research. It may also be because the final adjustment and wrapping up of dispensationary priesthood chains is best left for the Millennium.

169. Wilford Woodruff left a space in his journal for the text of the revelation, but never recorded it there and there is no known copy. *WWJ*, 9:296. See also Stapley, "Adoptive Sealing Ritual in Mormonism," 109.

170. Woodruff, "The Law of Adoption," *The Deseret Weekly*, April 21, 1894, 543.

171. *Conference Report of The Church of Jesus Christ of Latter-day Saints*, Sixty-Eighth Annual Conference, 89–90 (April 10, 1898).

172. Alexander, *Things in Heaven and Earth*, 329–330.

173. *Deseret Evening News*, "President Woodruff Is Dead," September 2, 1898, 1.

174. "While some will ever associate him with missionary work, his most long-lasting contributions to the history of the Church may well have occurred within temple walls," historian Richard E. Bennett said. (Bennett, "Line upon Line, Precept upon Precept," 57.)

175. *Conference Report of The Church of Jesus Christ of Latter-day Saints*, Sixty-Eighth Annual Conference, 92 (April 10, 1898). Four months before April conference, at the Salt Lake stake conference, President Woodruff said something similar: "I do not want to go into the spirit world and meet with my progenitors who never heard the Gospel in their day and generation, and have them tell me, 'You held in your hand the power to go forth and redeem me, and you have not done it.' I do not want to meet that. I do not want the Latter-day Saints to meet it." (Woodruff, "Remarks Made at the Salt Lake Stake Conference," *Deseret Evening News*, December 18, 1897, 9.)

176. Puls, *Samuel Adams: Father of the American Revolution*, 156.

177. Ibid. Compare *FF*, 49. This particular bribe story comes from the memory of Adams's daughter Hannah and was told in 1818.

178. Puls, *Samuel Adams: Father of the American Revolution*, 1, 22. Under the Julian calendar used at the time he was born, Adams's birthdate was September 16, 1722.

179. Puls, *Samuel Adams: Father of the American Revolution*, 22.

180. *WW*, 6; *FF*, 46; *R*, 39.

181. *SDB*, 18; Puls, *Samuel Adams: Father of the American Revolution*, 23, 25.

182. Puls, *Samuel Adams: Father of the American Revolution*, 25–26.

183. Ibid., 27; *SDB*, 18; *FF*, 46.

184. Rakove, *Revolutionaries: A New History of the Invention of America*, 39; *FF*, 46; Puls, *Samuel Adams: Father of the American Revolution*, 28.

185. *SDB*, 18; Puls, *Samuel Adams: Father of the American Revolution*, 28.

186. Rakove, *Revolutionaries: A New History of the Invention of America*, 39.

187. Puls, *Samuel Adams: Father of the American Revolution*, 29.

188. Puls, *Samuel Adams: Father of the American Revolution*, 29; *SDB*, 22.

189. *SDB*, 18.

190. *SDB*, 18; *WW*, 6; Rakove, *Revolutionaries: A New History of the Invention of America*, 39.

191. Puls, *Samuel Adams: Father of the American Revolution*, 31; *SDB*, 22.

192. *FF*, 47; *WW*, 6. In 1763 the Boston tax collection was under target by 4,000 pounds. Adams was short 2,200 pounds in collections. (Puls, *Samuel Adams: Father of the American Revolution*, 34.)

193. *SDB*, 22.

194. Puls, *Samuel Adams: Father of the American Revolution*, 36.

195. *SD*, 37.

196. *SDB*, 21–22.

197. *FF*, 47.

198. Puls, *Samuel Adams: Father of the American Revolution*, 62–63.

199. Ibid., 16.

200. Ibid., 67.

201. Ibid., 68.

202. *WW*, 7.

203. *SD*, 37.

204. Puls, *Samuel Adams: Father of the American Revolution*, 77.

205. *SDB*, 18.

206. *SD*, 37.

207. Ibid.; *FF*, 47.

208. *FF*, 48.

209. "Condescending" means talking down to people.

210. *FF*, 48.

211. *WW*, 7.

212. *SDB*, 19.

213. *WW*, 7.

214. *SD*, 37.

215. *SDB*, 20; *WW*, 7.

216. *WW*, 7.

217. Puls, *Samuel Adams: Father of the American Revolution*, 146; *SDB*, 20.

218. *WW*, 7; *SDB*, 20.

219. *SD*, 38; *SDB*, 20; *WW*, 7; Rakove, *Revolutionaries: A New History of the Invention of America*, 49; *FF*, 48; Puls, *Samuel Adams: Father of the American Revolution*, 154.

220. *SD*, 38.

221. *FF*, 49.

222. Rakove, *Revolutionaries: A New History of the Invention of America*, 59. Joseph Galloway was the Pennsylvania assembly's speaker and later became a refugee loyalist in Britain, where he made this assessment.

223. *WW*, 7; *SDB*, 20.

224. *SD*, 38, *SDB*, 20–21, *FF*, 49.

225. *FF*, 51.

226. *FF*, 46, 49; Puls, *Samuel Adams: Father of the American Revolution*, 171.

227. After recounting the events of the battles of Lexington and Concord, Gage said: "In this exigency of complicated calamities, I avail myself of the last effort within the bounds of my duty to spare the effusion of blood, to offer, and I do hereby in his Majesty's name offer and promise, his most gracious pardon in all to who shall forthwith lay down their arms, and return to the duties of peaceable subjects, excepting only from the benefit of such pardon, Samuel Adams and John Hancock, whose offences are of too flagitious a nature to admit of any other consideration about than that of condign punishments." *FF*, 49. "An American Time Capsule: Three Centuries of Broadsides and Other Printed Ephemera," Library of Congress website.

228. *SDB*, 21; *WW*, 7.

229. *WW*, 7.

230. *FF*, 46

231. *WW*, 7.

232. *SDB*, 21; Puls, *Samuel Adams: Father of the American Revolution*, 2.

233. *FF*, 51.

234. *SD*, 39; *STL*, 32; *FF*, 51.

235. *FF*, 51.

236. *SD*, 39; *STL*, 33; *FF*, 51; *WW*, 7.

237. Puls, *Samuel Adams: Father of the American Revolution*, 2.

238. FF, 51.

239. Puls, *Samuel Adams: Father of the American Revolution*, 2; WW, 7; SD, 39; FF, 46.

240. FF, 51; Puls, *Samuel Adams: Father of the American Revolution*, front matter.

241. FOF, 65–66. Emphasis in original.

242. McCullough, *John Adams*, 179.

243. Ibid., 188.

244. Ibid., 181.

245. Ibid., 186.

246. Ibid., 187.

247. WW, 5; SDB, 12. October 19, 1735 Old Style, Julian calendar.

248. FF, 34.

249. WW, 5.

250. SDB, 8.

251. SD, 33.

252. FF, 34.

253. WW, 5; SDB, 8; FF, 34.

254. IL, 130.

255. SDB, 12; FF, 34.

256. IL, 132.

257. WW, 5; FF, 34; SDB, 8.

258. FF, 34; WW, 5; SD, 34.

259. WW, 5; FF, 34–35.

260. FF, 35.

261. Ibid.

262. SDB, 9.

263. FF, 36.

264. FOF, 22. Letter to Abigail Adams, October 7, 1775.

265. FF, 37.

266. Ibid., 38.

267. Smith, *Letters of Delegates to Congress, 1774–1789*, 4:60–61 (May 22, 1776, John Adams to Abigail Adams).

268. FF, 38,

269. WW, 5; FF, 38; SDB, 9; Scheer, *Rebels and Redcoats: The American Revolution Through the Eyes of Those Who Fought and Lived It*, 150. On that committee were John Adams, Benjamin Franklin, Thomas Jefferson, Robert Livingston, and Roger Sherman.

270. WW, 5.

271. FOF, 60. Conversation with Daniel Webster, 1824.

272. Smith, *Letters of Delegates to Congress, 1774–1789*, 4:374–375 (July 3, 1776, John Adams to Abigail Adams).

273. Ibid., 4:376 (July 3, 1776, John Adams to Abigail Adams).

274. FF, 38.

275. FOF, 24. Letter of Benjamin Rush, September 16, 1776.

276. SD, 34.

277. SD, 35; WW, 5.

278. Adams, *The Works of John Adams, Second President of the United States: with a Life of the Author, Notes and Illustrations, by his Grandson Charles Francis Adams*, 3:189 (February 11 1779).

279. WW, 5; FF, 40.

280. FF, 41.

281. FOF, 31–32. A disenchanted Alexander Hamilton in 1800 said these were not compliments but were an example of the French having "a very dexterous knack of disguising a sarcasm."

282. WW, 6.

283. FF, 42.

284. WW, 6.

285. McCullough, *John Adams*, 436–437; FF, 42–43.

286. FF, 43.

287. Ibid.

288. SDB, 11.

289. FF, 44.

290. Ibid.

291. SDB, 12; FOF, 2.

292. FOF, 60.

293. FF, 44.

294. WW, 6.

295. SD, 35.

296. McCullough, *John Adams*, 645.

297. FF, 52.

298. WW, 38.

299. Smith, *Letters of Delegates to Congress, 1774–1789*, 4:351 (Josiah Bartlett to John Langdon, July 1, 1776).

300. People who look at the written document may assume the column on the left had the first signatures. It is the opposite and begins with Bartlett's signature in a column on the right. The delegates signed as state delegations, some adding their signatures later.

301. SD, 42.

302. FF, 56.

303. FF, 55; *Biographical Directory of the United States Congress 1774–Present*.

304. Green, *Wives of the Signers: The Women Behind the Declaration of Independence*, 258; SDB, 33; FF, 55

305. Brown University Steering Committee on Slavery and Justice, *Repository of Historical Documents*.

306. SDB, 32; WW, 59; Rakove, *Revolutionaries: A New History of the Invention of America*, 178–179.

307. Find a Grave website.

308. Burke, *American Connections: The Founding Fathers. Networked*, 223.

309. SDB, 32; FF, 57.

310. FF, 57.

311. SDB, 38. Goodrich tells a slightly different version of the events. Goodrich, *Lives of the Signers to the Declaration of Independence*, 359.

312. SDB, 39; Rakove, *Revolutionaries: A New History of the Invention of America*, 187.

313. John Carroll eventually became the first Catholic Bishop in America, and Daniel Carroll was a signer of the Constitution and a member of the first United States Congress. FF, 58.

314. FF, 58.

315. Rakove, *Revolutionaries: A New History of the Invention of America*, 187.

316. FF, 58; SD, 43; Burke, *American Connections: The Founding Fathers. Networked*, 196.

317. FF, 58.

318. Ibid., 59–61.

319. Goodrich, *Lives of the Signers to the Declaration of Independence*, 362; FF, 61.

320. FF, 61.

321. Hagerty, "Charles Carroll of Carrollton."

322. WW, 85; SD, 44.

323. FF, 62.

324. Burke, *American Connections: The Founding Fathers. Networked*, 196.

325. *FF*, 64.

326. Ibid., 63.

327. *SDB*, 44.

328. *FOF*, 103.

329. Ibid., 101.

330. Ibid., 102.

331. Ibid., 105.

332. *FF*, 65.

333. *FOF*, 107.

334. Ibid., 106.

335. Goodrich, *Lives of the Signers to the Declaration of Independence*, 345.

336. *FF*, 69.

337. Burke, *American Connections: The Founding Fathers. Networked*, 112.

338. *FF*, 68.

339. *FOF*, 476.

340. *WW*, 96.

341. *FF*, 69.

342. Sanderson, *Sanderson's Biography of the Signers to the Declaration of Independence*, 261.

343. *FF*, 71.

344. Ibid., 70.

345. *FF*, 71; *WW*, 103; *SDB*, 52.

346. *FF*, 71; *SDB*, 52.

347. *FF*, 72–73.

348. Ibid., 73.

349. Ibid., 76.

350. Scheer, *Rebels and Redcoats*, 303.

351. *FF*, 75. Compare Matthew 10:37: "He that loveth father or mother more than me is not worthy of me: and he that loveth son or daughter more than me is not worthy of me."

352. *WW*, 151.

353. *FF*, 77.

354. *FF*, 78; Sanderson, *Sanderson's Biography of the Signers to the Declaration of Independence*, 194.

355. *WW*, 165.

356. *FF*, 78.

357. *FF*, 79; Goodrich, *Lives of the Signers to the Declaration of Independence*, 185.

358. Judson, *A Biography of the Signers of the Declaration of Independence and of Washington and Patrick Henry with an Appendix Containing the Constitution of the United States and Other Documents*, 109.

359. *WW*, 165; The General William Floyd House website.

360. Fire Island National Seashore—William Floyd (U.S. National Park Service) website.

361. *FF*, 79; Judson, *A Biography of the Signers of the Declaration of Independence and of Washington and Patrick Henry*, 111.

362. The General William Floyd House website; Goodrich, *Lives of the Signers to the Declaration of Independence*, 185; *FF*, 79; *WW*, 165.

363. Judson, *A Biography of the Signers of the Declaration of Independence and of Washington and Patrick Henry*, 111; *FF*, 79.

364. Josiah Franklin had seven children by his first wife, Anne. After she died, he married Abiah and had ten more children—one of whom was Benjamin. (Gaustad, *Benjamin Franklin: Inventing America*, 9.) Under the Julian calendar used at the time, Benjamin was born on January 6, 1706.

365. *SDB*, 67.

366. *FF*, 81.

367. *SDB*, 76.

368. Ibid.

369. *IL*, 77–78.

370. *SDB*, 69.

371. Ibid., 67.

372. *FF*, 83. Some people have expressed doubt that the kite experiment ever took place. They base their skepticism mainly on their own personal difficulty of making a kite fly that matched the simple description Franklin gave. This may have more to do with their own expertise than Franklin's. Similar-sized kites fly all the time with minor adjustments to the bow of the crossbars, harness, tail, and so forth.

373. *SDB*, 69.

374. *FF*, 84.

375. *IL*, 85.

376. *SDB*, 75.

377. *FF*, 85.

378. *FF*, 85; *SDB*, 71.

379. *FF*, 85. Franklin's pamphlet, "Rules by Which a Great Empire May be Reduced to a Small One" is one example of his attempts to persuade Britain of its folly.

380. *FF*, 85; *SDB*, 71.

381. *IL*, 95.

382. Ibid.

383. *FF*, 85.

384. Although the idiom "Go fly a kite" is dated to the twentieth century, some people think it refers to Franklin's famous experiment that his son William helped him with.

385. *SDB*, 71.

386. *FOF*, 141–142.

387. *BFS*, 219.

388. *FF*, 86.

389. *FF*, 86; *SDB*, 71.

390. *FOF*, 142.

391. *FF*, 86.

392. Ibid., 87.

393. *IL*, 112–113.

394. *SDB*, 73.

395. *SDB*, 73; *IL*, 118.

396. *SDB*, 73–74.

397. *FF*, 87.

398. De Groote, "Patriotic Patriarch: Benjamin Franklin at the Constitutional Convention."

399. Ibid., 20.

400. *FF*, 88.

401. Ibid., 89.

402. *FOF*, 140.

403. Ibid., 163–164.

404. *SDB*, 75.

405. *FF*, 89.

406. Ibid.

407. ColonialHall.com; *FF*, 90. Menotomy is currently named Arlington, Massachusetts.

408. Rakove, *Revolutionaries: A New History of the Invention of America*, 381.

409. *WW*, 185.

410. *FOF*, 177.

411. Ibid., 171.

412. Bennett, *Our Sacred Honor: Words of Advice from the Founders in Stories, Letter, Poems, and Speeches*, 30.

413. *FOF*, 172.

414. *FF*, 93; *FOF*, 181.

415. *FF*, 93.

416. *FOF*, 183.

417. *FF*, 94.

418. *WW*, 203.

419. Burke, *American Connections: The Founding Fathers. Networked*, 270; *WW*, 203.

420. Delegates signed and voted in geographic order from the north to the south.

421. *WW*, 203.

422. *FF*, 95.

423. Some sources say he lingered for only three days.

424. *SDB*, 90.

425. *SD*, 66.

426. *FF*, 96.

427. *WW*, 208; *SDB*, 90; *SD*, 65.

428. *SDB*, 91.

429. Ibid., 90.

430. Ibid.

431. *WW*, 208; *FF*, 96.

432. *FF*, 96.

433. *SDB*, 90; *WW*, 208.

434. *SD*, 67.

435. *FF*, 96.

436. Unger, *John Hancock: Merchant King and American Patriot*, 110–111; *SDB*, 96–97.

437. Unger, *John Hancock: Merchant King and American Patriot*, 4.

438. *FF*, 98. Under the Julian calendar used at the time, he was born on January 12, 1737. *SDB*, 98.

439. *FF*, 98.

440. *FF*, 98; *WW*, 211.

441. Adams, *The Works of John Adams*, 10:259 (June 1, 1817, John Adams to William Tudor).

442. *FF*, 98; Unger, *John Hancock: Merchant King and American Patriot*, 60–62.

443. *SDB*, 98; *FF*, 100.

444. Unger, *John Hancock: Merchant King and American Patriot*, 119.

445. Ibid., 120–121.

446. *FF*, 100.

447. Unger, *John Hancock: Merchant King and American Patriot*, 168.

448. Ibid., 169.

449. Adams, *The Works of John Adams*, 2:415–416.

450. Adams, *The Works of John Adams*, 2:417; *WW*, 211; *FF*, 101.

451. *SDB*, 98; *FF*, 102.

452. *WW*, 212.

453. *SD*, 69.

454. *FOF*, 59.

455. *FF*, 103.

456. Ibid., 105.

457. *FOF*, 241. Five years later, Adams made a similar statement: "I can say, with truth, that I profoundly admired him, and more profoundly loved him. If he had vanity and caprice, so had I. And if his vanity and caprice made me sometimes sputter, as you know they often did, mine, I well know, had often a similar effect upon him. But these little flickerings of little passions determine nothing concerning essential characters. I knew Mr. Hancock from his cradle to his grave. He was radically generous and benevolent." (Adams, *The Works of John Adams*, 10:259, [June 1, 1817, John Adams to William Tudor]).

458. *FF*, 106; *WW*, 214; *SD*, 70; *SDB*, 103.

459. *SDB*, 104.

460. *STL*, 170; *SD*, 405.

461. *FF*, 106.

462. *FF*, 106; *SDB*, 104.

463. *SD*, 70.

464. *STL*, 27.

465. Ibid., 171.

466. *SDB*, 103.

467. Ibid.

468. *STL*, 172.

469. *FF*, 108.

470. *WW*, 215.

471. Ibid., 106.

472. *FF*, 109.

473. *WW*, 216.

474. *FF*, 109; *SDB*, 109.

475. Valis, "New Jersey During the Revolution."

476. *FF*, 109.

477. Valis, "New Jersey During the Revolution."

478. *SDB*, 109.

479. *STL*, 87; *FF*, 109; Valis, "New Jersey During the Revolution."

480. *STL*, 87.

481. *WW*, 227.

482. *FF*, 112.

483. *SD*, 73; *FF*, 111.

484. *FF*, 111; *WW*, 227.

485. *FF*, 112; *STL*, 196; *SD*, 73.

486. Burnett, *Letters of Members of the Continental Congress*, 1:83.

487. *STL*, 197.

488. Burke, *American Connections: The Founding Fathers. Networked*, 235.

489. *SDB*, 112.

490. Scheer, *Rebels and Redcoats*, 152; *SD*, 74; *STL*, 197.

491. Scheer, *Rebels and Redcoats*, 152.

492. *STL*, 197.

493. *WW*, 227; *FF*, 112.

494. *STL*, 198.

495. Ibid.

496. *WW*, 227; *SDB*, 116.

497. *FF*, 114; *SDB*, 116.

498. *FF*, 113; *SDB*, 117.

499. *FF*, 113; *WW*, 227; *SDB*, 117.

500. Edwards, "Stories of Old St. Augustine."

501. 1779 Pennsylvania Packet; *SD*, 76; *WW*, 227.

502. *SDB*, 117.

503. *WW*, 232; *FF*, 115.

504. *WW*, 232.

505. Goodrich, *Lives of the Signers to the Declaration of Independence*, 423.

506. Descendants of the Signers of the Declaration of Independence website.

507. *FF*, 115; *WW*, 233.

508. *FOF*, 247.

509. *FF*, 116.

510. *WW*, 233; Burke, *American Connections: The Founding Fathers. Networked*, 229.

511. Descendants of the Signers of the Declaration of Independence website.

512. Ibid.

513. *FF*, 119.

514. *FF*, 117; *SDB*, 126.

515. *FF*, 117.

516. *WW*, 234; *FF*, 117.

517. *FF*, 117; *SDB*, 124–125.

518. *SDB*, 124.

519. The Voyage of the Slave Ship Sally: 1764–1765 website at Brown University.

520. *FF*, 117.

521. *SDB*, 125.

522. *STL*, 52.

523. *SDB*, 126; *STL*, 52.

524. *FF*, 119.

525. *WW*, 235; Axelrod, *The Real History of the American Revolution: A New Look at the Past*, 240.

526. Axelrod, *The Real History of the American Revolution: A New Look at the Past*, 241.

527. *FF*, 120; *SDB*, 130; *FF*, 120.

528. *FF*, 120.

529. *SDB*, 130–131; *FF*, 120.

530. *FF*, 120.

531. Ibid., 122.

532. Ibid., 120.

533. Ibid.

534. *STL*, 89–92; *SDB*, 130; *FF*, 120.

535. Huges, *The Artful Rebel: Francis Hopkinson*, 49; Goodrich, *Lives of the Signers to the Declaration of Independence*, 225.

536. *FF*, 121.

537. Burke, *American Connections: The Founding Fathers. Networked*, 100.

538. *SDB*, 130.

539. AmericanMusicPreservation.com

540. *FF*, 120.

541. *FF*, 123; *WW*, 245.

542. *WW*, 245.

543. *FF*, 124.

544. *WW*, 123.

545. See Sanderson, *Sanderson's Biography of the Signers to the Declaration of Independence*, 183–184. The name of the person who lived with the Huntingtons is not mentioned by Sanderson, although he says the witness was still alive when the book was written circa 1846.

546. Under the Julian calendar used at the time, he was born on April 2, 1743.

547. *FF*, 127; *SD*, 86; *WW*, 257.

548. *FF*, 127.

549. Ibid., 128–129.

550. *IL*, 274–275.

551. *FF*, 129.

552. *SD*, 88.

553. *FOF*, 287.

554. Ibid., 288.

555. *FF*, 130. Underlining is in the original letter from Jefferson to Madison (August 30, 1823).

556. *SDB*, 141.

557. *IL*, 280.

558. *IL*, 281; *SDB*, 141.

559. *FF*, 282.

560. SD, 88.

561. FF, 133.

562. IL, 287.

563. Ibid., 288–289.

564. SDB, 144.

565. IL, 289.

566. Ibid., 291.

567. FOF, 290; IL, 289–290.

568. FOF, 290.

569. Ibid., 291.

570. FF, 134; IL, 292.

571. IL, 294.

572. Ibid., 294–295.

573. FF, 134.

574. Ibid., 135.

575. FOF, 301.

576. FF, 136.

577. FOF, 303. In a letter to John Jay (May 7, 1800). Emphasis in original.

578. FOF, 304. From a letter from Fisher Ames to Rufus King (September 24, 1800).

579. SDB, 141.

580. IL, 316. By this time, Mary used the name Maria.

581. FF, 138.

582. Ibid.

583. FOF, 316.

584. SD, 90.

585. IL, 325.

586. IL, 326–327.

587. STL, 186.

588. FF, 141.

589. SDB, 150.

590. FF, 141.

591. SDB, 150.

592. SD, 91.

593. STL, 185.

594. Burke, *American Connections: The Founding Fathers. Networked*, 217; Axelrod, *The Real History of the American Revolution: A New Look at the Past*, 234.

595. STL, 185.

596. FF, 141.

597. SDB, 150; FF, 141.

598. STL, 180; FF, 142–143.

599. FF, 142.

600. Ibid.

601. SDB, 156; FF, 143.

602. FF, 143.

603. FF, 143; SDB, 156.

604. FF, 144.

605. SDB, 155.

606. Ibid., 156.

607. FF, 144.

608. Ibid., 145.

609. Ibid., 142.

610. FF, 146; Burke, *American Connections: The Founding Fathers. Networked*, 300.

611. FF, 146.

612. STL, 182.

613. Ibid., 183.

614. FF, 146–147.

615. *SD*, 94; *FF*, 146.

616. *FF*, 144.

617. *STL*, 76.

618. *FF*, 148.

619. *Dictionary of Canadian Biography*.

620. *SDB*, 160.

621. Ibid.

622. *FF*, 148; *SD*, 95.

623. *SD*, 95.

624. *FF*, 149.

625. *STL*, 77; *SDB*, 160; *FF*, 148.

626. Green, *Wives of the Signers: The Women Behind the Declaration of Independence*, 122.

627. *FF*, 149; Goodrich, *Lives of the Signers to the Declaration of Independence*, 196; *STL*, 77; Green, *Wives of the Signers: The Women Behind the Declaration of Independence*, 122–124.

628. *STL*, 77. *WW*, 293; *SDB*, 160–161.

629. *STL*, 77.

630. *FF*, 149.

631. Goodrich, *Lives of the Signers to the Declaration of Independence*, 196; *FF*, 149.

632. *SDB*, 161.

633. *STL*, 69.

634. *FF*, 150; *STL*, 68.

635. *FF*, 150; *SD*, 97.

636. *FF*, 150; Goodrich, *Lives of the Signers to the Declaration of Independence*, 187.

637. *FF*, 150.

638. Goodrich, *Lives of the Signers to the Declaration of Independence*, 190. Emphasis in original; *FF*, 150–151.

639. Barrett, Walter. *The Old Merchants of New York City*, 4:265.

640. *FF*, 151–152.

641. *WW*, 297.

642. *STL*, 69.

643. *FF*, 152; *WW*, 297.

644. *STL*, 70.

645. *STL*, 70; *WW*, 297.

646. Goodrich, *Lives of the Signers to the Declaration of Independence*, 191.

647. *FF*, 152; *STL*, 70; Goodrich, *Lives of the Signers to the Declaration of Independence*, 192.

648. *FF*, 153.

649. *SDB*, 168–169.

650. *WW*, 304.

651. *FF*, 153.

652. *FF*, 153; South Carolina Plantations, "Peachtree Plantation—McClellanville—Charleston County."

653. *FF*, 153; *WW*, 304.

654. Burke, *American Connections: The Founding Fathers. Networked*, 259.

655. *STL*, 207.

656. Ibid., 208.

657. *FF*, 154; *WW*, 304; *STL*, 208; Goodrich, *Lives of the Signers to the Declaration of Independence*, 446.

658. *SDB*, 169; South Carolina Plantations, "Peachtree Plantation—McClellanville—Charleston County."

659. Goodrich, *Lives of the Signers to the Declaration of Independence*, 326. Emphasis in original.

660. *FF*, 155; *SDB*, 172.

661. *WW*, 309.

662. *FF*, 155; *SDB*, 172.

663. *SDB*, 172; *FF*, 155; *WW*, 309.

664. *FF*, 156; *STL*, 138.

665. *SDB*, 174.

666. *WW*, 309; *SDB*, 173; *STL*, 23; *FF*, 156.

667. *FF*, 156–157.

668. Ibid., 157.

669. *FF*, 157; *STL*, 55. Americans consider George Washington to be the first president of the United States, and rightly so, because he was the first under the Constitution—a document that had a strong federal government and an executive branch with power. Under the Articles of Confederation, the "president of the United States in Congress Assembled" was basically the president of the Congress. He was the highest officer of the land but had no real executive power.

670. *FF*, 157; Scheer, *Rebels and Redcoats*, 495.

671. Scheer, *Rebels and Redcoats*, 495.

672. *FF*, 159.

673. Ibid.

674. *SDB*, 174.

675. Burke, *American Connections: The Founding Fathers. Networked*, 265; *FF*, 160; *WW*, 326.

676. Sanderson, *Sanderson's Biography of the Signers to the Declaration of Independence*, 695.

677. *FF*, 160.

678. *FF*, 161; Find a Grave website.

679. Sanderson, *Sanderson's Biography of the Signers to the Declaration of Independence*, 703.

680. *FF*, 162.

681. *WW*, 336.

682. *FF*, 162; *SDB*, 182.

683. *STL*, 80.

684. *WW*, 336.

685. *FF*, 163; *SD*, 105; *STL*, 80; Burke, *American Connections: The Founding Fathers. Networked*, 83.

686. *SD*, 105.

687. *FF*, 163.

688. *FF*, 166; Rappleye, *Robert Morris: Financier of the American Revolution*, 34.

689. *SDB*, 189.

690. Rappleye, *Robert Morris: Financier of the American Revolution*, 7.

691. *FF*, 164.

692. *FF*, 164–165; *SDB*, 186; Rappleye, *Robert Morris: Financier of the American Revolution*, 13.

693. *FF*, 166; Rappleye, *Robert Morris: Financier of the American Revolution*, 22.

694. *FOF*, 429.

695. *FF*, 166.

696. *FOF*, 428.

697. Rappleye, *Robert Morris: Financier of the American Revolution*, 71.

698. *FF*, 166; Rappleye, *Robert Morris: Financier of the American Revolution*, 71.

699. Rappleye, *Robert Morris: Financier of the American Revolution*, 74.

700. *FOF*, 445–446.

701. Rappleye, *Robert Morris: Financier of the American Revolution*, 30; *STL*, 118.

702. Rappleye, *Robert Morris: Financier of the American Revolution*, 93.

703. *FF*, 167.

704. Rappleye, *Robert Morris: Financier of the American Revolution*, 173–177; *FF*, 167.

705. STL, 119.

706. FF, 169.

707. WW, 337.

708. FF, 170.

709. FF, 172; SDB, 108.

710. Rappleye, *Robert Morris: Financier of the American Revolution*, 493.

711. IL, 173.

712. STL, 119.

713. Rappleye, *Robert Morris: Financier of the American Revolution*, 507.

714. STL, 120.

715. Rappleye, *Robert Morris: Financier of the American Revolution*, 507.

716. FF, 172; Rappleye, *Robert Morris: Financier of the American Revolution*, 510.

717. Rappleye, *Robert Morris: Financier of the American Revolution*, 508.

718. Ibid., 510.

719. Ibid., 510, 512.

720. STL, 118.

721. FF, 172; SDB, 187; Rappleye, *Robert Morris: Financier of the American Revolution*, 515.

722. FF, 173.

723. STL, 103.

724. STL, 103; FF, 173.

725. WW, 338.

726. SDB, 194.

727. STL, 104.

728. SD, 110.

729. SD, 112; FF, 175.

730. FF, 175.

731. SDB, 199.

732. STL, 188.

733. Ibid., 27.

734. WW, 347.

735. SD, 111.

736. FF, 176. Emphasis in original.

737. Ibid., 176–177.

738. Ibid., 177.

739. SD, 111.

740. FF, 179.

741. SDB, 198–199.

742. FF, 180–181.

743. Ibid., 180.

744. SDB, 205.

745. FF, 180–181.

746. Ibid., 181.

747. Adherents.com.

748. Burke, *American Connections: The Founding Fathers. Networked*, 31.

749. Adherents.com; FF, 182.

750. Burke, *American Connections: The Founding Fathers. Networked*, 31.

751. FOF, 238.

752. FF, 183.

753. Adherents.com.

754. FOF, 59.

755. STL, 202.

756. Descendants of the Signers of the Declaration of Independence website.

757. Ibid.

758. *WW*, 374.

759. *FF*, 184.

760. *STL*, 203.

761. *FF*, 184.

762. *FF*, 187; *WW*, 402; *STL*, 144; Read, *Life and Correspondence of George Read: A Signer of the Declaration of Independence; with Notices of Some of His Contemporaries*, 276, 295.

763. Adherents.com.

764. *WW*, 402.

765. *FF*, 187; *SD*, 118; *SDB*, 218.

766. *FF*, 187; Read, *Life and Correspondence of George Read*, 11.

767. *FF*, 187.

768. Read, *Life and Correspondence of George Read*, 22.

769. *WW*, 402.

770. Read, *Life and Correspondence of George Read*, 29–30.

771. Ibid., 36. Emphasis in original.

772. Ibid., 37.

773. *SDB*, 218.

774. Read, *Life and Correspondence of George Read*, 164–165.

775. *STL*, 143.

776. *FF*, 187.

777. Read, *Life and Correspondence of George Read*, 165–166.

778. *FF*, 187.

779. Read, *Life and Correspondence of George Read*, 280.

780. Ibid., 292.

781. *SD*, 119.

782. *FF*, 189.

783. Ibid.

784. Read, *Life and Correspondence of George Read*, 456–457.

785. *SDB*, 219.

786. Pickett, "Delaware's Hero for all Times: 'Soldier, Judge, Governor, Patriot' Caesar Rodney: 4th President of Delaware."

787. *SD*, 120.

788. *FF*, 190.

789. *WW*, 413.

790. *FF*, 190.

791. *SD*, 121.

792. *WW*, 413.

793. *SDB*, 222.

794. Burnett, *Letters of Members of the Continental Congress*, 1:534 (Thomas McKean to Caesar A. Rodney, September 22, 1813); Smith, *Letters of Delegates to Congress, 1774–1789*, 4:388 (Caesar Rodney to Thomas Rodney, July 4, 1776).

795. *SDB*, 222.

796. Smith, *Letters of Delegates to Congress, 1774–1789*, 4:388 (Caesar Rodney to Thomas Rodney, July 4, 1776).

797. *WW*, 414.

798. *SD*, 121.

799. Pickett, "Delaware's Hero for all Times: 'Soldier, Judge, Governor, Patriot' Caesar Rodney: 4th President of Delaware."

800. Wilbor, *Werner's Readings and Recitations*, No. 6, 136–137.

801. *FF*, 192.

802. Sanderson, *Sanderson's Biography of the Signers to the Declaration of Independence*, 437; *WW*, 418.

803. *WW*, 418.

804. Burke, *American Connections: The Founding Fathers. Networked*, 162.

805. *FOF*, 460. Compare *SDB*, 231.

806. *FF*, 195; *SDB*, 230.

807. *FF*, 196; *WW*, 419.

808. *SDB*, 230.

809. *FF*, 196.

810. *WW*, 419.

811. *FF*, 196–197.

812. *WW*, 419.

813. *STL*, 128.

814. Wright, *The Continental Army*, 82–83.

815. *SDB*, 230.

816. *WW*, 419–420; *SDB*, 231.

817. *FF*, 197–198.

818. Ibid., 198.

819. *SDB*, 231.

820. *FF*, 198.

821. Ibid., 199.

822. Ibid., 198.

823. *FOF*, 462.

824. *SDB*, 231.

825. *SD*, 126.

826. Burke, *American Connections: The Founding Fathers. Networked*, 123.

827. *FOF*, 464.

828. Ibid., 464.

829. *FF*, 200.

830. Ibid., 201.

831. *FF*, 201; *STL*, 213.

832. *SDB*, 237.

833. *WW*, 42.1

834. *FF*, 201.

835. *WW*, 421.

836. Ibid.

837. *FF*, 202.

838. Ibid.

839. *STL*, 214.

840. *FF*, 202.

841. *FOF*, 469.

842. Signer Josiah Bartlett's father was also a shoemaker.

843. *STL*, 57.

844. *FF*, 203.

845. *SD*, 130.

846. *FF*, 205.

847. Scheer, *Rebels and Redcoats*, 150.

848. *FF*, 205.

849. Ibid., 203.

850. Ibid.

851. Ibid., 208.

852. *WW*, 442.

853. *SDB*, 241.

854. *FOF*, 467.

855. McClure, "Smith Brought Declaration to York"; McClure, "1776 Declaration of Independence Reading in York Town Re-enacted in Annual Ceremony."

856. *SD*, 132.

857. *SDB*, 246. Two other Signers, McKean and Read, were also educated there.

858. *FF*, 209.

859. *WW*, 446.

860. *SDB*, 246.

861. Hagaman, *The Old Martyrs' Prison, New York; An Historical Sketch of the Oldest Municipal Building in New York City*; Cornelius, *Journal of Dr. Elias Cornelius, a Revolutionary Surgeon: Graphic Details of His Sufferings While a Prisoner in Provost Jail, New York, 1777 and 1778, with Biographical Sketch*.

862. Smith, *Letters of Delegates to Congress, 1774–1789*, 5:706 (December 30, 1776, Benjamin Rush to Richard Henry Lee).

863. *FF*, 211; *SDB*, 251.

864. Annis was the sister of Elias Boudinot, one of Stockton's law students who later signed the peace treaty in 1783 that finished the Revolutionary War.

865. *SDB*, 250.

866. *FF*, 211. It was two years before Witherspoon accepted. *SD*, 134.

867. *WW*, 456.

868. *SDB*, 250. Compare *STL*, 93.

869. *FF*, 212.

870. *STL*, 94.

871. *FF*, 212.

872. Smith, *Letters of Delegates to Congress, 1774–1789*, 4:529 (July 23, 1776, Benjamin Rush to Julia Rush).

873. *WW*, 456.

874. *STL*, 94; *SDB*, 251.

875. *STL*, 94.

876. *SDB*, 251.

877. Smith, *Letters of Delegates to Congress, 1774–1789*, 6:9 (January 1, 1777, William Hooper to Joseph Hawes).

878. Ibid., 5:706 (December 30, 1776, Benjamin Rush to Richard Henry Lee).

879. "Whereas Congress hath received information that the honorable Richard Stockton, Esq. of New Jersey, and a member of this Congress, hath been made a prisoner by the enemy, and that he has been ignominiously thrown into a common goal, and there detained; Resolved, That General Washington be directed to make immediate enquiry into the truth of this report, and if he finds reason to believe it well founded, that he send a flag to General Howe, remonstrating against this departure from that humane procedure that has marked the conduct of these states to prisoners, who have fallen into their hands; and to know of General Howe, whether he chuses that this shall be the future rule for treating all such, on both sides, as the fortune of war may place in the hands of either party." (Ford, *Journals of the Continental Congress, 1774–1789*, 7:12–14. See also, Smith, *Letters of Delegates to Congress, 1774–1789*, 6:40 [January 6, 1777, John Hancock to George Washington]): "Make Enquiry whether the Report which Congress have heard of Mr. Stockton's being confined in a Common Jail by the Enemy, has any Truth in it, or not."

880. Smith, *Letters of Delegates to Congress, 1774–1789*, 6:39–40 (January 6, 1777, John Hancock to the Executive Committee).

881. Knight, "Prisoner Exchange and Parole in the American Revolution," 205.

882. Ibid., 214.

883. Ibid., 213–214.

884. "The Howes' Proclamation of November 30, 1776."

885. *STL*, 95.

886. Rush, *The Autobiography of Benjamin Rush*, 130.

887. Smith, *Letters of Delegates to Congress, 1774–1789*, 6:240–241 (February 8, 1777, Abraham Clark to John Hart).

888. Ibid., 6:246–247 (February 9, 1777, John Hancock to Robert Treat Paine).

889. Ibid., 6:454–456 (March 17, 1777, John Witherspoon to David Witherspoon). Witherspoon then talked about a further rumor: "Mrs. Cochran was sent to the Enemies Lines by a flag of Truce and when Mr. Cochran came out to meet his wife he said to the Officers that went with the flag that Judge Stockton had brought Evidence to General Howe to prove that he was on his Way to seek a protection when he was taken. This he denies to be true yet many credit it but Mr. Cochrans known quarrel with him makes it very doubtful to candid Persons."

890. Smith, *Letters of Delegates to Congress, 1774–1789*, 6:240–241 (February 8, 1877, Abraham Clark to John Hart).

891. "Minutes of the Council of Safety of the State of New Jersey," 178. On Monday, December 22, 1777, "Richard Stockton Esq., was called before the Board, and the Oaths of Abjuration & Allegiance being tendered to him, he took & subscribed the Same, & was thereupon dismissed."

892. FF, 213; STL, 95.

893. FF, 213. From his funeral sermon: "For nearly two years he bore with the utmost constancy and patience, a disorder that makes us tremble only to think of it. With most exquisite pain it preyed upon him, until it reached the passages by which life is sustained: yet, in the midst of as much as human nature could endure, he always discovered a submission to the will of heaven, and a resignation to his fate, that could only flow from the expectation of a better life. Such was the man, whose remains now lie before us, to teach us the most interesting lessons that mortals have to learn, the vanity of human things; the importance of eternity; the holiness of the divine law; the value of religion; and the certainty and rapid approach of death." (Goodrich, *Lives of the Signers to the Declaration of Independence*, 210–211.)

894. Smith, *Letters of Delegates to Congress, 1774–1789*, 4:49 (May 20, 1776, Thomas Stone to James Hollyday).

895. FF, 214.

896. Smith, *Letters of Delegates to Congress, 1774–1789*, 4:47 (May 20, 1776, Thomas Stone to James Hollyday).

897. SDB, 258.

898. FF, 216.

899. STL, 132.

900. Smith, *Letters of Delegates to Congress, 1774–1789*, 6:118–119 (January 17, 1777, Executive Committee to John Hancock).

901. WW, 468.

902. Because we don't know his birth month, we cannot be sure he was twenty-six at the time he started practicing medicine. He could have still been twenty-five at the time.

903. Adams, *Matthew Thornton of New Hampshire: A Patriot of the American Revolution*, 19–20.

904. Ibid., 25. Emphasis in original.

905. Farmer, *Collections, Topographical, Historical and Biographical, Relating Principally to New-Hampshire*, 1:88–89. Emphasis in original.

906. STL, 22.

907. STL, 23; Adams, *Matthew Thornton of New Hampshire*, 60.

908. Adams, *Matthew Thornton of New Hampshire*, 48.

909. Ibid., 57. Compare with Farmer, *Collections, Topographical, Historical and Biographical, Relating Principally to New-Hampshire*, 1:90.

910. Farmer, *Collections, Topographical, Historical and Biographical, Relating Principally to New-Hampshire*, 1:90.

911. Lamplugh, "George Walton, Chief Justice of Georgia, 1783–1785," 83. Emphasis in original.

912. Bridges, "George Walton." Other sources place his birth as early as 1741. SD, 141; WW, 493.

913. Bridges, "George Walton."

914. Bridges, "George Walton"; *WW*, 493.

915. *FF*, 219.

916. *SDB*, 272.

917. Bridges, "George Walton"; *FF*, 219. Walton could have been admitted to the bar in 1774; the exact year is unclear.

918. *FF*, 219.

919. Smith, *Letters of Delegates to Congress, 1774–1789*, 4:259 (June 17, 1776, George Walton to Lachlan McIntosh),

920. Bridges, "George Walton." *SDB*, 272 says Walton was first mentioned in *Journals of Congress* on July 17, 1776. *FF*, 220 says he was only thought to be the youngest because of his size and places his age at thirty-five.

921. Smith, *Letters of Delegates to Congress, 1774–1789*, 7:431–432 (August 5, 1777, George Walton to George Washington). Because his birthdate is unknown, he could have been slightly older than Rutledge.

922. Bridges, "George Walton"; *SDB*, 273.

923. *SD*, 141–142.

924. Cashin, "George Walton and the Forged Letter," 133.

925. Ibid.

926. *WW*, 494.

927. Lamplugh, "George Walton, Chief Justice of Georgia, 1783–1785," 83; *FF*, 221; Sanderson, *Sanderson's Biography of the Signers to the Declaration of Independence*, 719.

928. Lamplugh, "George Walton, Chief Justice of Georgia, 1783–1785," 83.

929. Button Gwinnett.

930. *SD*, 142.

931. *FF*, 221.

932. Bridges, "George Walton."

933. Sanderson, *Sanderson's Biography of the Signers to the Declaration of Independence*, 718.

934. *WW*, 506.

935. *FF*, 222.

936. *SDB*, 276.

937. Vaughan, "This Was a Man: A Biography of General William Whipple," 5.

938. *FF*, 222.

939. *FF*, 223.

940. Rakove, *Revolutionaries: A New History of the Invention of America*, 232.

941. *SDB*, 276.

942. *FF*, 223; *WW*, 507.

943. Goodrich, *Lives of the Signers to the Declaration of Independence*, 178. Emphasis in original.

944. *FOF*, 224.

945. *FF*, 225; Goodrich, *Lives of the Signers to the Declaration of Independence*, 177.

946. Goodrich, *Lives of the Signers to the Declaration of Independence*, 179.

947. Ibid., 178.

948. *SD*, 146.

949. *SDB*, 286.

950. *SD*, 146.

951. *FOF*, 529.

952. *FF*, 226.

953. *WW*, 515.

954. Rappleye, *Robert Morris: Financier of the American Revolution*, 191.

955. Ibid., 193.

956. *FF*, 229. Emphasis in original.

957. *FOF*, 531.

958. Ibid., 532.

959. Ibid., 533–534.

960. *STL*, 115.

961. *SDB*, 288.

962. *STL*, 98.

963. Woods, *John Witherspoon*, 216.

964. Ibid., 294.

965. Dwight, *The Lives of the Signers of the Declaration of Independence*, 122.

966. *FF*, 234.

967. Ibid, 233.

968. *FOF*, xvii.

969. Various secondary sources give different dates in September or October for when Wolcott signed. *FF*, 234 says September, for example. *WW*, 518 and Burke, *American Connections: The Founding Fathers. Networked*, 306 say October.

970. *WW*, 518.

971. *FF*, 234.

972. *STL*, 191.

973. *FF*, 237.

974. *SDB*, 304.

975. *FF*, 237.

976. *STL*, 194; Chadwick, "The Mysterious Death of Judge George Wythe."

977. *FF*, 235.

978. *WWJ*, 7:367.

979. Ibid.

980. Ibid., 7:367–369.

981. McAllister, *John D. T. McAllister Journal*, 3:48.

982. Ibid.

983. Ibid.

984. Ibid., 6:153.

985. Ibid., 6:154–155.

986. Smith, *Journal of Joseph West Smith*, 77–78.

987. Woodruff, "Remarks Made at the Salt Lake Stake Conference," *Deseret Evening News*, December 18, 1897, 9.

988. *Conference Report of The Church of Jesus Christ of Latter-day Saints*, Sixty-Eighth Annual General Conference, 89–90 (April 10, 1898). Emphasis added.

989. Marvel Ruth Bleak Spiering was born September 30, 1916 to James Alonzo Bleak and Violet Ruth Reynolds Bleak. James's father was Joseph Gosnold Bleak, who was a son of James Godson Bleak. Marvel died December 17, 1997.

990. Compare listing to Stuy, "Wilford Woodruff's Vision of the Signers of the Declaration of Independence," 83–90; see incorrect order in *WWJ*, 7:367–369 and compare with Woodruff's actual journal.

991. Identified as "Lawrence Washington Augustine's father" in the St. George Temple records.

992. Polk won the election of 1844. Joseph Smith Jr. was a candidate in this election until he was assassinated on June 27, 1844.

993. When Woodruff was compiling names from Duyckinck's *Portrait Gallery of Eminent Men and Women of Europe and America*, he probably scanned through the biography for "Benito Juarez," looking for Juárez's wife. On page 125, he saw the phrase "He had been for some years married to the Princess Charlotte, daughter of King Leopold of Belgium" and assumed this was Juárez's wife. She was not. The paragraph was about Juárez's enemy, Emperor Maximilian I of Mexico. Princess Charlotte was Maximilian's wife and went by the name "Carlota of Mexico." Princess Charlotte died in 1927, and since she was alive in 1877, she would be a poor candidate

for baptisms for the dead. Woodruff's intent, however, was to do the work for Juárez's wife, even if he got her name wrong, so I list it here. Duyckinck's book did not mention Margarita Maza Juárez. This particular baptism done using Princess Charlotte's name instead of Juárez's wife's became moot in 1921 when Margarita Maza Juárez's work was done correctly in the Salt Lake Temple.

994. The connection between Elijah Gibbs and Lucy Bigelow Young was pointed out by Jennifer Mackley to the author. Personal e-mail, November 7, 2013. Mackley is the author of *Wilford Woodruff's Witness: The Development of Temple Doctrine*.

995. Lydia Knapp was only identified as "Mrs. Elijah Gibbs" in the St. George Temple records of 1877. Her baptism was eventually redone under her name in 1891.

996. Identified as "Mrs. John Washington" in the St. George Temple records. She was the first wife of John Washington. After she died, he married Anne Gerrard, and after she died, he married Anne Gerrard's sister, Frances.

997. Even though she is identified as "Mrs. Washington" in the St. George Temple records, the journal of John D. T. McAllister from August 23, 1877, helps identify her: "Also acted for Augustine Washington & my Wife Ann for his 1st wife & 2nd Mary Ball in the Sealing." McAllister, *John D. T. McAllister Journal*, 3:48.

998. McAllister, *John D. T. McAllister Journal*, 3:48 (August 21, 1877).

Go to MichaelDeGroote.com for other information about this book, including signings, speaking events, and corrections and updates to the text. Please notify the author of any historical errors by e-mailing WoodruffSigners@gmail.com. Follow Michael De Groote on Twitter: @DeGroote.

ABOUT THE AUTHOR

Michael De Groote was born and raised in the Midwest until his family decided to move away from the cold to Arizona during his senior year of high school. He served a mission in Belgium and Holland. He has a BA in Secondary Education, with an emphasis in history from Arizona State University and a law degree from J. Reuben Clark Law School at Brigham Young University. In addition to being a recovering attorney, his work experience includes being the director of communication and marketing for the Salt Lake Chamber of Commerce and an award-winning journalist for the Deseret News. He currently lives in the Salt Lake Valley with his wife and daughters.

ABOUT THE AUTHOR

Ronald L. Fox is an author and historian and owns a public affairs firm in Salt Lake City. His firm specializes in marketing, public relations, and government advocacy. Fox has also provided collectors, antique dealers, the LDS Church, and the Utah State Historical Society with historical research and information on various photographs, artifacts, paintings, and books. He has at times been likened to a modern-day Indiana Jones in his ability to find lost treasures. In his career, he has worked for the California Senate, FHP Health Care, and American Medical International.

For three years, beginning in 2008, he was a contributor to the Deseret News, providing a weekly article on Utah photographic history. In 2011 he coauthor his first book with Mike Winder, When the White House Comes to Zion. Currently he is working on three additional books, John Bernhisel: Utah's first Congressional Delegate, Marsena Cannon: Utah's first photographer, and Famous Visitors to the Salt Lake Tabernacle. He has also produced or appeared in four commercial video presentations for television.

Fox has managed large ceremonies, such as the opening of the Winter Olympic Games in 2002 at Utah's Capitol, Utah Inaugurations in 1993, 1997, 2001, 2003, and 2013. He has traveled with and for five U. S. presidents: Nixon, Ford, Reagan, and both Bushes, as well as their first ladies; six vice presidents; and members of the Cabinet. He also served on the Dole, McCain, and Romney campaigns in one capacity or another. Attended eight Republican National Conventions since 1972, several times as a delegate. He has assisted with the planning and execution of numerous visits of foreign heads of state, including the presidents of China, Ecuador, Brazil, and the Philippines; the king of Sweden; the queen of England; the secretary general of the United Nations; the Dali Lama; and the Pope for the State Department. He has been tasked to work the NATO Summit in Prague and the Czech Republic and the G-8 Summit in Sea Island, Georgia, were he was responsible for the visit of the president of Iraq and president of Uganda.

His efforts have been recognized by resolutions from the Senate of California, the House and Senate of Utah, and several city and counties governments. He has served on the board of the Fort Douglas Military Museum, was the chairman and member of the Salt Lake County Library Board, the Legacy Film Foundation, and the Colonial Flag Foundation. He assisted his wife in founding Mothers Against Drunk Drivers, with Candy Lightner in 1980.

Fox attended El Camino College and California State University at Fullerton and currently resides in Salt Lake City. He has been married to his wife, Linda, for thirty-nine years. They have three daughters: Jennifer, Elizabeth, and Kari, who, with their husbands, have given Fox and his wife grandchildren Oliver, Kiera, and Gwen, with one more to be added this year.